The Complete
IRISH WOLFHOUND

by
Alma J. Starbuck

Third Edition
Illustrated

Eighth Printing

1984

HOWELL BOOK HOUSE INC.

230 Park Avenue
New York, N.Y. 10169

Dedicated in memory of
CH. GARTHA OF AMBLESIDE
*"... a majestic Hound ... claiming a very
special kind of beauty all her own ..."*

The late L. O. Starbuck with Ch. Killabrick.
Killabrick, whelped July 1927 out of Ch. Mona of Ambleside,
was the sire of Ch. Brannish of Ambleside, Ambleside Finn of
Erin, Kilshane of Ambleside, Padraic of Summerhill, Ch.
Killary of Ambleside, and Ch. Gartha of Ambleside.

ACKNOWLEDGMENTS

FOR EARLY historical references I am indebted to the writings of Father Edmund Ignatius Hogan, S.J., in his book, *The Irish Wolfdog,* published in 1897, and to Captain George Augustus Graham's book, *The Irish Wolfhound,* published in 1885; and I am indebted to Delphis Gardner for permission to use woodcuts and quote from her late sister's book, *The Irish Wolfhound,* by Phyllis Gardner.

I wish to express my appreciation for information furnished me by Dr. R. J. May in Ireland, and by Mrs. Florence Nagle and Miss Esther M. Croucher in England.

I have drawn heavily for dates and information from the books of the Irish Wolfhound Club of England, from the "Biennial Reports" of the Irish Wolfhound Club of America, and later from the club's quarterly, *Harp and Hound.*

And I am deeply grateful for all the material available now and for all time, contained in *Fifty Years of Irish Wolfhound Registrations in America,* compiled and edited by LeRoy E. Fess and published by the Irish Wolfhound Club of America, carrying, as it does, full particulars of the pedigrees of all registered Hounds included therein.

Alma J. Starbuck

The publisher wishes to express thanks to Mr. Samuel Evans Ewing, III and to Mr. and Mrs. Gordon Graham for their assistance in bringing the information for this third edition up-to-date.

TABLE OF CONTENTS

PART I

by Alma J. Starbuck

PART II

General Care and Training, by E. S. Howell,
  Milo Denlinger, A. C. Merrick, D.V.M.

Ch. Ambleside Edain of Edgecliff, best of breed at Westminster, 1952, and best of opposite sex at Club Specialty, 1952.

Early History of the Breed

THE STORY of the Irish Wolfhound, "like all Gaul," may be divided into three parts: the data regarding the ancient wolfdog with his romantic historical background; the extraordinary feat of Captain G. A. Graham in reviving the breed in the nineteenth century; and the dog among us today.

Though the Wolfhound's origin is lost in antiquity, he is famous both in legends and in the written pages of history.

Arrian, writing in the second century A.D., mentions that swift Hounds were brought to Greece during the invasion of the Celts, who sacked Delphi in 273 B.C. Evidence of this is borne out by statues, jewelry, and paintings which are described in detail, and some of which have been recovered along with other artifacts of the period.

One of the woodcuts by Phyllis Gardner is from a picture of a fresco at Tiryns in Northern Greece, and shows a man with a pair of horses and a dog. Miss Gardner says the artists of this period were given to fairly accurate representations and the scale of the man and horses is reasonable; yet, the highest part of the dog's back is nearly up to the man's waist, while the tip of the dog's ear is actually level with the man's shoulders. The Hound in this picture is of Greyhound type, though enormous, and is of good weight and power.

To Father Edmund Ignatius Hogan, S.J., is due the credit for much of the information concerning the Irish Hound. Father Hogan devoted years of a busy life searching modern and ancient classics for all references to this great Hound and evidences of his character, size, and appearance. He published his findings in Dublin in 1897 in a monograph he called *The Irish Wolfdog,* but a disastrous fire destroyed almost the entire edition. Only a few copies were saved and Father Hogan was unable to have the book reprinted. About ten years later, Joseph A. McAleenan of Long Island, a sportsman and lifelong friend of the dogs of Ireland, had two hundred copies printed privately. Some of these were presented to friends, others found their way into libraries.

Mr. McAleenan says, "I believe this, the only authoritative book on the subject, will excite interest and be the means of spreading an intimate knowledge of a dog that typifies the greatest in stature, intelligence, courage, loyalty, and affection of all the dog family."

In the preface of his book, Father Hogan writes, "To the blessed Edmund Campion, S.J., we owe the first description of the form, size and use of the great Irish greyhound. In the year 1571 he wrote at Turvey, near Dublin: 'The Irish are not without wolves and greyhounds to hunt them, bigger of bone and limb than a colt.' In the light of these words we understand that 'his' big wolf-hunting greyhounds were identical in breed with 'the Irish dogs,' 'big dogs of Ireland,' 'Greyhounds of Ireland,' 'Wolfdogs of Ireland,' which were sent as highly prized presents to Roman Consuls; to Kings of England, Scotland, France, Spain, Sweden, Denmark and Poland; to Emperors, Great Moguls, Grand Turks, the Shahs of Persia; Ambassadors, Papal Nuncios, French Princes and Dutch Noblemen; to Prime Ministers, Noblemen and highborn beauties in Great Britain."

The breed was well known in Roman days. The first authentic record was made in A.D. 391 when the Roman Consul, Quintus Aurelius Symmachus, mentions them in a letter to his brother, Flavianus, in thanking him for a gift of Irish dogs which he had contributed to their solemn "Shows and Games," saying, "All Rome viewed them with wonder." The dogs sent to Symmachus were seven in number—the usual number presented by one king or chief to another.

The Irish Wolfhound was the most valued and sought after hunting dog of the early centuries, not only because of his hunting prowess but because he was an exceptional guardian and companion.

We read of Cu-Chulainn, the bravest hero of the Irish in the first century of our era, who derived his name from an incident of his youth, writes Miss Gardner. I quote: "As he approached to the house of the smith Culann, the great hound that was Culann's guardian set upon him and in the ensuing struggle he slew it—no mean feat for a boy of fifteen. He was overcome with remorse and offered to take the place of the slain hound for a year, while he should train a pup of its begetting. His name up to this time had been Setanta, but he is much better known as Cu-Chulainn, 'the Hound of Culann.'"

Father Hogan says the admiration and love of the Irishmen for their Greyhound is evidenced by the fact that Cu (Greyhound) or Mil-Chu (Greyhound that hunted large game) was part of the name of many chieftains and warriors.

Cu-Chulainn says of himself:

"I was a greyhound (Cu) of catching a deer,
I was a greyhound strong for combat,
I was a greyhound of visiting troops . . ."

About the third or fourth century there flourished the mighty warrior and huntsman, Finn, son of Cumall, celebrated in the cycles of the poet Oisin. Finn was chief of the household of King Cormac, commander of the armies and master of his Hounds. We are told his Hounds numbered three hundred and his puppies, two hundred. Finn had a favorite Hound named Conbec, and not in all Ireland might any stag whatsoever, at which he was slipped, find covert before Conbec would head him off and run him right back

*Marble statue found on the
Acropolis at Athens.*

Head of above.

Diamhar-Geal of Coolafin, head.

**Man leading a hound before a pair-horse chariot.
From a fresco at Tiryns.**

10

up to Finn's main pack, and to their attendants. And it is said that neither did Hound other than Conbec "ever sleep in the one bed with Finn." At Traig Chonbicce, Conbec was drowned by Goll, a rival of Finn, and on him Cailte, a warrior serving Finn, uttered the lay:

> "Piteous to me was Conbec's cruel death,
> Conbec of perfect symmetry,
> I have not seen a more expert of foot
> In the wake of wild boar or stag.
> A pang to me was Conbec's tragic fate,
> Conbec of the hoarse deep voice;
> Never have I seen one more expert of foot
> At killing buck without delay.
> A pang to me was Conbec's death,
> Over the high, green billows,
> His cruel death was a cause of strife,
> His fate was most pitiful."

Fighting the Romans along Hadrian's Wall in Britain were bands of Scots and others from Northern Britain, who were known as Fianna. There are various descriptions of great hunts organized by the Fianna. They tell how the chiefs of heroes, with their Hounds, would take their places on commanding heights, while their followers with lesser dogs sought out and drove the game over a large area. When the game came in sight, the chiefs would slip their Hounds at it. Sometimes as many as two hundred stags would be taken in one hunt.

Miss Gardner writes, "Many hill-tops still bear names which mean the seat of such and such a hero, *i.e.,* a place from which he conducted his hunting. Suidhe Fergus, in Arran, is a case in point, being a hill with a very wide view in the centre of a district full of Celtic legend. Finn is said to have conducted certain hunts from the top of Ben Edair (Howth) and there are many other 'Finn's seats' in Ireland."

The powerful Irish dogs were used not only in hunting wolf, stag, and boar, but also in hunting the gigantic Irish elk which stood six feet at the shoulder. Some of the Hounds were to be found in Iceland in the early days, and also in Scandinavia, with the result that we find early Irish influence in the folk tales from those two cultures.

According to the *Saga of the Burnt Njal,* in the tenth century, Olaf, a Norwegian, son of an Irish princess, says to his friend, Gunnar, "I will give thee a hound that was given to me in Ireland; he is big and no worse than a stout man. Besides, it is part of his nature that he has a man's wit, and he will bay at every man whom he knows to be thy foe, but never at thy friends. He can see, too, in any man's face whether he means thee well or ill, and he will lay down his life to be true to thee. This hound's name is SAMR."

After that Olaf speaks to the Hound: "Now shalt thou follow Gunnar, and do him all the service thou canst." The Hound went at once to Gunnar, and laid himself down at his feet. Later, history relates, when Gunnar's enemies plotted to kill him, they found it necessary to kill the Irish Hound first.

King John of England presented an Irish Hound to Llewellyn, Prince of Wales, about the year 1210. A dog of this breed is referred to thus, in the Hon. W. R. Spencer's verses on Beth Gelert:

> "The flower of all the race,
> So true, so brave—a lamb at home,
> A lion in the chase.
> 'Twas only at Llewellyn's board
> The faithful Gelert fed.
> He watched, he served, he cheered his lord,
> And sentinelled his bed.
> To sooth he was a peerless hound,
> The gift of Royal John."

The poem goes on to tell how Gelert killed a gaunt wolf and so saved his master's child.

A curious old manuscript from the twelfth century, mentions a certain Mesrodia, King of Leinsternien, who had a Wolfhound named Aibe, whose fame filled all Ireland. For this Hound six thousand cows and various other possessions

12

Ch. Sulhamstead Fella at 6 months. Winner of Challenge Certificate and Brewers Cup at Birmingham at 10 months, also Puppy Criterion, all breeds. (By Ch. Fonab of Ouborough ex Ch. Sulhamstead Fiana.)

Ch. Clodagh of Ouborough, winner of the Graham Shield, 1925.

were offered by the King of Connacht. At that, the King of Ulster made approximately the same offer. Feeling ran so high over the dog that the kings and their retainers betook themselves to their swords and a mighty battle ensued. History does not relate who won the dog.

There are many references to the Hound in Spain. In 1596 the great Spanish poet, Lope de Vega, wrote a sonnet on the Irish Wolfhound, in which he describes one surrounded by an army of curs, barking at him, and says:

"This high born greyhound, without heeding them,
Lifted his leg, wet the projecting angle of the wall,
And through the midst of them went on quite at his ease."

From the twelfth to the sixteenth centuries hunting continued to occupy the attention of the Irish nobles and their chieftains, and their Wolfhounds continued to aid in their great hunts. By the seventeenth century, due to the disappearance of the wolves and elk and the steady depletion of the breed resulting from excessive exportation, a serious shortage of Wolfhounds became apparent in their native land—so much so that an order was passed at a Parliament sitting in Kilkenny in 1652, prohibiting all persons from exporting them.

Some years ago Fredson T. Bowers wrote in the *Gazette:*

"That the history of the Irish Wolfhound is by no means complete as yet is shown by a reference, previously unrecorded, which I recently came upon in a play by William Wycherley, 'The Gentleman Dancing Master,' published in 1672 in London. In this play a Spaniard and a Frenchman are satirically describing each other, and the Frenchman says to the Spaniard: 'And your Spainish hose, and your nose in the air, make you look like a great, grizzled, long Irish greyhound reaching a crust from a high shelf, ha! ha! ha!'

"This is one of the most fruitful references I have read in the past. It comes at a time when the hound has just about finished his work of exterminating the Irish wolves,

14

and before the period of his decline has set in. Therefore, the date is a date when the hound is in his full flower and relative purity of blood, and should be close to the type of the traditional ancient breed. With these considerations in mind, now note the specific words. The hound is 'great,' that is, he is a huge hound, as he is today and has always been. This word is most frequently in the mouths of older writers of the breed.

"The next word is 'grizzled.' Without a doubt this word describes the various colored hairs which go to make up the peculiar characteristic of the hound's color which we know as 'brindle.' Probably Wycherley means also that the total effect is grey, as a person's hair is described as grizzled when its color is changing. More important, this grizzle is almost certainly to be applied only to a long coated dog; and Wycherley has in mind a hound of the present type.

"The next word is 'long,' a singularly appropriate word to describe the rangy conformation of the Wolfhound, especially when he is stretching—as he is in the portrait here—to his full height, and probably on his hind legs, to reach up to the high shelf. This last detail is of the highest interest, for it is meant to emphasize the especial size and length of the dog, in short his great reaching ability, as the most vivid simile Wycherley could employ. Every detail confirms a dog of the characteristics known today, and all are peculiarly pertinent to the special qualities in the hound as we have him at the present time."

Huntsman and hound with dead hare. From Jean de Tournes (1556)

IRISH GREYHOUND, by Reinagle, from Toplin's *Sportsman's Cabinet* (1803). The original is owned by R. Montagu Scott. It was reproduced in Father Hogan's edition of *The Irish Wolfdog*.

Revival of the Breed

THE *Sportsman's Cabinet,* published in 1803, is illustrated by very good engravings, after drawings from life by Reinagle, a Royal Academician. Included is a spirited drawing of an Irish Wolfdog, which, though faulty in minor points, gives an admirable idea of what this grand dog was at that time. The drawing shows a gigantic, rough Greyhound of great power. The text says: "The Irish greyhound is of an ancient race, is still to be found in some remote parts of the kingdom, though they are said to be reduced in size even in their original climate." The original of the engraving is owned by R. Montagu Scott, one of the early supporters of the breed in the twentieth century, whose Ifold Kennels sent many fine Hounds into many lands.

There is evidence that at one time both smooth and rough coated Irish Hounds existed. Father Hogan gives a series of extracts on this and then leaves the reader to judge for himself. A number of breeds have both smooth and rough coated varieties and have evolved that way (for example, the St. Bernard and the Collie). However, in the nineteenth century the rough coated Irish Wolfdog predominated, and after Graham's work, the rough coat was standardized.

The Irish conquered Scotland centuries ago and took their

17

dogs with them. It may be said that the Irish and Scottish Hounds were really two strains of the same breed, altered by circumstances, use, and environment. Of the two, the Irish Hounds were probably the older, with the Scottish claiming the more direct descent. They have been distinct since the twelfth century.

By 1800 the old race was thinning out and comments regarding "the last of the race" were to be heard. There existed, indeed, three or four strains whose owners claimed for them the geniune Irish Wolfdog blood.

In 1841 H. D. Richardson wrote an article on the breed for an Irish journal and illustrated it. He was tremendously enthusiastic and set out to prove that despite claims to the contrary, the Irish Wolfhound was still to be found in Ireland. He collected and continued the breed and handed down not only the actual tradition but the actual strains to Sir John Power of Kilfane, Sir John and Mr. Baker of Ballytobin, and Mr. Mahoney of Dromore.

It was from these strains that Captain George Augustus Graham of Rednock, Dursley, secured specimens and by judicious outcrosses, chiefly with the Scottish Deerhound, sought to rehabilitate the breed. He kept up a constant inquiry for whatever animals could show a descent from the right Irish forebears.

Sir John Power and Mr. Baker were breeding from 1842 to 1873. The Kilfane strain came directly from the Richardson dogs and if it is true that these possessed the ancient ancestry, then the breed never became entirely extinct. Captain Graham fully believed in the authentic antiquity of these strains, and "in their day," these men, who said they had some of the true blood, were known as gentlemen of integrity. Had their beliefs been false, it could easily have been established then, and they proven guilty of misrepresentation. Therefore, it is undoubtedly true that the breed was not extinct in 1800, but that a remnant survived.

We know that there are always dissenters and that ugly rumors find their sustenance in politics, ignorance, and plain avarice. But when rumors have nothing on which to live, they ultimately die. We can agree with Father Hogan's

18

quotation of the proverbial saw that "If it be not Bran, it be his brother."

Captain Graham began his work in 1862, and he deserves *unlimited* credit. He worked for twenty years before his ideal was attained, and the present Standard, to which the modern Hound subscribes, was drafted under his supervision in 1885. The Standard's continued validity is justified inasmuch as it was drawn up after exhaustive study of all old prints and historical references to the Wolfhound, and the findings carefully sifted. The Standard describes the ancient Hound, and the present day effort is to breed the old Wolfdog in fullest perfection.

Patience and persistence marched with Captain Graham, and his work is an inspiration in the history of dog breeding. At first he concentrated on size, but it was long before he could secure uniformity of type. Toward the end of the last century a distinct improvement was achieved and finally O'Leary was whelped. A splendid dog, O'Leary's contribution to the breed is apparent, even to the present day.

In 1885 a club was founded to look after the interests of the breed, to protect and promote it. In the same year Captain Graham revised and completed his book on the Irish Wolfhound, which he had originally compiled in 1879.

In reference to outcrosses, Graham replied to his critics by saying, "I hardly think the breed will be any more 'manufactured' than has been the case with many that are now looked on as pure. 'Recovered' would strike me as a more appropriate term and had it not been for this recovery many of our best national breeds would have disappeared altogether and it has not been accomplished without resorting freely to outcrosses."

This is true. Should it prove disturbing to new breeders of dogs, I can only say it behooves them to study the art of breeding and no better text book can be suggested than Kyle Onstott's book, *The Art of Breeding Better Dogs,* recently revised, and published by Howell Book House. I have often told breeders about Lord Orford's crossing a Bulldog with one of his famous English Greyhounds, and how he had attempted endless experiments to improve the blood but had been disappointed until he made this Bulldog cross. It took seven generations before he obtained by this cross the finest English Greyhounds of the day, dogs with "small ears, rat-tails, and skins almost without hair, together with that *innate courage* . . . rather to die than relinquish the chase."

We know that in rebuilding the Wolfhound breed, Captain Graham used Deerhounds, but they are so closely allied in type as to hardly constitute an outcross. Captain Graham also introduced a single cross of Tibetan Wolfdog. He did not himself use a Dane cross, but the Earl of Caledon, from whom Captain Graham procured some Hounds, had used a Dane, as had Major Granier.

I hold no brief for outcrosses—the work that was needed has been done. It is finished. I mention Kyle Onstott's book as a matter of enlightenment, for I have run into confusion on the part of many breeders. Mr. Onstott explains Mendelism by saying, "It is an inescapable law. Used, it will lead to better dogs; abused, it will wreck any strain."

Captain Graham never forgot the type to which he was trying to keep true, and by breeding in and in on the true strains, he established their predominance over others. The first requisite in such a breeding plan is to form an ideal, which Captain Graham obviously did. Today, the knowledge of inheritance as transmitted by means of the genes and chromosomes renders absurd our former attitude towards the pedigree and methods of analyzing it.

Miss Gardner says, "The fact that Graham's strains bred true in remarkably few generations proves not only that he must have done his work very cleverly, but that the type he was working on was a definite and potent one."

This part of the Hound's history can well close with the advice of the late Joseph A. McAleenan, sent to Walter A. Dyer in 1920 when the latter was about to write a new article on the breed: "I hope you are not going to write of the dog of past centuries. Write of the present dog. The field is large enough and the breed holds an interest that is purely modern. The old Irish dog has had his day and the bards of ancient Ireland have endowed him richly in their songs, weaving a romance about him that will never die.

20

These old pagan songs are well worth reading and the wild rhythm of their cadence bespeaks strong men and momentous events. But *it is the modern dog that counts now.*"

Hound of the Heroes

Huge hound
Great hound
Gray hound and gaunt
Royally imperial
You tower above taunt.

Comrade of chieftain
Grim dog of war
Your fame has been heralded
And hailed from afar.

From Rome of the Caesars
From Spain's classic bard
You've won kingly praises
And knightly award.

The elk of old Erin
You brought to his knees
At the roar of your challenge
The timber wolf flees.

Yet noble descendant
Of fierce fighting sire
You are playing tonight
With my child by the fire.

                —William J. Dammarell

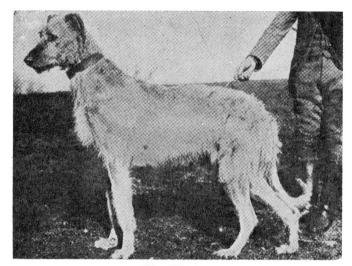

Ch. O'Leary

Brian II

All present-day Irish Wolfhounds can trace direct male-line descent, either to Brian II or to Bran II. The latter was the sire of Ch. O'Leary, and it is through Ch. O'Leary that nearly all the descent from Bran II comes.

Development of the Breed

WITH THE FOUNDING of the Irish Wolf-
hound Club in 1885, the way was paved for orderly growth
of the breed, for members of the club agreed to exercise
care in selecting and breeding from existing specimens.

At the Dublin Show in 1885, a class was scheduled for
Irish Wolfhounds. Twelve Hounds were entered. Since that
year, Irish Wolfhounds have been represented at all principal championship shows in England and Ireland, except,
of course, during the war years.

Among the early sponsors of the breed was John F. Baily,
Esq., of County Dublin, one of the gentlemen mentioned by
Father Hogan in his *History of the Irish Wolfdog*. In en-
deavoring to help the breed, Mr. Baily bought stock of R. T.
Martin of Artane, County Dublin, one of the prominent
breeders and exhibitors.

Mr. Martin owned Ch. Marquis of Donegal, Connaught,
Nuala, Leinster, and others. Donegal was a tall dog, standing some thirty-five to thirty-six inches, and from him
descended many good Hounds. Mr. Martin also owned Ch.
Dhudesia, whom he later sold to Major P. S. Shewell, who
started a successful career from the exhibition point of
view. About this same time, Mr. Bolton started with the

breed. During his many years as a Wolfhound breeder, he bred, among others, a very noted bitch named Cheevra, who went to Mr. A. E. Gerard. Her name can be seen today in some of the old pedigrees.

Mr. George Crisp stayed at the top for many years and bred and owned many notable Wolfhounds, including Ch. O'Leary. 1902 was the year of O'Leary's death. That same year also marked a sort of turning point, at which the breed passed its most difficult time, and after which good conformation was generally to be found, and size was easily attainable in males.

Captain Graham served as the club's first president and held office from 1885-1908; Major Shewell was president from 1910-1915; and J. W. Booth, Esq., J.P., from 1922-1925.

In 1924 an Irish Wolfhound Association was formed and the following year the Association published a "Club Report." Also in 1925, the Association amalgamated with the Irish Wolfhound Club, making a unified front, and the first "Year Book" of the Irish Wolfhound Club was published in 1926. Officers were: President-General, The Earl of Cavan, K.P., G.C.M.G., G.C.V.O., K.C.B.; Vice-Presidents, Mrs. T. H. Barr, Major C. E. W. Beddoes, Captain T. H. Hudson, Miss M. S. Kearns, N. Nagle, Esq., and H. Pemberton, Esq.; Honorary Secretary and Treasurer, K. P. Strohmenger, Esq.

The names of some of the earlier breeders, together with their kennel names, may be useful for reference. Some are still active, some have retired from breed activities, and a few have passed on. We know, of course, that the two devastating wars greatly depleted the ranks of Wolfhoundry.

The list of early breeders is headed by I. W. Everett, for he is credited by many as having carried the breed through World War I, and his *Felixstowe* Hounds were famous all over the world. Mr. Everett passed on in 1950, but he left a heritage of work well done.

Others who were actively successful in the interim between the two world wars were: R. Montagu Scott—*Ifold;* Captain and Mrs. T. H. Hudson—*Brabyns;* Mrs. Barr—*Grevel;* Mrs. Nagle—*Sulhamstead;* Miss M. S. Kearns—*Southwick;* K. P. Strohmenger—*Coval;* Mr. D. le B. Bennett—*Chu-*

lainn; Mrs. Beynon—*Bournstream;* Rev. C. H. Hildebrand—
Clonard; Esther M. Croucher—*Rippingdon;* James V. Rank
—*Ouborough;* Miss N. I. Nichols—*Bradfield;* Phyllis Gard-
ner—*Coolafin;* Miss Ansel—*Pentavalon;* H. Pemberton—
Comberford; Mr. and Mrs. H. L. Crisp—*Hindhead;* H. R.
Fisher—*Lindley;* Mr. T. B. Bolton—*Steyning;* Mrs. M. V.
Massy—*Wealdstone;* E. G. Trousdale—*Lynstone;* Mrs. Knox
—*Raikeshill;* and Dr. R. J. May—*Ballytobin.*

In the 1926 "Year Book" of the club, the late Miss M. S.
Kearns wrote with authority on the "Parental Influence on
Type." We shall quote the first part, which begins with
pre-World War I Hounds:

"I will go back to Brian II and Bran II, the founders of
the two principal strains. Taking Brian II first. Captain
Graham mated him to Nookoo which mating produced
Mrs. G. Williams' Ch. Dermot Asthore, a fine wheaten
hound with black shading, a good rough coat, but just
lacking quality. This dog mated to Mrs. Gerard's Cheevra
produced Ch. Marquis of Donegal, Ch. Sportella and Princess Patricia of Connaught (dam of Ch. Cotswold). They
were not of such good type as their sire, lacking his coat
and outline. Mated to Mr. A. J. Dawson's Tynagh (s. Ch.
O'Leary, d. Lady Kathleen) Dermot Asthore sired quite
another type of hound or rather Tynagh gave the type—
Brian Asthore, Iseult, Wildcroft, Dermot Dhulert and Ch.
Gareth, were all better type than Cheevra's progeny,
showing plainly that in both these cases the bitch gave
the type, as in neither litter were they Dermot Asthore's
type.

"Going back to Brian II. Mated to Mr. Birtill's Tuefella
he produced Mrs. G. Williams' Ch. Wargrave and Mr. W.
Williams' Ch. Daireen and Ballyhooley. I never saw Teu-
fella but have heard that she was beautiful. Captain
Graham gave Ch. Daireen the prize for best type in a big
entry at the Kennel Club Show 1902. This was my first
K. C. Show, and I knew very little about it, of course, but
admired Daireen immensely. She and her two brothers
I considered the most beautiful dogs I had ever seen. They

25

were all three wheaten, the two dogs light like their sire Brian II, Daireen red. Ch. Wargrave mated to Miss Pope's Laragh sired Mrs. G. Williams' Ch. Artara, a very beautiful bitch and one of the best Wolfhounds of her day of either sex. Captain Graham awarded her the bitch challenge certificate at that same K. C. Show (1902). Mated to Mr. Allen's Acushla (s. Ch. O'Leary, d. Lady Kathleen) Wargrave produced Aughrim, a very beautiful type like his sire, but with more quality and the most perfect head of his day, and I have never seen a head to equal it yet, though some of his descendants have run it close. It is wonderful how this type persists in this line, it has even come down through Ch. Ivo Dennis (s. Aughrim, d. Ivo Drogheda) a son of AUGHRIM and rather like him. His grandson, SULHAMSTEAD PEDLAR, sired Mr. Everett's Ch. Felixstowe KILCULLEN (s. Sulhamstead Pedlar, d. Sarah) who is also wonderfully like her great, great grandsire. Aughrim mated to Mr. C. E. Palmer's Hibernia sired perhaps the most beautiful Wolfhound we have had —the huge Donegal who stood 37½ inches and was a larger edition of his sire, not quite such a beautiful head but the same lovely quality. He died of distemper when only 16 months old, before he had attained his full development or lost his awkward puppy movement and nervousness. He raised a storm of jealous criticism, as all extra beautiful dogs do, and his detractors would not allow anything for his youth, I suppose because they knew that if he lived he could beat anything they ever bred. His dam, Hibernia, was quite a small light wheaten bitch but very beautiful and remarkably like Aughrim, which I suppose accounts for the wonderful likeness in their puppy. Sulhamstead Pedlar was descended from Aughrim's son Ch. Ivo Dennis and this beautiful Hibernia, and thus we get Ch. Felixstowe Kilcullen, about the same size as Donegal and with a good deal of his beauty. A daughter of Aughrim, Wyck Biddy (s. Aughrim, d. Wyke Mark Colleen) rather like her sire with his beautiful head, passed on the type to all her puppies, particularly to Mr. F. E. Dawson's Llantarnam Tara (s. Conn, d. Wyck Biddy) and

26

Biddy's, *i.e.,* Aughrim's type appears to a striking degree in her great-grandchildren, proving that a bitch certainly can transmit type, and this is a purer strain than Pedlar's as down to Biddy's sons and daughters there is no trace of the Felixstowe Dane cross.

"Going back to Ch. Wargrave, mated to Mrs. Herbert Compton's Wolfe Colleen, he produced Wolfe Tone and Dr. Pitts Tucker's Juno of the Fen. These two hounds were quite a different type to any of Wargrave's other progeny, again proving that they took their type from their dam. Wolfe Tone mated to Major Shewell's Princess Patricia of Connaught (s. Ch. Dermot Asthore, d. Cheevra) produced Ch. Cotswold Patricia. Juno of the Fen mated to Mr. Walter Williams' Finn (s. Bran II, d. Roseen Ruaidh) produced Felixstowe Dromore, dam of Ch. Felixstowe Kilronan (s. Ch. Cotswold, d. Felixstowe Dromore).

"Now we will take Bran II, founder of the second strain. Mated to Princess Oona he produced Ch. O'Leary. I never saw O'Leary alive, but I have seen him in the Natural History Museum, South Kensington. One cannot tell much from this what he was really like, but Captain Graham, when I first joined the Irish Wolfhound Club, told me to go and study him for type. I would have liked better to study him in life. I believe he was a very typical hound, by no means big, but with plenty of quality. He gives quality wherever he appears in a pedigree. Mated to Princess Patricia of Connaught, he sired Ch. Cotswold, a beautiful wheaten hound full of quality and type. Born in 1902 he was first shown at Cruft's 1903, he retired after the C. C. Show, October, 1908, and in that time was never beaten, and held the Graham Shield for six years. He has not given his type to his progeny in any great degree. Mated to Mr. Pemberton's Frona (s. Thady O'Flyn, d. Brenda) he produced two bitches, one Mr. Pemberton's Cynethrith, dam of Bolebrook Frona (s. Ch. Lindley Hector, d. Cinethrith) and grand dam of Comberford Mick (s. Wyke Mark Dan O'Hagarty, d. Bolebrook Frona). The other Major Shewell's Cotswold Kelpie, a beautiful

27

wheaten bitch sold abroad when quite young. These two bitches took their type from Frona, who never bred a bad puppy. Mated to Miss McCheane's Wolf Watch, Cotswold produced Cotswold Watch, a small brindle hound, sound but very ordinary. Mated to Felixstowe Dromore he produced Cotswold Bloom and Ch. Felixstowe Kilronan. Cotswold Bloom was a very tall, good-looking brindle bitch who mated to Mr. Pemberton's Cenwulph (s. Ch. Gareth, d. Frona) produced Thommond, a very tall, lightly built hound of good type. Ch. Felixstowe Kilronan, a red wheaten hound, was the tallest dog of his day until Donegal appeared. Mated to Mr. Pemberton's Frona, in one litter he sired Mr. Pemberton's King Offa and Ch. Creoda and Dr. Fisher's Lindley Biddy and Ch. Lindley Lupin. All this litter had their dam's type. Frona's second litter by him produced Mr. Pemberton's Andy, a tall red dog very like Kilronan. This dog should have done much better than he did, but had the misfortune to appear when the judges had a mania for the coarse, heavy Dane type, and was again and again beaten by dogs who could not hold a candle to him for type and soundness. Kilronan mated to Miss Windley's Good Hope (s. Ivo O'Niel, d. Adel Colleen) sired Mrs. Heywood's Wyke Mark Dan O'Hagarty. Born in February, 1914, he is the sire of many present day hounds. Mr. Pemberton's Comberford Mick (s. Wyke Mark Dan O'Hagarty, d. Bolebrook Frona) is not like Dan and most of Mick's puppies have a distinct likeness to Ch. Lindley Hector, Bolebrook Frona's sire. Dan mated to the Rev. C. H. Hildebrand's Sarah, sired many good hounds, among them Mr. Hildebrand's Ch. Rachel, Mr. Bradbury's David, Mrs. Southey's Crewkerne Georgie, Mrs. Bennett's Deborah, Captain Hudson's Colleen of Brabyns, and many others. Mated to Mr. Montagu Scott's Deirdre of Ifold, he sired Ch. Patrick of Ifold, Mrs. Massy's Wolf of Ifold, Mrs. Ellis' Gerg of Ifold and Mr. Butler's Findchoem of Ifold. None of these hounds take their type from their sire.

"The two hounds that have done the most to rescue the breed after the war are Hindhead Mollie (s. Hy. Niall, d.

Norah) and Sulhamstead Pedlar (s. Bryan, d. Lady Alma of Sheepey). Mollie appears in most present day pedigrees. She was bred by Mrs. H. L. Crisp, and was a light grey bitch, not very big, but very nice type."

Mrs. Nagle gives us an insight into conditions during World War I when she says:

"I had my first Irish Wolfhound in 1913. I bred one litter during the first World War, at that time the Kennel Club would not register any pedigreed dogs except bred by their special permissions, which was rarely given owing to the food position. In that litter was Sulhamstead Pedlar, who later made a great name as a sire. He sired Mr. Everett's unbeaten 37½ inch Ch. Felixstowe Kilcullen and was the grandsire of Sulhamstead Dan exported to America, who became the ancestor of many famous American hounds. The line from Kilcullen was carried on by his brother, a large, very plain hound, Felixstowe Kilbarry, who sired Ch. Sulhamstead Conncara, out of Caragh, a great brood bitch, dam of Int. Ch. Sulhamstead Thelma, Ch. Acushla of Ouborough and Ch. Clodagh of Ouborough. These were all top class hounds.

"Ch. Sulhamstead Conncara was one of the greatest sires in the breed, and his name is in nearly every Irish Wolfhound pedigree many times over. He had size, 36 in., quality and soundness and type. His was a romantic story, as he was born blind and his breeder Mrs. Lockhart was going to put him down but I had pick of the litter and went to see him and I thought he was the best Irish Wolfhound puppy I had ever seen, so I brought him home at six weeks old. He was blind but so outstanding I showed him and he got his title and nobody ever knew he was blind until I told them after he retired from the bench. He sired many great Champions including Ch. Galleon of Ouborough and never produced a blind puppy.

"During the last war very few Irish Wolfhounds were bred but the breed was just kept going, and just before that war I had another great dog Ch. Sulhamstead Fella

Mr. Montagu Scott's Ch. Patrick of Ifold. Winner of Irish Guards Shield, Lord Waring Model and challenge certificate, K. C. Show, 1924, challenge certificate, Richmond, 1924, and LKA, 1925.

Ch. Sulhamstead Mary

Ch. Rippingdon Rathgelert, whelped September 1, 1950, by Ch. Kerryman of Boroughbury ex Rippingdon Tessa of Boroughbury.

Ch. Sulhamstead Manna, winner of Graham Shield, 1956; champion certificate, Crufts, 1955; Green Star, Dublin, 1956; challenge certificate and best of breed, W.E.L. K.S. By Ch. Sanctuary Rory of Kihone ex Ch. Sulhamstead Mesa.

who at ten months won the Challenge certificate and the Brewers Cup for the Best Hound at Birmingham. His sister Sulhamstead Fara was sent to America at the beginning of the war, became a champion and the dam of some great hounds.

"Clonboy of Ouborough, a son of Ch. Chulainn Casey, was the sire that produced the best hounds during the last War. He sired Ch. Artel Ballykelly Sandy, his brother a great sire out of a daughter of Ch. Sulhamstead Fella. Clonboy also sired Int. Ch. Mulligan of Boroughbury, and Ch. Ouborough McCarthy of Boroughbury, both bred by Mrs. James."

Ch. Mulligan of Boroughbury sired Ch. Kerrymand of Boroughbury, the sire of Rippingdon Gelert.

In writing of the Hounds that had the most influence on the breed, Miss Croucher comments that Hindhead Mollie had a lot to do in stabilizing the breed but that none can get away from the influence of Ch. Sulhamstead Conncara and his descendant, Ch. Rippingdon Dan of Southwick. The two bitches whose names appear in most pedigrees are Ch. Biddy of Ouborough and Sweetbriar of Rippingdon; they, again, are in every present day pedigree if traced back far enough.

The recent English club book covers the seventeen years prior to publication, and in an article about the Hounds since the war, Mrs. Nagle says: "Things were now getting crucial, as every hound traced straight back to Clonboy of Ouborough and it was imperative to have an outcross. Thanks to the kindness of Miss Jeannette McGregor of America, who gave Rory of Kihone to the Irish Wolfhound Club, the situation has been saved. Rory was selected by Miss Croucher during her visit to America as being suitable to mate with English bitches. She went for quality, conformation and soundness. The result of his mating to Sulhamstead Felcara has been Sulhamstead Freda, winner of two C.C.'s and best of breed at Crufts, and Sulhamstead Fellus, winner of Ch. Certificate, the Graham Shield and best of breed at the L.K.A. Rory's mating to Sulhamstead

31

Mesa produced Sulhamstead Manna, winner of two Challenge Certificates, and Sulhamstead Melba, winner of C.C. at Birmingham. His mating to Sedlestan Sandra produced Sedlestan Rosalie, reserve Certificate at the L.K.A., and to Spark of Boroughbury he produced Sanctuary Symbol and Sanctuary Serene, good winners in the Junior Classes." Mated to Rippingdon Rhapsody, Rory produced Rippingdon Brackenbury Rhythm, a winner at ten months of age.

Rory of Kihone now belongs to Miss Harrison and Miss Atfield. He has won his championship and has made good use of great opportunities offered him, the pick of the winning bitches visiting him.

Mrs. Nagle adds, "We now have Mrs. Van Brunt's Ch. Barney O'Shea over here, which will provide more valuable outcross blood. He will be the second Cragwood Irish Wolfhound imported from America, as many years ago Cragwood Darragh came over, and his best daughter Ch. Iduna of Hindhead bred many Champions and left a great mark on the breed.

"It is to be hoped that now the breed is on its feet again, more people will take them up. Actually they are not big eaters for their size and do not require any more exercise than other dogs."

The lifeblood of any successful breed club is an active, interested, capable secretary, since all else will then fall in order. It's interesting to note that K. P. Strohmenger served as secretary until 1930, when he continued on as treasurer and Mrs. Nagle assumed the secretaryship; and in 1937 Mrs. Nagle was both secretary and treasurer. World War II brought changes, since everyone was busy winning the war. From 1939 to 1954 Miss E. M. Croucher was the secretary and Miss Marion Clark was treasurer—a position she still holds. In 1955 Major J. H. L. Godfrey became the honorary secretary, a post he held until 1960, when ill health forced him to resign. He was succeeded by William Marriott.

In 1664 Katherine Phillips, otherwise known as "The Matchless Orindo," wrote a poem about an Irish Greyhound. Katherine Phillips was born in London but went to Dungan-

non, Ireland, as a child. Although there are various versions
of this poem, this is the original:

"Behold this Creature's Form and State
Which Nature therefore did create
That to the World might be exprest
What mien there can be in a Beast,
And that we in this shape may find
A Lion of another kind,
For this Heroick beast does seem
In Majesty to rival him;
And yet vouchsafes, to Man, to show
Both service and submission too.
From when we this distinction have,
That Beast is fierce, but this is brave.
This Dog hath so himself subdu'd
That hunger cannot make him rude,
And his behaviour doth confess
True Courage dwells with Gentleness.
With sternest Wolves he does engage
And acts on them successful rage.
Yet too much courtesie may chance
To put him out of countenance.
When in his opposer's blood
Fortune hath made his vertue good,
This Creature from an act so brave
Grows not more sullen, but more grave.
Man's Guard he would be, not his sport,
Believing he hath ventur'd for't;
But yet no blood or shed or spent
Can ever make him insolent."

Ch. Finbarr Boroimhe, model for the Irish six-penny
piece, and winner of the Irish Guards Shield, 1928.

Ch. Mulligan of Boroughbury (whelped 1944) and his son
Kerryman of Boroughbury at 14 months (whelped 1947).

The Irish Wolfhound Club of Ireland

THE LATE T. W. Corcoran, Esq., of Dublin was the founder of the Irish Wolfhound Club of Ireland and his Hounds were well known. He was the owner of Int. Ch. Finbar Boroimhe, who was used as a model by the artist who designed the Irish sixpenny piece.

In 1939 a conjoint reprint of the original editions of Father Hogan's *The Irish Wolfdog* (1897) and Captain Graham's *The Irish Wolfhound* (1879) was published by the Irish Wolfhound Club of Ireland (affiliated with the Irish Kennel Club). President of the club at that time was R. J. May, Esq., F.R.C.S.I., of Glenview, Swords, County Dublin.

The editing of the volume was deputed by the club to a subcommittee consisting of the president, Dr. May, and Phyllis Gardner, with the added help of the secretary, Mrs. Lait.

"This mass of evidence about the history of the Irish Wolfdog will probably never appeal to a very great number of readers," comments Miss Gardner, "but those few who do want it, want it very keenly. By its aid they should be able to dispel many false ideas, and to uphold the proud position of our noble hound as the worthy successor of a long continuity of blood and tradition from the remote past."

The Standard for the Irish Wolfhound is the same in Ireland and England, so there are no appreciable differences in the qualities of the dogs from the two countries. There were also good Hounds to be seen in Austria, Holland, and Belgium before World War II. Many Hounds were lost during the war, although everything was done by soldiers on both sides of the line to help the dogs along.

Dr. May, in his article "The National Dog of Ireland," tells us this story:

"At evacuation of the British Expeditionary Forces from the beach at Dunkirk in June, 1940, one was found straying on the sands by a soldier, an Ulsterman. He recognized it to be an Irish Wolfhound and with the permission of his officer, another Irishman, he brought the hound with him in a boat to England. After the necessary quarantine, the hound was brought to a military camp in Co. Antrim, and became the mascot of the regiment and the good friend of all the people in a nearby town. He responded to the name of Paddy and was made welcome in every house in the neighborhood.

"His history is bound up with the history of Ireland. He lived before history was born. He goes back to the mystic period of charmed romance, of legend, myth and fairy tale. His name is linked with round towers, ancient harps and shamrocks. He was the faithful companion and devoted friend of our Irish Saints (St. Patrick, St. Kevin and St. Brigid) as well as that of Kings, Warriors and Chieftains of Ireland." The Wolfhound has made his way into museums, and Mr. Crisps' Ch. O'Leary is to be seen in the London Museum of Natural History, while Mr. Richard O'Mahony's Kilcullen is to be found in the National Museum in Dublin.

The following is from an article by Macneill of Colonsay on the ancient Scottish and Irish Hound:

"An eye of sloe, with ear not low
With horse's breast, and breadth of chest,
With breadth of loin, and curve in groin,
And nape set far behind the head,
Such were the hounds that Fingal bred."

Monmouth County Show, May 25, 1957. Barbara O'Neill's Ch. Sir Gelert of Ambleside (l), and Celeste Hutton with her Ch. Cristel of Ambleside (r).

Irish Wolfhound Club Specialty, 1957. Left, Suzanne Bellinger's Ch. Owen of Killybracken, winners dog and best opposite sex; right, Mrs. Mary Britcher's Ch. Sweet Kathy of Kilrain, best of breed.

An old group picture taken at Halcyon Farms,
as Halcyon Kennels was starting in Wolfhounds (probably about 1929).
To the left of the late Mrs. E. T. Clark is Ch. Felixstowe Kilgarth. To the right is Ch. Felixstowe Kilbagie.
In front are Felixstowe Kilmichael, Princess of Coval, and Chulainn Dauntless.

The Irish Wolfhound in America

NO ONE KNOWS the exact time the first Irish Wolfhound was brought into the United States. We know Father Hogan, in his book, refers to some exportations to America, and from time to time other references to such exportations are made in articles by various writers on "both sides." And we do know when the first one was registered by The American Kennel Club. The Newry Hounds of Joseph A. McAleenan on Long Island were among the pioneer registrations from 1912 and, close on these, were the Wolfhounds registered by the Toyon Kennels of Horace Hill.

In 1926 Mrs. Norwood B. Smith wrote an article for the English club book on the breed in the Unitel States. In it she says:

"There are two distinct groups of Irish Wolfhounds in America. Both are registered in the American Kennel Stud Book, yet they are as different as a Collie and a Shetland Sheep Dog. These little Irish Wolfhounds seem to have originated in a Polyglot Kennel, well known to almost every American breeder. We have seen a number of these dogs and many of their pedigrees, but have failed to find a familiar name. . . . The bitches weigh around 75 pounds and the dogs occasionally reach a hundred. They are more a small rough coated greyhound than what is demanded by the Irish Wolfhound Club Standard.

"These little hounds are apparently produced in great numbers and find a ready market at $25.00. Naturally the buyer feels that a registered dog will qualify as to standard. They are bought by ranchers for coyote dogs, for which purpose they are no doubt well suited. Many buy them for pets and later seeing a typical hound, wonder why their 'dog is so small when he is so well-bred.' Their idea of well-bred being a five generation pedigree.

"Until about 5 years ago (written in 1926—Ed.), it was not necessary for a dog's sire and dam to be registered in order to register a dog. Merely a five generation pedigree and one dollar placed his name on record as a dog of this or that breed. However it happened, these weird creatures are masquerading as Irish Wolfhounds and have been for ten or fifteen years.

"Fortunately the true Irish Wolfhound, dogs that boast the best blood of England, is a great and ever increasing band and the time is not far distant when these little counterfeits will be crowded out. No sane man could doubt for an instant which was the true dog."

In 1926 we started to exhibit a few or our Wolfhounds and we "met" some of these little imposters. We had known about them, since we had corresponded with one of the kennels producing them, but just happened not to have been taken in by their elaborate brochure and a picture of a truly BIG Wolfhound, which they did not own, and the usual backdrop of romantic aura.

The judges at shows proved a great help in establishing true Wolfhound type. When real Wolfhounds started to appear in the show rings, judges were alert to notice the difference and they started handing out second and third prize ribbons to the small Hounds when there was only one in the class. When the exhibitor remonstrated, the judge had only to bring into the ring one of "the true race" and things were soon settled. For YEARS they didn't reappear.

Then someone in the Southwest started breeding dogs that LOOKED like these. The breeders CALLED them Irish Wolfhounds, but would tell their customers they could NOT give papers. That cleared the breeders from misrepresentation—but the club is aware that only eternal vigilance will keep the imposters from cropping up again, so the subject rates notice here.

While we can give a list of early Wolfhound owners and the names of their dogs, the important part is to note the Hounds that have "done something" for the breed. I have already mentioned Mr. McAleenan. His Newry Hounds are found in many of the earliest pedigrees in this country. A few found their way into Long Island homes.

About the time Mr. McAleenan was exhibiting his early Wolfhounds, Albert J. Davis of Jericho, Long Island, imported some good ones and bred a few, using the name Jericho in registering the dogs. Mr. Davis also bought some of Mr. McAleenan's Newry Hounds. Several Hounds carrying the prefix of Dr. and Mrs. H. R. Fisher were imported, as were some of the early Felixstowe Hounds. Felixstowe was a name that was to carry considerable weight in America for many years to come.

Through Mr. Mason of Southport fame in England, one of these early Felixstowe Hounds was imported by Horace Hill, and the dog's name became Toyon Southport St. Patrick. Toyon, the kennel name taken by Mr. Hill, is the Indian name for "California Holly" and was also the name of Mr. Hill's ranch.

I have tried but failed to get a picture of Toyon Southport St. Patrick. I saw a picture years ago, but have been unable to get a duplicate. He was a beautiful Hound and his name is in the pedigrees of many of our present day American Hounds. He was whelped in 1913, bred by Mr. I. W. Everett of Felixstowe Kennels, and came to this country when not quite a year old.

The pedigree of Toyon Southport St. Patrick can be found in *Fifty Years of Irish Wolfhound Registrations in America,* the book by LeRoy E. Fess which was published by the Irish Wolfhound Club. This book gives full particulars of the pedigree of each of the 2,265 Wolfhounds registered in America by The American Kennel Club from the first one in 1897, up to and including those registered in 1955.

To those who love to compile extended pedigrees, this book is a "must." Having kept one for our personal use, we have found such ready reference a source of satisfaction many times. We do need to remember that many fine dogs are never shown—so their history remains unsung. Records can but give the names of the Hounds that have done considerable winning, and with their listed pedigrees, one can find the Hounds that have contributed in a large measure to the continuance of the breed.

Of the earlier Eastern breeders, Robert M. Barker of Syracuse, New York, built up a fine, exclusive kennel of Hounds, housing some imports from England and from France, as well as his home-bred Rudraighe Hounds. Mr. Barker was good publicity material and many articles were written about him and his Hounds by well known authors, and appeared in some of the class magazines of that period—from 1916 to 1920.

Mrs. Glen Stewart of Cape Centaur, Maryland, imported a few and established a select kennel. Her Bally Shannon affix was well known.

In California, Sylvester Spaulding, who imported Felixstowe Magee, occasionally bred a litter. And G. G. Moore had an ambitious kennel and bred from descendants of his imported Gweebarra.

It was in 1915 that Mrs. Norwood B. Smith visited the Toyon Kennels of Mr. Hill and found Wolfhounds to be "all she had imagined them to be—and then some." Mrs. Smith was interested in St. Bernards at the time and did not feel she could launch out on a new breed at once, but the desire was born. When she did become active in the breed, her first Hounds were Toyon Bridget and Toyon Irish Elegance; the latter was bred by Mr. Hill and the former by Mr. McAleenan. Then Mrs. Smith purchased Toyon Diana, who became her first champion of the breed. It was in June 1921 that the first litter of Wolfhounds was registered under the Cragwood name in The American Kennel Club Stud Book.

Frank Hall of Piedmont was active in the breed and Mrs. H. S. Bonestell had one of his dogs, sired by Cragwood Egan, as did Mrs. A. T. Pettey. The Bonestell dog was exceptionally large and sound and his picture appeared from coast to coast in a Sunday-supplement feature.

Mrs. Smith was shipping some of her stock East, and Robert Hare Davis of Philadelphia acquired some, as did Robert Barker. In March 1924, Mrs. Smith shipped a pair to Mr. and Mrs. L. O. Starbuck, which marked the beginning of the Ambleside Kennels in Michigan.

In the fall of 1926 The American Kennel Club held a "model" show during the Sesqui-Centennial in Philadelphia, and Mrs. Smith contacted all the new owners of Wolfhounds as well as all the owners of long standing, and urged them to come to the Sesqui-Centennial and show their Hounds. Fourteen Wolfhounds were entered, and although it was one of the biggest dog shows, with close to three thousand dogs entered, Wolfhounds had but two classes and in these they were not divided by sex. It was just this sort of thing that had inspired Mrs. Smith to get together a group of people who were interested in Wolfhounds, and to try to promote the breed's interests and to acquaint the public with their grand qualities.

A meeting was held. E. Francis Riggs was appointed chairman and L. O. Starbuck became the temporary secretary. Two hundred dollars was subscribed at once and the wheels were started to form a club and apply for membership in The American Kennel Club.

The exhibitors in attendance at this meeting were Mr. and Mrs. R. Hare Davis, Mr. and Mrs. Charles Daly, Mr. and Mrs. Francis Riggs, Miss E. Frances Jones, Mr. and Mrs. L. O. Starbuck, and Mrs. Norwood B. Smith. The next meeting was scheduled to be held at the following Westminster Show—in February 1927.

Mrs. N. T. Bellinger's Ch. King Lir of Ambleside.
Best in show, all breeds, 1931. First American-bred Wolfhound to go best in show.

Ch. Barn Hill Dan Malone, owned
by Killybracken Kennels. A best
in show, all breeds, Hound, 1950.

Edgecliff Kennels' Ch. Brian Boru
of Edgecliff. A best in show,
all breeds, four times in 1950.

The Irish Wolfhound Club of America

THE WESTMINSTER SHOW of 1927 saw sixteen Hounds benched, and the club meeting, which had been planned at the Sesqui-Centennial, took place. A charter had been granted by The American Kennel Club, so the Irish Wolfhound Club of America took its place in the governing body of The American Kennel Club. Officers were elected and a delegate to the AKC was appointed. The officers were: President, Mrs. Norwood Browning Smith, and Governing Committee, Mr. Charles Daly, Mr. Robert Hare Davis, Mr. E. Francis Riggs, Mrs. N. B. Smith, and Mr. L. O. Starbuck. Mr. Monson Morris was then appointed delegate to The American Kennel Club, and Mr. L. O. Starbuck was appointed honorary secretary-treasurer.

The club patterned itself a great deal after the Wolfhound Club in England. The same Standard was adopted, and it was decided that a committee would be elected annually, but that the president and vice-president would be elected for three-year terms. All officers were to serve ex-officio on the committee. We were "feeling our way" and at the time didn't even have any elected vice-presidents. Later, as we grew, this changed and the vice-presidents were elected to try to cover the country regionally. But people

45

have a way of moving about, so this idea did not always work out as it had been planned.

New and important Wolfhound enthusiasts joined the club. Among them were Mr. and Mrs. Edward T. Clark of Goshen, New York, who brought in some of England's best Wolfhounds, and their Halcyon Kennels became as famous for their Irish Wolfhounds as it already was for their Welsh Terriers.

Our first "Club Report," with the usual club data, appeared in our 1927-28 club book. This first book brought the first "President's Message" by Mrs. Smith and it is as good today as when first written. There is no age nor time to this message. Mrs. Smith was a leader of vision. Omitting the opening paragraphs and the closing, we quote it as it was written:

"The Irish Wolfhound has improved much within the last ten years. Our judges are coming more and more to demand soundness. The time was when a St. Bernard won by his head, so it seemed, and it was suggested that some of the exhibitors provide themselves with wheelbarrows to bring in the rear of their dogs. How much more important that the Irish Wolfhound, a sporting breed, should be sound and able to move with ease and grace. Soundness and a conformation suitable to its purpose in life is one of the prime requisites of all breeds. Size is intriguing. The untrained eye can recognize and appreciate bigness, a beautiful color and a fine coat, just as all register pleasure in hearing a simple musical air. To catch all the nuances in a great masterpiece the ear must have received technical training. This is the recognition of quality and the lack of ability to define quality is the reason that so often those along the side lines cannot follow the judging. We must guard against catering to the applause of the gallery and being content if we merely produce a huge, spectacular hound. Our Irish Wolfhound belongs in the classical, not the jazz class. He is more than just the largest breed of dog, he is the greatest.

"Many of our hounds now measure thirty-six inches and

46

over and weigh one hundred and fifty pounds at one year. I doubt if the breed can with safety stand more size unless by some miracle we can lengthen the growing period. As it now is, Jack's Bean Stalk is the only thing that has the edge on him.

"Points to be stressed are shoulders, stifles, back line and hocks. No horse or dog with a straight shoulder can really run. The straight shoulder belongs to the draught animal. Let us watch our stifles that they are well bent, giving a graceful sweep to the hind legs and enabling the dog to push himself along when running instead of just pounding the ground. The back must arch to act as a sort of spring which recoils with every bound. The loin furnishes the motive power for driving the hind legs so must be broad and strong. The lung cavity must be large but not too wide. Given this big, useful frame we may turn our attention to ears which sadly need 'fixing.' We meet all sorts of ears. Three quarters of them are wrong. The Standard is quite clear on the subject. They should be small and folded like a greyhound's. Many of our hounds when relaxed carry them Dane fashion. Eyes over here as a rule are good. The coat seems to vary from the almost smooth coat to something akin to the Old English Sheepdog. Whatever its length it should be coarse. A fine silky or fuzzy coat is an abomination as it soaks up water and all sorts of burrs stick to it. Brows, eyelashes and whiskers are necessary to impart the true Irish expression and these should adorn a long, rather lean head with plenty before the eyes and showing strength to the end of the muzzle."

Due to the great area of the United States, the club decided at the 1927 meeting to support two shows each year: the Westminster classic at Madison Square Garden, New York City, and one other show, preferably an out-of-doors show, where the classes might be considered "Our Specialty." Club members were to work for entries and offer a club plate at each fixture.

At that time the greater entries normally came to Westminster and, as it was a three-day show, the club decided to hold the annual business meeting at that time. This worked very well for a few years and a drive was made to encourage members to take their Hounds to Westminster. These efforts brought the first big entries. The club was also fortunate in that several good sized kennels were located within a reasonable distance of New York. This helped the entry, particularly in the puppy class.

The first biennial club book, published for 1927-28, carried the club's by-laws, the breed Standard, membership list, and the list of trophies that were donated through the efforts of enthusiastic and unselfish members. The membership list does not, of course, include all of the Wolfhound owners of the time. Not all Wolfhound owners show, but owners who enjoy showing, and especially breeding a few of the good ones, usually become club members.

A complete list of trophies and their winners is a part of the club's records and such information comes to the members through their club books. No trophy lists are given here. They often vary or change in name, as they are won outright. The rules governing them are subject to change by The American Kennel Club and many of the fine trophies we used to have are no longer permissible.

It was much fun "while they lasted." But I also appreciate the complex judging problems that arise when we are sponsoring classes at an all-breed show and calling it "Our Specialty." Perhaps now that the club is having its own specialty, divorced from any other show activity, with its own superintendent, judge, catalogue, etc., it may be possible that some of the trophies that have been discontinued can again be found at our specialty. That, of course, will be in accordance with the will of the club members. We used to have cups for the most typical Hound, the tallest, the soundest and best moving, and I recall at one show we even had a cup for the best eyes and best ears. We may have outgrown some of this. I still think the cup awarded for best type, and the cup for best-moving Hound serve a purpose.

Before continuing with the club's subsequent growth, further records of the Hounds and owners that were to contribute to the breed's history should be considered.

48

One of the very early owners and breeders, so far not mentioned, was Neil O. Broderson, of New Jersey, whose Trailmoor Kennels was active as far back as 1917. He had some of Dr. and Mrs. Fisher's Lindley stock, and he had Hounds from G. G. Moore and others. Beginning about 1935 the name reads Edwin C. Broderson, but still with the Trailmoor prefix. Trailmoor Wolfhounds are found in many of the earlier pedigrees and one whelped in 1935 became Ch. Trailmoor Lady Colleen after she was purchased by Paul F. Paine. She has been very useful to the breed. Mated to Mr. Paine's Conbec Tailteann, she produced Ch. Barn Hill Daisy, and mated to Padraic of Summerhill, she became the dam of the illustrious Ch. Barn Hill Hilda, who was an outstanding show Hound and perfect matron, raising such sons as Ch. Barn Hill Dan Malone and the Pacific Coast winner, Ch. Barn Hill Gilda.

In 1924 Mrs. Eloise Butler Duncan on Long Island had Wolfhounds. The first were from Centaur Kennels, bred by Mrs. Stewart, but for many, many years Mrs. Duncan kept a few Wolfhounds in her home and gardens and was a quiet but capable member of the Irish Wolfhound Club after it was formed.

In 1926 Herbert B. Shaw of Boston was active, and his imported Torna of Brayyns did considerable winning. Also in Massachusetts was Malcolm B. Stone, who bred a litter in 1927, and Eben Draper, who did some breeding too. In Maryland the E. F. Riggs were developing their Chillum Kennels.

Also in 1927, Mr. and Mrs. Edward T. Clark made a trip to England and France to bring back to their Halcyon Kennels stock that was outstanding from the breeding and showing angles. Some of the best in the breed came to reside in their kennels and the fact that they continued to import the best for many years, did a great service to the breed. They first brought in the French Hound Chialiapine du Prieure, and Ch. Chulainn Dauntless, a Hound that won the "type cup" in England. In August 1928, Dauntless produced Halcyon's first Irish Wolfhound litter, sired by the French import. At this time the Clarks brought in Ch. Felixstowe Kilbagie.

In 1928, Charles D. Burrage, Jr., of Boston, brought home one of Mr. Draper's Hounds, Beowulf, and Rathain Kennels came into being. From 1944 until his death in June 1960, Charles Burrage served as honorary secretary-treasurer of the Irish Wolfhound Club, and the club's success is due in great measure to his unceasing work on the club affairs, to which he devoted so much of his time. Besides his activities as secretary-treasurer of the club, Mr. Burrage held a license to judge all Hound breeds.

In these years history was constantly being born. In late 1928, Mr. and Mrs. C. Groverman Ellis, who were then living in Chicago, purchased their first Wolfhound for their son Leonard Ellis. A mate joined the first Hound and their first litter was whelped in Chicago. Then they purchased a large farm near Wayne, Illinois, and the Wolfhounds became a real part of Killybracken Farms. Both Wolfhounds and Cairn Terriers are sponsored at Killybracken Kennels, and both are well known from coast to coast.

Mr. Arthur G. Wyman of Los Altos, California, purchased Wolfhounds at this time from Ambleside and Cragwood and from Mr. Moore. Mr. Wyman was active on the Pacific Coast for a few years before his untimely death.

In 1929 Eugene Lilly's Lilly Pond Kennels sent out some very excellent stock and later there was a partnership there with Frank J. Cusak. Mr. Lilly started the successful Boyer Ranch Kennels in Wyoming and three times he shipped bitches from his Colorado Springs place to Augusta, Michigan, to be bred in Ambleside Kennels.

In the early thirties there were several owners who showed and bred and devoted real effort to promoting the breed. The Whippoorwill Kennels of the late Mrs. Amory L. Haskell was one of these. I seem to recall hearing Mr. Haskell tell me that a Wolfhound puppy was one of the gifts he took Mrs. Haskell when he was courting her. The puppy was very young and I believe he presented it in a hat box. I know their interest and affection for the Irish Wolfhound is a "long-time thing." Eventually some Hounds came to Woodland Farms and some of Captain Hudson's best were imported. The Haskells' Ch. King Shane of Brabyns can be found back in the pedigree of some of the present day winners. I believe Mr. Haskell still feels King Shane typified what an active Hound should be—a potential hunter.

Another owner who established a fine kennel at this time is Miss F. Jeannette McGregor. Her Kihone Kennels have been, and still are, a great contribution to the world of Wolfhounds. She purchased Sulhamstead Flute, when his owner had to part with him after his importation, and she showed him successfully at major shows. Miss McGregor brought back Ch. Chulainn Casey one year when she returned from Europe. Casey was a son of Rippingdon Dan of Southwick and a great-grandson of Ch. Felixstowe Kilmorac and Ch. Galleon of Ouborough. He sired some stock in England before he came over, which was a fortunate thing as he sired but one litter in this country after he arrived. He made a rapid championship but died very suddenly. His death was a great shock for he was well one day and gone the next, with no history of illness. But a "post" showed he had been functioning on one-third of a heart. The veterinarian said that at some time in his growing period he must have had an infection which caused this condition. Along with Ch. Felixstowe Kilmorac, Chulainn Casey was one of the great ones imported to the United States.

From Casey's one litter two great studs appeared, and they can be found in pedigrees of many present day winners. Casey was at Ambleside and had just served Fair Finnelda the day before the tragedy, so both kennel names were used on the entire litter. The two males became Ambleside Failinis of Kihone and Ambleside Meac Casey of Kihone. Two bitches also have carried on, one at Kihone Kennels. The other, Fair Fand, eventually went to William J. Williams in Cincinnati. Later, Mr. Williams returned Fand to Ambleside to be mated to Padraic of Summerhill. She produced a fine litter and one son, Fair Patrick, sired the first litter at the Clontarf Kennels of Mr. Dammarell in Cincinnati.

In this period of the early thirties, David Ingalls in Chagrin Falls, Ohio, was breeding and he bred one litter by the imported Ch. Chulainn Connacht, owned by Charles A. Otis. Eventually, Connacht as well as his mate was sent to New

51

Mexico and the last person to own him was, I believe, Captain Arthur Bell.

Fredson Thayer Bowers became active at this time with his "of the Fen" Wolfhounds. Mr. Bowers was a great force in helping spread Wolfhound knowledge and the club was fortunate that his scholarly articles on the breed were published. He bred some good Hounds, and had both imported dogs and home-breds. Mr. Bowers was an authority on the breed, and judged some of the important fixtures.

No one knows better than The American Kennel Club how kennels "come and go," hence their ruling which now grants kennel names for but five years, subject to renewals. This is well demonstrated in our breed, where there are many, many attempts to breed the Wolfhound. But it is a breed requiring special attention in rearing and kenneling. The Wolfhounds' size precludes their being handled as are some breeds, and their mental characteristics very definitely preclude their being reared as kennel Hounds. Unless one practically lives with his Hounds, a kennel, *per se*, is doomed to failure. Wolfhounds are *not* like other breeds and the breeder who fails to recognize this cannot be successful. He may start to establish a kennel, but after a few years decide it is best to buy, from time to time, Hounds to meet his requirements. I know once you have a Wolfhound, you usually keep some in the family and I am still shipping out puppies to people to whom I first sent Hounds more than twenty or twenty-five years ago; and in some cases where I am not still shipping to the original purchasers, I am shipping to their children, who want their own children to have the advantage of growing up with a Wolfhound about.

This accounts for the "in and out" of breeding kennels, in a breed that holds the loyalty of its owners from one generation to the next. In the period of the thirties, we find many who contributed with limited breeding, but for reasons mentioned, after a few years remained as owners, not as breeders.

The Brom Bones Kennels of Mr. J. T. deBlois Wack, the Ambrose Kennels of Richard K. Lackey, the Barrington Kennels of Thomas N. Howell, the Inverdale Kennels of Mrs. Grant Small and the El Dorado Kennels of James MacKenzie

52

were in evidence about 1930. Mrs. Small's Inverdale Kennels stayed with the breed for some time and her Cragwood Hy-On was a specialty winner. And Mr. Burrage did very well with his Ch. Inverdale Dawn and Ch. Inverdale Trouble.

At this time the Rathmullan Kennels of Miss Martha R. White and Miss A. Elizabeth White, under the capable management of Alex Scott, made breed history for a few years and exhibited all through the Mid-West, Southwest, and Pacific Coast areas. They even made one trip to Westminster when Mr. L. M. McCandlish came to judge. They bred some champions and raised a few litters, but it was Ch. Balbricken of Ambleside that set a record in best in show wins. After Miss Martha died there was no more active breeding in Wolfhounds, although Miss A. E. White has remained a very active supporter of the breed.

In 1927 Mr. and Mrs. Northrup T. Bellinger bought King Lir of Ambleside. He became the second Irish Wolfhound to go best in show, all breeds, and the first American-bred one to do so. The Bellingers enjoyed dogs and had some great stories about their English Bulldogs and Lir after he arrived. Mrs. Bellinger had a kennel of Kerry Blues, later known as Belcrest Kennels. After Mr. Bellinger passed on, Mrs. Bellinger talked of having another Irish Wolfhound. Though she died without realizing her wish, Mrs. Bellinger's desire for another Irish Wolfhound had a great influence on her daughter, Suzanne Bellinger, who was a child when Lir was in his prime. In due time Suzanne purchased Roise of Ambleside in memory of her mother's wishes. So Belcrest had its Wolfhound and Suzanne commenced to experience what her mother had some years before: the hold a Wolfhound has on an understanding owner. As a result, Belcrest is today an important and helpful member in the Wolfhound world.

In 1930, Charles H. Morse, Jr., brought Ch. Moran of Ouborough to his Rimwold Kennels. A limited breeding program has continued there since.

The Avonwood Kennels of Mrs. Victor Mather left some worthy stock, of which Bournstream Lorna and Bournstream Peter were the best known. Bournstream Peter is in Dark

53

Kathleen of Rathbunwood's pedigree, for he was the sire of Cragwood Sheenagh, the dam of Ch. Gaellic Gift. R. Pryor Comba was interested in the breed for a time, as was Mrs. John Ekern Ott, who still is in a limited way. She got her first, Dermot of Ambleside, in 1930 and she soon added Patsy of Killybracken to breed a few Hounds under her Janesway name.

Max Friedman was loyal to the breed for many years, raising his "of Granville" Hounds. But at his passing, the kennels were closed.

Mr. and Mrs. W. L. Blackett of Atlanta, Georgia, obtained their first Hound in 1934. At that time they had just returned to this country after many years in the Orient. They fell in love with the breed and have had Wolfhounds ever since and have bred a few litters. From one of these came Ch. Killesandra of Ambleside. They then named their next few Hounds with the name *Samarkand* and one can find them not far back in some pedigrees.

Dr. and Mrs. McCormick of Reynoldsville, Pennsylvania, purchased a pair of Hounds, Kilshane of Ambleside and Finnola The Fay of Ambleside, and bred two litters, which were registered under the affix "of Summerhill." Our Padraic of Summerhill came from them, as did Jonathan E. Pierce's Michael of Summerhill. When I went to see their dogs, there were NINE of them, all males but one. They were from two litters and it had not occurred to the McCormick's to sell any of them.

Walter Roehrs, Jr., bred a little and showed considerably. And in the late thirties we find Jonathan E. Pierce in Houston, Texas, with his Toyone Kennels. Mr. Pierce stayed with the breed after he moved to California. He has been active in club affairs for many years, both with the parent club and the West Coast association.

The earlier kennels of Cragwood, Halcyon, Killybracken, Whippoorwill, and Ambleside were very active during these years and until World War II, when Halcyon Kennels, after Mrs. Clark's passing, was no longer active. The Clarks had been importing some of England's best. Felixstowe Kilfree, Felixstowe Kilgarth, and Felixstowe Kilcully were among

Rathmullan Kennels' Ch. Balbricken of Ambleside. Best in show, all breeds, four times in 1934 and once in 1935.

Ch. Roonagh of Ambleside, whelped February 1931. By Sulhamstead Dan ex Ch. Kathleen of Ambleside. BOS, 1934 Specialty; WB, Westminster, 1933 and 1935; BOB, Westminster, 1936.

Branwen Kennels' Ch. Timber of Ambleside. A best in show, all breeds, winner, 1954.

Taraledge Kennels' Ch. Shamus Failinis of Ambleside. A best in show, all breeds, winner, 1949.

some of the notable ones brought over. And from the early crop of youngsters at Halcyon came Halcyon Tamara and Halcyon Baronet and later the American-bred Halcyon Alannah of Ambleside, who won at Westminster and the Specialty in 1938 and 1939. Also, there were several Chulainn-bred Hounds that came to live at Halcyon.

Felixstowe Kilbrew had come to Cragwood Kennels, and Ambleside Failinis of Kihone was at Killybracken. During the war years three good Canadian-bred dogs sired by Gui of Pentavalon came in. I lost mine from the effects of a rattlesnake bite and I do not know whether Mrs. Ellis bred hers or not, but the male that went to Mr. Paine for his Barn Hill Kennels prospered and became a champion, and for a few years the Barn Hill's sent out a number of Hounds.

In the focus of breed activity at this time, "to be and to do," loom Mr. and Mrs. LeRoy E. Fess and Colonel and Mrs. John W. Wofford, who in the mid-thirties arrived in the breed.

The late Roy Fess "liked dogs," and when I first met him he was knee-deep in helping the St. Bernard Club in this country reorganize itself. He had had some Saints and he did have a Great Dane or so. This contributed to his attraction to the Irish Hound, which is not unusual, for I have many times sold a Wolfhound to a Dane owner. The breeds are unlike in character, but there is something that brings a mutual attraction. For instance, one of the largest kennels of Great Danes in England was also a stronghold for Irish Wolfhounds. This was the celebrated kennels of the late James V. Rank, of Ouborough fame.

Roy and Margaret Fess had Wolfhounds before their "Tara" arrived in 1940, but she changed their kennel from "Cour de Lion" and their home from "The Ledge" to become the combination, *Taraledge*. This was no small thing. Tara led them into more work for Wolfhounds than any other two people have had to face up to. Both Margaret and Roy were feature writers, and up to his death in April 1958, Roy wrote a "Dogality Column" for the *Buffalo Courier* and other papers. He was so capable he was literally drafted into Wolfhound publicity work, and was the originator and editor of the club's official magazine, *Harp and Hound*, which has done such an amazing job for the breed. Since these posts are all honorary, true appreciation goes beyond the reach of words.

Colonel and Mrs. Wofford had their interest stimulated with the arrival of Sheila of Killibeg from a friend. Whenever possible she was taken with them wherever the Colonel was stationed; otherwise, she went to their Rimrock Farm in Kansas. All of the puppies in Sheila's first litter were registered with the Rimrock name. Later, official consent from The American Kennel Club to register "Rimrock" as the kennel name was denied, and the name Rathrahilly was chosen for future registrations. The Woffords' place is close to Fort Riley, and since Rath means "fort" and Rahilly is the Gaellic for "Riley," the name is a natural. After Colonel Wofford passed on, the place at Milford continued with its kennel of Wolfhounds and fine stable of horses.

I think it is of interest to note here that from their first Rimrock litter, a male named Dermot, whelped in 1940, went to Charles Elmers in Pittsburgh and some years later when Mrs. Wofford returned from England with Bacara of Spean, she wanted her bred to Dermot to hold "her first line" if possible. Dermot was then nine years old and had never stood in stud, but the mating was successful and the first of the Rathrahillys were whelped.

Robert Button of California brought in some Hounds, and he helped in the forming of a West Coast Association. Also in the early forties, the Clontarf Kennels of William Dammarell were active, as was Colman O'Shaughnessy, for a time. When we entered the war years, with gasoline curtailment and so many Wolfhound owners busy in the war effort, conditions changed. The Amblesides in Michigan and Killybracken in Illinois no longer traveled their usual distances to shows, since even the railroads discouraged the taking of space in baggage cars that might be needed, and all war materials had priority. Dogs bred during this time were frequently referred to as "war-babies," since some of the best were never shown, and breeding was limited.

Mrs. Peter Van Brunt was able to show her Erin II and later her Cragwood Victoria. The Riverlawn Kennels were

57

then in New Jersey, and when they moved to Lake Placid, greater activity was enjoyed and the kennel is well known today. Also during this time, Mrs. Winifred Little Heckman, long interested in the breed, started to breed a few and to judge.

In 1949 the Misses Helen Dalton and Catherine Cram purchased Fair Fingal of Ambleside as a puppy and he was to change a certain department of their lives. He traveled everywhere with them and in early 1952 they found him a mate. Later, their first litter arrived and was named after their place in Northern Minnesota at Hackensack. So the *Hillaways* came into being, and the kennel is well known today.

By 1950 Cynthia Madigan (Mrs. Thomas F.) purchased Timber of Ambleside. He became a champion in 1952 and a best in show winner in 1954. Although Mrs. Madigan was well known in Poodles, this was the beginning of a lively interest in Wolfhounds in her Branwen Kennels.

We need to turn back again, for we are tempted to tell about the individuals and can hardly leave a thought in mid-air, dangling, so we carry it along and then we must return to pick up a related event. This at times precludes continuity, but it also saves us from just plain statistics.

We are trying to give the names of Hounds and owners that have carried on in the breeding field. The dog show triumphs have their very important place in the breed missionary work, else how could the public see them? With records here of the specialty wins and Westminster placings for a few years, the general public, breeders and owners can check individuals. But it's the field of breeding where the heirs apparent are found.

We must not overlook Mr. and Mrs. H. Rathbun Hees, who owned and showed Ch. Cragwood Gaelic Gift in 1941, winners in bitches at the specialty at Madison, New Jersey, one year. She had but one litter, but it should be counted here. Gift was mated to Ch. War Buckler of Ambleside and Mr. and Mrs. Hees used the name of *Rathbunwood* in registering the litter. Several of the dogs were shown but there is one that left more than a memory. First owned by Mrs. Smith

58

(Cragwood), Dark Kathleen had a litter sired by Cragwood Bard, and Cragwood Hogan is a son of this mating. He is also the grandsire of the litter brothers Ch. Cragwood Mark O'Mahoney and Ch. Cragwood Barney O'Shea, the latter exported by Mrs. Van Brunt to England.

Dark Kathleen changed hands by going from Cragwood to Jonathan Pierce, who mated her to Ch. Arnold of Edgecliff. She became the dam of Ch. Monahan of Tyrone, later campaigned so well by Mrs. Laura L. Thomas to become a "Hound of the Year" winner. Unfortunately, Ch. Monahan left no progeny. We run into these blind alleys, where the line seems to stop, but in the next litter of Dark Kathleen some bitches were whelped that have contributed mightily. Among them are the Fess's Judy of Tyrone, who has given some wonderful stock; Ambleside's Moya of Tyrone, who also pleased us so much and gave us a male that we felt was the best we ever had; Mr. Pierce's own Ch. Maureen of Tyrone; and also Darcie of Tyrone, owned by Henry E. Britcher of Homeplace Kennels.

Of course, writing of Ch. Arnold of Edgecliff's first mate leads us to the Edgecliff Kennels of Thomas B. Wanamaker, Jr. Edgecliff was the Pasadena home of Douglass Montgomery's family and Mr. Wanamaker also had a house there. Douglass had been attracted to the breed and had purchased his first Wolfhound some years previously from Halcyon Farms. Later he bought Padraic of Ambleside, and still later, a very young pair went down; the female was Isolde of Ambleside, who lived to a ripe old age. About this time the Marshall Westcotts bought a pair of Irish Wolfhounds. The male was Eber Finn of Ambleside and when he was offered for sale when the Westcotts were moving, Mr. Wanamaker bought him and started showing him. Finn lacked but one point of the title when Mr. Wanamaker was called into military service in the Pacific. Unfortunately, he did not finish Finn, and thinking he would be back in a comparatively short time, he put him in boarding with instructions not to campaign further. While Finn was at Gladys Shipman's Dude Ranch for dogs in the mountains, he was used at stud for a bitch owned by Miss Shipman.

59

After the litter arrived, one of Mr. Wanamaker's friends went to the kennel to pick out a puppy to hold for him. Alas, Finn died just a few days before his master docked on his return, so it was grievous news that greeted Mr. Wanamaker. He had been eager to get back to the Hounds but instead he found a young son of Finn's waiting for him. However, as Mr. Dammarell says in one of his wonderful poems, "Kings Never Die."

Mr. Wanamaker enjoyed Arnold, as the puppy was called —a sort of namesake after the lady who picked him out. And much later Mr. Wanamaker brought in two Hounds from England. The oldest was Tara of Ouborough, to whom the breed owes much. She proved a perfect mate for Arnold and her first litter came at a time when stocks were very low. Practically all of these puppies found their way into the hands of real breeders. It was not because they were lucky—they were good! Two males became champions, Ch. Brian Boru of Edgecliff and Ch. Finn mac Cool of Edgecliff, later to go to Mrs. Wofford. Both Hounds became best in show, all-breed winners and were shown from coast to coast. Three females annexed the title and deserved it, and all became important brood matrons. Ch. Erin of Edgecliff went to Mrs. Ellis at Killybracken, Ch. Deirdre of Edgecliff to Mr. Burrage's Rathain Kennels, and Ambleside Edain of Edgecliff came to live with me at Ambleside.

One more import, Kinsale of Boroughbury, came to Edge-cliff, but after one more litter, Edgecliff reluctantly closed its kennels, as Mr. Wanamaker was taking residence in the Islands.

Mr. Joseph A. Coll, who passed on in 1951, always had Wolfhounds about, but not until he imported his Ballymac of Boroughbury and Patrick of Ballytobin, did he find himself showing. Ballymac was only two months old when he was shipped over. In 1949 he started a great show career, handled by Albert H. Smith, huntsman for the Monmouth County Hunt, of which Mr. Haskell is the M.F.H.

Albert Smith used to handle Mrs. Haskell's Whippoorwill Hounds so it is interesting to see Clyde B. Smith, Albert's son, with The McGillacudy, a fine son of Ch. Patrick of Ballytobin. The McGillacudy was winners at the Westminster Kennel Club Show in Madison Square Garden, *three* years in succession.

In 1947 Colonel William D. Dana became a partner in the Ambleside Kennels of Alma J. Starbuck. He brought to the kennels an understanding of the breed, tested over the years, for "way back when," he had bought Wolfhounds from Halcyon and Ambleside. After a year in Santa Fe, New Mexico, where we had the use of Miss White's lovely kennels that had originally been scaled to Wolfhounds, we moved into their permanent home on Colonel Dana's Ranch at Healdsburg, California, in the Redwood Empire. After five years I thought I might like living farther south, so the partnership was dissolved. It had been a wonderful five years for Wolfhounds, due to Colonel Dana's generous support. He did a tremendous amount of good for the breed, and although not breeding now, his interest in Wolfhounds remains, as it always has been, at a very high level.

One of the importations we made for Ambleside was in mid-April of 1948 when Tralaigh of Boroughbury arrived. He was selected by Elsie James, in England, but partly reared by Miss Croucher, for food in Britain was still rationed and anyone having a cow and milk helped with the puppies, I was told. Tralaigh was a magnificent Hound. We bought him at three months of age but he was to be held for later delivery. He then had distemper at five months, which left him a little weak behind. However, at nine months we let him come in. He could stand perfectly; he had a slightly weak movement in rear quarters, but if you ran him and stopped quickly, he stood well and was not "cowhocked." We showed him twice to help with entries and he won a four-point show each time. For the sake of his off-spring it is a pity he was not shown more. He died at four and one-half years of age—the distemper had impaired the kidneys. Everyone loved him and admired him, for he had one of those fine, steady dispositions.

I brought out a three-months-old puppy in 1947 when I motored to Santa Fe, New Mexico, with Gartha of Ambleside. This puppy became Ch. Finn-mac-Cumaill of Amble-

61

side and he and Tralaigh were so close in age they made a fine pair of Hounds, though they were quite unrelated. Ch. Finn-mac-Cumaill of Ambleside carried the blood of a long line of Ambleside-breds, back to the first in 1924. He was a tall Hound, typical and sound, and he sired six champions.

Tralaigh eventually sired four champions: Ch. Dian of Ambleside, who went to Killybracken Kennels; Ch. Cheevers of Ambleside, who went to Rathain Kennels; Ch. Cullykilty of Ambleside, originally purchased by Jack McKenna; and Ch. Lance of Ambleside, still on the Dana Ranch with Colonel Dana, who says he is the most satisfactory dog he ever had. He liked them all, but Lance is special. He has sired five champions, all of which went out as puppies to be reared and shown by their owners. Ch. Talgarth of Ambleside, the "Hound of the Year" for 1956, shown and owned by Dorothy L. Ellis (Killybracken Kennels) is one. And Ch. Tralee of Ambleside (sired by one of the above, Ch. Cullykilty), was a "Hound of the Year" for two successive years. If I make considerable over these "Hound of the Year" wins, it is, perhaps, because I'd like it to happen to me, for the credit goes to the rearing, conditioning, and showing of the owners.

In 1952, two events brought active owners into the club. Celeste W. Hutton received her Irish Ch. Fuath of Ulaid for her Greysarge Kennels in Maryland, and Dr. and Mrs. E. V. Kenneally purchased Sandra of Rathain for their Kilrain Kennels.

Miss Hutton started Fuath out at the shows, both here and in Canada, and he soon had his title. He was mated to Miss Hutton's Ch. Windale Killala, who has had some fine puppies.

Dr. Kenneally worked his Sandra of Rathain in obedience and she won her C.D. Then she was mated to Ch. Timber of Ambleside and had a very satisfactory litter. One exceptional youngster, Sweet Kathy of Kilrain, ran off with top honors at the 1956 specialty, taking winners bitch for her owner, Mrs. Britcher, and at the 1957 specialty, Sweet Kathy was best of breed. Best of opposite sex that year was Suzanne Bellinger's Ch. Owen of Killybracken. Forty-two

Irish Wolfhounds were present and competing at the 1957 specialty, again held at Amory L. Haskell's Woodland Farms out of Red Bank, New Jersey.

In 1953 Mr. Haskell extended an invitation to the club to hold a real specialty at his place, which has *everything* to make a perfect show, and the thoughtfulness and kindness of everyone there brings a wonderful afterglow when it is over.

Each year since 1953 Mr. Haskell has repeated this invitation. It accounts for growth of entries and has put the breed in an enviable position nation-wide. No man works alone— it's a "we" world. The club has made the most of the advantages coming to it through Mr. Haskell's generosity and it has been able to offer the best in leadership through sincere and capable people. The club at present is headed by Jeannette McGregor, president, who for several years previous to taking office in 1958, had served as chairman of the bench show committee. Her meticulous, careful planning made her a golden link in the chain of show-giving responsibilities. She now devotes the same enthusiasm to guiding the club's affairs.

We have to have owners, breeders, and a steady improvement in stock, and we also have to "tell the story." The club supports shows, its members do a limited amount of advertising, but the publication of a club organ—call it what you will—becomes the backbone of any organization.

First we published *Biennial Books,* bound; four such volumes were published before Mr. Starbuck passed on, and I carried on with them afterwards. We changed the size and color and continued until the *1942-43 Book,* which was paper bound. It was at this time I asked to be relieved of the secretarial duties. This is an appointive position and I felt Mr. Burrage was the one to take over and do a still better job. He finally accepted the appointment from the committee but I confess it was not his choice. He was being pressured into it and felt duty bound to accept. I do not think he was sorry, because work well done carries its own reward and he certainly improved the office he took over.

In 1946 the membership had a general meeting at Katonah,

New York, where the club had sponsored classes for a specialty, and an election of officers took place. I accepted the presidency. The vice-presidents elected were Mrs. C. Groverman Ellis, Miss Jeannette McGregor, Paul Paine, Mrs. Norwood B. Smith, and Miss A. Elizabeth White.

The committee consisted of Miss Suzanne Bullard, Edward T. Clark, LeRoy E. Fess, Charles H. Morse, Jr., Mrs. Peter Van Brunt, and William J. Williams.

The delegate elected to The American Kennel Club at that time was Amory L. Haskell and he has held the office ever since.

It became apparent that the club books were "too far apart"—it would be hard to keep your interest in a continued story if you got the new chapter every two years, yet club work is a continued story. There was new enthusiasm —we wanted to grow and be of service. The last club book issued was a *1946-47 Report,* bringing all club affairs up to date. It was then decided to issue a bulletin at regular intervals, seeking closer membership contact, and Mr. Burrage issued the first in 1947.

Some time after this, it was decided to divorce the bulletin and its responsibility from the secretary's office and to expedite the news angle. LeRoy Fess was appointed editor of the bulletin and given a free hand. It was in the experimental stage, but the bulletin moved swiftly in popularity and the conservative element was soon recognizing and joining the enthusiastic trend. New members joined and the bulletin found itself outgrowing its ability to meet the demand.

The shape of things to come demanded a new policy. The club could NOT expand its bulletin and continue to publish the expensive *Biennial Books* of former years. Hence, at our annual club meeting in September 1949, it was enthusiastically voted to continue the bulletin as a printed quarterly and to christen it *Harp and Hound,* with an extra copy retained for each member by the club. Every year these copies can be bound in a book as a service for those who desire such permanent record. All the features of the former books were preserved but with that "something added" the bulletin brought.

What happened after *Harp and Hound* got rolling is the good news of increased membership, for one thing. With the enthusiasm it generated, more people started "taking them up," and today the Club has a breed publication second to none; in fact, it is exclusive in its field. It has not been easy, though, to get a quarterly out on time, with all the nagging details to handle, dealing with people who are unfamiliar with the business field and who have little concept of the necessary cooperation. Getting out the bulletin has to be a labor of love, as the demands made can ultimately be an intrusion on one's daily work and life. Roy Fess was a man to meet an emergency. He was also a perfectionist—an artist for details—and he organized *Harp and Hound* into an efficient publication. He appointed associate editors who were capable and had the heart to work.

The future of *Harp and Hound* has now passed into the efficient hands of Gordon F. Graham, and these past years have seen a fantastic growth. As to *where* it is going, we cannot say. We do know that it is going *on*.

Framingham Kennel Club Show, August 1940. Judge, Mr. Eskrigge.

Ch. Felixstowe Kilgarth, winners dog at
1929 Club Specialty, Cornwall, N. Y.

Club meeting at Halcyon Farms after second Specialty.

66

Specialty Show Notes

THE FIRST Wolfhound Club Specialty Show was held at Cornwall, New York, in conjunction with the Storm King Show in September 1928. The second specialty show was held in the same place on September 8, 1929, At the second show about fifty people, enthusiastic members or just owners of the breed, accepted an invitation from Mr. and Mrs. Edward T. Clark to enjoy the hospitality of their place, Halcyon Farms, at Goshen, New York.

About 10:30 A.M. a program was started and Dr. Leon F. Whitney, the eugenics authority, addressed the gathering. At noon a luncheon was served at the main house, after which everyone gathered near the tennis court to resume participation in the activities of the day.

The afternoon speaker was Freeman Lloyd. The breed Standard was read and then Ch. Felixstowe Kilgarth and Ch. Killabrick were brought to the court to be used as examples in Mr. Lloyd's talk and the discussion that was to follow. At the close, an informal question and answer session was conducted—both Mr. Whitney and Mr. Lloyd answering the questions directed to them.

In 1930 there was a sorry entry in numbers, when only nine appeared for the specialty, held this time at Devon,

67

Pictured across these facing pages is the impressive *Specials Only* competition at the 1955 Specialty, under Judge Alva Rosenberg (left). From
l. to r. are Ch. Cristel of Ambleside, with Miss Mary Jane Ellis; Ch. Rathain
Deirdre of Edgecliff, with Chas. D. Burrage, Jr.; Ch. The McGillacudy
(BOS), with A. H. Smith; and Ch. Owen of Killybracken, with Lloyd M. Case.

Ch. Ballykelly Colin, bred by Sheelagh Seale (Ireland), and owned by
Mrs. H. Sheppard Musson. Handled by Clint Harris. Winner of six BIS
all-breeds. Pictured winning 1967 Specialty under judge Kenneth Given.

Continuing the 1955 IWCA Specials Only parade: Ch. Sandra of Rathain, C.D., with Dr. Elmer V. Kenneally; Belcrest Harp of Ambleside (BOW) with Mrs. Winifred L. Heckmann; Ch. Tralee of Ambleside (the BOB winner, owned by C. H. Morse, Jr.) with Miss Virginia Hardin; Int. Ch. Fuath of Ulaid, imp., with Miss Celeste W. Hutton, and Ch. Gilmichael of Ambleside, with Mrs. Constance M. Ayer.

A group of yearlings, 1956. The "Hounds of Hillaway" waiting to be taken into the ring by their owners, Misses Helen Dalton and Catherine Cram.

Pennsylvania. Actually, there WAS a good entry, but there were too many absentees.

In 1931 we were granted permission to consider the classes at the Morris & Essex Show at Madison, New Jersey, as our specialty. *This* was a turning point in entries. We had a judge from England, Miss Mabel S. Kearns, and we had forty-two Hounds entered, with forty on the bench. For eleven years our Specialty continued this way at Morris & Essex, from 1931 through 1941.

Many things happened in 1931. Our president, Mrs. Norwood B. Smith, resigned the office and it was not filled until 1933 when Edward T. Clark was elected. He served until 1942, when, being very busy with Red Cross work for the Government, he resigned; during these years Mrs. Clark passed on and Halcyon Kennels for Wolfhounds was closed.

In the 1930's there was considerable sponsoring by the Club of other shows. Cups were put up in Detroit, Chicago, Boston, and on the Pacific Coast. In 1930 there were eight Hounds at Chicago and a similar number in Detroit; Cleveland drew a few and Denver had an excellent entry. In 1931, just before the biggest entry at Morris & Essex, Westminster Kennel Club Show drew an entry of thirty-five Hounds. Comparing that with what is happening there today leaves one breathless. Wolfhounds have moved away from indoor, two-day shows to the one-day, out-of-doors fixtures. Even when Westminster changed from a three-day show to a two-day show, it did not change the trend in the breed. The Wolfhound Club ceased to have its annual meeting at Westminster and held it at the specialty where it always belonged and where entries were now beginning to arrive.

In 1935 Mr. L. O. Starbuck passed on and I was asked to fill his place in the club.

In 1942 the specialty was held at Katonah, New York, then for three years there were *no* specialty shows. In 1946 the club was able to become active and again the annual meeting was held at Katonah, New York. In 1947, 1948, and 1949, the club sponsored the classes at Rye, New York. In 1950 the club sponsored the classes at Framingham, Massachusetts, and the evening before the show, Miss F. Jeannette McGregor entertained the committee at her home, "Oldfields," at Sherborn, Massachusetts.

In 1951 we again were privileged to have a judge from England, when Miss Esther M. Croucher came over to judge the breed at the Harbor Cities Show in Long Island Beach, California. It was not a show large in numbers of our breed, but Miss Croucher was wonderful. I probably erred in thinking the East would show in the West. The West goes East (they always have), but the reverse is not true except in isolated cases. Of course, Long Beach was not exactly next door to most of the members in the West, either; those that came down from San Francisco had to travel 500 miles by motor and I came 600 miles from the Ranch, and Mrs. Wofford traveled a thousand or so from Kansas City. Mrs. Ellis did drive out from Chicago with Mary Jane and they had with them one of Jeannette McGregor's Hounds, but the rank and file of Eastern breeders made no attempt to attend or participate. Mr. Coll had promised me that participants could use the company plane, but when the time came, the East stayed more or less East. Like Kipling—East and West do not meet too well at dog shows.

Miss Croucher could have judged many places, but the idea was, in subscribing to this, to hold the show in Long Beach in the effort to get an entry for the specialty there. It didn't work. We thought fanciers might travel the distance to show under her, but she would have had to go to them. We had three large kennels and quite a few Hounds out in the Western area, so it should have worked out. Mrs. Smith, of Cragwood Kennels, came down with two; we were right in Edgecliff's home grounds and Thomas B. Wanamaker, Jr., sent over all the Hounds he had. We brought what we could down from Ambleside, and the Killybracken entry traveled in another car along with us. Our own pet at that time, Ambleside Edain of Edgecliff, was at home having a family. Mr. Pierce (Tyrone) entered and so did others.

Then in 1953 the specialty was held at Woodland Farms by invitation of Mr. Haskell in Red Bank, New Jersey, and everything seemed to come right side up again. Good entries have been in evidence ever since. The Parent Club is definitely an Eastern club and those wishing to show at it should plan that way. We know that branch associations throughout the land constitute the answer to breed development, and many clubs function most successfully with this setup. I had hoped successful branch organizations could be established in the West. But only time will tell whether this is possible.

The Bugle Blows for Boru

The Master of the Hunt has called
The mightiest of hounds
The bugle for the hosting blows
And leaving all his worldy woes
Brian of Edgecliff gladly goes
With gay and eager bounds.
    —William J. Dammarell

O'LEARY.
From a photo, also from the stuffed figure
in the Natural History Museum,
South Kensington.

72

Ch. Lacey of Ambleside, Best of Breed at 1958 West Coast Specialty. BOS in 1957. Owned by Mrs. Starbuck.

Ch. Sean Craig of Ambleside, winner of 1959 and 1960 West Coast Specialties. Owners, Kennett W. and Dorothy H. Patrick.

Cragwood Mark O'Mahoney, Winners Dog and Best of Breed at 1953 West Coast Specialty. (BOS in 1952). Owned by Mrs. N. B. Smith.

Ch. Ambleside Coppersmith II, winner of three consecutive West Coast Specialties (1961, 1962, and 1963). Bred and owned by Mrs. Starbuck.

Ch. Fleetwind Roonagh, two-time winner of the West Coast Specialty, 1964 and 1967, and BOS in 1963. Owned by Mr. and Mrs. Norman Hall.

Ch. Fleetwind Fingal, Best of Breed at the 1966 West Coast Specialty, and BOS in 1967. Fingal is by Ch. Fleetwind Finn MacCool ex Mona Macushla of Ambleside, and is owned by Andrew B. and Phyllis Talbot.

Irish Wolfhound Association on the West Coast

THE WEST COAST ASSOCIATION was organized February 11, 1941. The by-laws were submitted, and the Association was approved as a branch of the Parent Club. Mrs. Norwood B. Smith was elected president and Robert Button was secretary. The Parent Club provided the Pacific Coast Trophy for best Irish Wolfhound; also, the Arthur C. Wyman Memorial Trophy for best of opposite sex.

The Pacific Coast Trophy alternated between the Los Angeles show and the Del Monte Kennel Club show and was presented that way until won outright. In 1949 Cragwood Kennel's Barn Hill Gilda retired the cup. Other cups were forthcoming—there was the War Buckler Trophy for best of breed, and the Eber Finn Trophy for best of opposite sex. For the Pacific Coast Trophy for best of breed, the record reads as follows:

1935—Ch. Cragwood Muldoon, owned by Mrs. N. B. Smith
1936—Ch. Balbricken of Ambleside, owned by Rathmullan Kennels
1937—Shaun of Boyer Ranch (not owned by a member)

75

1938—Derek of Ambleside (not owned by a member)

1939—Void

1940—Eber Finn of Ambleside, owned by Mrs. Marshall Westcott

1941—Cragwood Casey II, owned by Mrs. N. B. Smith

1942—Eber Finn of Ambleside, owned by Thomas B. Wanamaker, Jr.

1943—Withdrawn ⎫
1944—Withdrawn ⎪
1945—Withdrawn ⎬ These were inactive years
1946—Withdrawn ⎪
1947—Withdrawn ⎭

1948—Arnold of Edgecliff, owned by Thomas B. Wanamaker, Jr.

1949—Cragwood Barn Hill Gilda, owned by Mrs. N. B. Smith

I have been unable to get complete records, but I do have the best of opposite sex, Wyman Memorial Trophy wins for a few years:

1937—Cragwood Brighde, owned by Mrs. N. B. Smith

1938—Void

1939—Cragwood Gaelic Gift, owned by Mr. and Mrs. H. Rathbun Hees

1940—Ch. Sulhamstead Fare of Cragwood, owned by Mrs. N. B. Smith

1942—Ch. Sulhamstead Rebecca, owned by Mr. Robert Button

1943—Void

1944—Void

1945—Void

1946—Void

1947—Void

1948—Cragwood Gaelic Harp (best of winners)
Cragwood Barn Hill Gilda (winners bitch)

In recent years the winning Hounds have been:

1952—Ch.—Tralee of Ambleside (best of breed), owned by Ambleside Kennels
Cragwood Mark O'Mahoney (winners dog), owned by Mrs. N. B. Smith
Cragwood Gold Rush (winners bitch), owned by Jonathan E. Pierce

1953—Cragwood Mark O'Mahoney (best of breed, winners dog), owned by Mrs. N. B. Smith
Cragwood Gold Rush (winners bitch, best of opposite sex), owned by Jonathan E. Pierce

1954—Ch. Cragwood Gold Rush (best of breed), owned by Mr. Pierce
Shamrock's Defending Foe (winners dog, best of opposite sex), owned by Paul W. Johnson

1955—Void

1956—Void

1957—Ch. Achris of Ambleside (best of breed), owned by Miss Louise Schwennesen
Lacey of Ambleside (winners bitch, best of opposite sex), owned by Mrs. Starbuck
Sean Craig of Ambleside (winners dog), owned by Mr. and Mrs. Kennett W. Patrick

1958—Ch. Lacey of Ambleside (best of breed), owned by Mrs. Starbuck
Clancy of Ambleside (winners dog, best of opposite sex), owned by John Scheiner
Hillaway's Cumaela (winners bitch), owned by Mrs. Starbuck

1959—Sean Craig of Ambleside (best of breed, winners dog), owned by Mr. and Mrs. Patrick
Ambleside Branwen Timberly (winners bitch, best of opposite sex), owned by Mrs. Starbuck

1960—Ch. Sean Craig of Ambleside (best of breed), owned by Mr. and Mrs. Patrick
Hillaway's Cumeala (winners bitch, best of opposite sex), owned by Mrs. Starbuck

Ambleside Coppersmith II (winners dog), owned by Mrs. Starbuck

1961—Ambleside Coppersmith II (best of breed, winners dog), owned by Mrs. Starbuck

Fleetwind Glentara (winners bitch, best of opposite sex), owned by Mr. and Mrs. Douglas N. Huntley

1962—Ch. Ambleside Coppersmith II (best of breed), owned by Mrs. Starbuck

Fleetwind Glentara (best of opposite sex), owned by Mr. and Mrs. Huntley

1963—Ch. Ambleside Coppersmith II (best of breed), owned by Mrs. Starbuck

Fleetwind Roonagh (best of opposite sex, winners bitch), owned by Mr. and Mrs. Norman Hall

McGavin of Ambleside (winners dog), owned by John J. Donohue

1964—Ch. Fleetwind Roonagh (best of breed), owned by Mr. and Mrs. Norman Hall

Ch. Ambleside Coppersmith II (best of opposite sex), owned by Mrs. Starbuck

Balbrigan of Balingary (winners dog), owned by Mr. and Mrs. Douglas N. Huntley

Fleetwind Balshauna (winners bitch), owned by Mr. and Mrs. Huntley

1965—Ch. Balbrigan of Balingary (best of breed), owned by Mr. and Mrs. Douglas N. Huntley

Ch. Fleetwind Chellis (best of opposite sex), owned by Mr. and Mrs. Norman Hall

Fleetwind Aran (winners dog), owned by S. Kessler

Fleetwind Balshauna (winners bitch), owned by Mr. and Mrs. Huntley

1966—Ch. Fleetwind Fingal (best of breed), owned by Andrew and Phyllis Talbot

Ch. Fleetwind Chellis (best of opposite sex), owned by Mr. and Mrs. Norman Hall

Fleetwind Rury Shaun (winners dog), owned by Mr. and Mrs. Erwin Rodemsky

Banshee of Balingary (winners bitch), owned by Mr. and Mrs. Douglas N. Huntley

Ch. Balbrigan of Balingary, winner of 1965 West Coast Specialty.
Balbrigan is by Ch. Fleetwind Finn MacCool ex Killarney Rose O'Killybracken, and owned by Mr. and Mrs. Douglas N. Huntley.

Ch. Fleetwind Chellis, BOS at West Coast Specialty, 1965 and 1966.
Bred and owned by Mr. and Mrs. Norman Hall, Fleetwind Kennels.

1967—Ch. Fleetwind Roonagh (best of breed), owned by Mr. and Mrs. Norman Hall
Ch. Fleetwind Fingal (best of opposite sex), owned by Andrew and Phyllis Talbot
Kelso (winners dog), owned by Donna Turman
Cori Callien of Ambleside (winners bitch), owned by Eugene and Georgia Meade
1968—Shannon of Keystone (best of breed, winners dog), owned by Murray Ehrenburg
Fleetwind Frona (best of opposite sex, winners bitch), owned by Fleetwind Kennels

Ch. Achris of Ambleside, BOB at 1957 West Coast Specialty, with judge, Dr. Frank Porter Miller, and owner, Louise Schwennesen.

Irish Wolfhound Association
of New England

THE IRISH WOLFHOUND ASSOCIATION
of New England was not "born yesterday." I believe Mr.
Burrage told me that Fredson Bowers first suggested to him
that they have a New England group. The Association has
had its ups and downs but is again on an even keel.

The only way the breed can be helped is to have a chain
of associations from coast to coast, wherever there are Wolfhounds. Such groups can manage to support at least one
show a year and the members are near enough one another
to have a good meeting and talk over needs and make plans.
When a club suffers a setback, as both of our Associations
have, it takes longer to get going again than if starting
"fresh." Just like a plant that's been frosted, it takes time to
recover.

The New England Club was organized in November 1934.
In 1940 at the North Shore Kennel Club Show at Hamilton,
Massachusetts, fifteen Hounds were benched. With parti-
tions removed, the benched entry made a splendid pic'ure
and a reproduction of it is in the *1940-41 Biennial Club Report*. Present in Hounds were: Maeve of Ambleside; Donogh
of Kihone; Ambleside Meac Casey O'Kihone; Ch. Taffy of
Ambleside; Finoaghal of Kihone; Ch. Baine of Kihone; Di-

81

anann of Kihone; Sulhamstead Rhoda; Bara of Ambleside; Ambleside Maida of Kincora; Ch. Sulhamstead Flute; Ch. Molly Kileen of Killybracken; Ch. Inverdale Dawn; Gara of Rathain; and Ian of Rathain.

During the years of 1951, 1952, 1953, and 1954, the Association was dormant, but it was reactivated in 1955. The organization now tries to sponsor about four shows a year, with trophies, in their territory.

King Size

One said: "How inappropriate
For living on the Modern Plan,
A sheer anachronism in
This century of Common Man.

A smaller dog for smaller times;
Neat, more efficient, scaled to size,
For pomp and pageantry no more
Find favor in the modern eyes."

A Wolfhound winked and gnawed a massive bone
A young Queen smiled, firm on a mighty throne.
—William J. Dammarell

Ch. Ballymacad of Ambleside, owned by S. E. Ewing, III, shown with Charles D. Burrage, Jr. at Westminster, 1958.

Harold Correll handling Am. & Can. Ch. Riverlawn Barnstorm at
Lawton-Fort Sill K.C., Lawton, Oklahoma, March 4, 1962.

Ch. Sanctuary Morne of Riverlawn, going BIS at Tidewater KC of Virginia,
March 28, 1964; owned by Mrs. Peter Van Brunt, Lake Placid, N. Y.

Eng. & Am. Ch. Boroughbury Brona, bred by Mrs. Elsie James, and owned by S. E. Ewing, 3rd. BIS all-breeds four times in 1968; BOB, Westminster KC 1968; BOS, IWCA Specialty 1968; Hound of the Year 1968.

Ch. Caragahoolie O'Killybracken, bred by Doris Hunt, owned by Killy-bracken Kennels, and handled by Roberta Campbell. BOB at IWCA Specialty 1968, followed by five BIS all-breeds within three months.

Comments on the Standard

SOME YEARS AGO there were a few attempts made to have the Standard either revised or amplified, but investigation proved the suggestions to have come from a small minority. It has been found in breed clubs that it is usually the new fancier who wants to change the Standard. The attempts to change the Standard may have been generated in part by our judge, C. R. Williams, who judged our breed at Madison, New Jersey, in 1932, "Our Specialty" that year, about which he wrote afterwards. He said, "Like most old-fashioned English Standards, that of the Irish Wolfhound is brief and sketchy. I prefer the precise and elaborate German Standard, represented by the Great Dane. . . ."

I believe Mr. Williams helped write the Dane Standard of the time, and I might say he was also a good judge. He regretted that when he came to the benches to talk about the Hounds, all that ensued was a pleasant conversation. He felt there should be a little give and take after the judging, and he commented, "I did not learn as much from the exhibitors as I think a judge has a right to expect." As I recall, the Dane Standard has gone through another change or so since that year, and it is this sort of thing many do not understand in Irish Wolfhounds. Our Standard is not the same in principle as the majority of other Standards, since our Standard describes the ancient Hound, and the endeavor is to breed a Hound that will approach as near as possible, in the fullest of perfection, that type of Hound. Many other breeds change from year to year and with the passing of the years the fanciers breed to meet present day requirements. They would be horrified if one were to suggest that they revert to the type of their breed described in the earliest data regarding it. I can almost say that such is true of the majority of breeds, but the opposite is true of the Irish Wolfhound. The desire is to again produce the old Hound in all his glory. So the premise is not the same. And we are not fettered by the Standard, for the Hounds are better all the time. Because the Standard is brief does not mean it is not adequate. All statements of truth are brief—and one may spend a lifetime understanding them.

At one time the subject of changing the Standard was under general discussion on "both sides," and all the older breeders were in accord that the Standard meets the requirements. The discussion was started when Mr. Starbuck wrote all the breeders in England and was able to print their replies. Mrs. Nagle said, "Hands off the Standard. I do not believe in too much amplification or giving the points in greater detail. It is a mistake to tie a Judge down to too many details that are not half as important as the dog as a whole. I think the Standard is a good one and perfectly adequate to convey to any Judge what an Irish Wolfhound should be.

"A sense of proportion is what is wanted in judging, but altering the Standard will not make bad judges into good ones. And the good ones can be safely left to interpret our present one to the best advantage."

K. P. Strohmenger wrote, "I am quite sure that the last thing any breeders and exhibitors of Irish Wolfhounds in this country would want is to alter our Standard of type. . . . Everyone when going into something new considers something ought to be changed, and it is always found that these people have very revolutionary ideas."

Ch. Tralee of Ambleside, owned by Charles H. Morse, Jr. BIS, all breeds, twice in 1954 and once in 1955; three times BOB, Irish Wolfhound Specialty (1954, 1955, 1956); BOB, 1952 West Coast Specialty; "Hound of the Year," 1954 and 1955.

Ch. Tyrone of Ballykelly, imp. Whelped July 8, 1956, by Casey of Bally-kelly ex Ch. Antostal of Ballykelly. Ch. Tyrone won the Irish Wolfhound Club's Hound Group Trophy for the most Group placements in 1960 and also went BIS at Watertown, New York in that year.

Miss Mabel Kearns, a successful and popular breeder, exhibitor, and judge of the breed for many years, says, "I think it would be a pity to change the Standard. It is a very good description of what we want and I do not think any amplification is needed for the novice."

I. W. Everett of Felixstowe wrote, "I sat on the Committee which was arranged to consider and discuss this subject in 1898 or somewhere then. It was in the latter days of Captain Graham. He, Major P. S. Shewell, the late J. F. Baily, and a few others, including myself, were on the Committee. The outcome was the present Standard.

"I have, every now and again, gone through it since that time, trying to find out if there were any points which needed correction in any way and I failed to find them. One thing I do feel about our breed is in some quarters there is a great effort being made to work into our bench Hounds a rather overdone condition of trimming up, which is in some cases pretty pronounced. This I feel should be severely dealt with. It very greatly detracts from the correct appearance—the actual Irish Wolfhound type."

Captain and Mrs. Huddon said it would be a mistake to interfere with the Standard and that if a Hound is good enough to conform perfectly to the sixteen points in the Standard of excellence, he will need no alteration. They felt this was the opinion of the breeders of any importance in their country.

"Judging is an art," says Mrs. Smith. "No Standard is foolproof. Ours is okay for a person with a 'doggy knowledge,' or an eye for a dog. A poor workman usually blames his tools. Our Standard was written for the future by men of vision and most of us do not feel we have outgrown it."

No matter what may be said of "each part," the most vital factor is viewing the dog in its entirety. Each part must be in perfect relation to the remainder. 'Tis said the strength of a chain is that of its weakest link and the chain is in no way improved by the addition of one or two links of excessive strength. Soundness is structural correctness for the job it is intended to do.

There is only *one true type,* in any breed—and the official

Standard defines it. Once you have that picture firmly in mind you cannot get away from it. And as John Kemps said, "You have an ace in the hole."

Since our Standard does not mention this, it should be said that today The American Kennel Club disqualifies in the ring, a specimen of any breed that is a monorchid (having but one testicle in the scrotum), or a cryptorchid (a condition where both testes fail to descend normally). This was a new ruling made for all dogs in 1957.

There are times when the measure of one's ability to appraise is found in knowing "how good is good"—for the rankest novice can see faults. As we develop and perfect our ability to appraise, we become more skillful breeders. When you are so busy hanging on the faults you see, the scale of balance tips destructively. It is perptual warfare to keep the picture of perfect symmetry and balance in the mind, and we must think *from* that.

There is too much reckless dilettantism in the breeding of good dogs. When we read the Standard, we are entering into the vestibule of the understanding of the breed. It is a prelude. Then we study anatomy in general, movement, and even breed temperament to clear the path for constant balance. We should try to keep the Wolfhound free from the stranglehold of dog-show barbering. To tidy up a coat, especially if half shed out and open, is one thing; to strip a Wolfhound like a Terrier is an abomination and unbecoming. Let the natural head remain a symbol of his heritage. Actual barbering, especially the use of clippers, should be sufficient cause to disqualify an entry in competition.

In training and showing, we need not violate the breed's natural tendencies in order to keep our Hounds strictly beautiful!

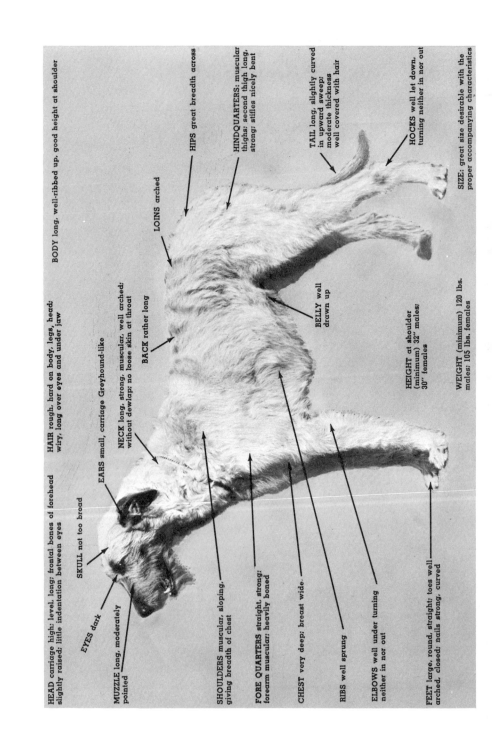

HEAD carriage high; level, long; frontal bones of forehead slightly raised; little indentation between eyes

HAIR rough, hard on body, legs, head; wiry, long over eyes and under jaw

BODY long, well-ribbed up, good height at shoulder

HIPS great breadth across

HINDQUARTERS: muscular thighs; second thigh long, strong; stifles nicely bent

TAIL long, slightly curved in upward sweep; moderate thickness, well covered with hair

HOCKS well let down, turning neither in nor out

SIZE: great size desirable with the proper accompanying characteristics

LOINS arched

EARS small, carriage Greyhound-like

NECK long, strong, muscular, well arched; without dewlap; no loose skin at throat

BACK rather long

BELLY well drawn up

SKULL not too broad

EYES dark

MUZZLE long, moderately pointed

SHOULDERS muscular, sloping, giving breadth of chest

FORE QUARTERS straight, strong; forearm muscular; heavily boned

CHEST very deep; breast wide.

RIBS well sprung

ELBOWS well under turning neither in nor out

FEET large, round, straight; toes well arched, closed; nails strong, curved

HEIGHT at shoulder (minimum) 32" males; 30" females

WEIGHT (minimum) 120 lbs. males; 105 lbs. females

The Standard of the Irish Wolfhound

General Appearance—Of great size and commanding appearance, the Irish Wolfhound is remarkable in combining power and swiftness with keen sight. The largest and tallest of the galloping Hounds, in general type he is a rough-coated, Greyhound-like breed; very muscular, strong though gracefully built; movements easy and active; head and neck carried high, the tail carried with an upward sweep with a slight curve towards the extremity. The minimum height and weight of dogs should be 32 inches and 120 pounds; of bitches, 30 inches and 105 pounds; these to apply only to Hounds over 18 months of age. Anything below this should be debarred from competition. Great size, including height at shoulder and proportionate length of body, is the desideratum to be aimed at, and it is desired to firmly establish a race that shall average from 32 to 34 inches in dogs, showing the requisite power, activity, courage and symmetry.

Head—Long, the frontal bones of the forehead very slightly raised and very little indentation between the eyes. Skull, not too broad. Muzzle, long and moderately pointed. Ears, small and Greyhound-like in carriage. *Neck*—Rather

91

long, very strong and muscular, well arched, without dewlap or loose skin about the throat.

Chest—Very deep. Breast, wide. *Back*—Rather long than short. Loins, arched. *Tail*—Long and slightly curved, of moderate thickness, and well covered with hair. *Belly*—Well drawn up.

Forequarters—Shoulders, muscular, giving breadth of chest, set sloping. Elbows well under, neither turned inwards nor outwards. *Leg*—Forearm muscular, and the whole leg strong and quite straight. *Hindquarters*—Muscular thighs and second thigh long and strong as in the Greyhound, and hocks well let down and turning neither in nor out. *Feet*—Moderately large and round, neither turned inwards nor outwards. Toes, well arched and closed. Nails, very strong and curved.

Hair—Rough and hard on body, legs and head; especially wiry and long over eyes and under jaw.

Color and Markings—The recognized colors are gray, brindle, red, black, pure white, fawn, or any other color that appears in the Deerhound.

Faults—Too light or heavy a head, too highly arched frontal bone; large ears and hanging flat to the face; short neck; full dewlap; too narrow or too broad a chest; sunken or hollow or quite straight back; bent forelegs; overbent fetlocks; twisted feet; spreading toes; too curly a tail; weak hindquarters and a general want of muscle; too short in body; lips or nose liver-colored or lacking pigmentation.

LIST OF POINTS IN ORDER OF MERIT

1. *Typical.* The Irish Wolfhound is a rough-coated Greyhound-like breed, the tallest of the coursing Hounds and remarkable in combining power and swiftness. 2. *Great size* and commanding appearance. 3. Movements easy and active. 4. Head, long and level, carried high. 5. Forelegs, heavily boned, quite straight; elbows well set under. 6. Thighs long and muscular; second thighs, well muscled, stifles nicely bent. 7. Coat, rough and hard, specially wiry and long over

eyes and under jaw. 8. Body, long, well ribbed up, with ribs well sprung, and great breadth across hips. 9. Loins arched, belly well drawn up. 10. Ears, small, with Greyhound-like carriage. 11. Feet, moderately large and round; toes, close, well arched. 12. Neck, long, well arched and very strong. 13. Chest, very deep, moderately broad. 14. Shoulders, muscular, set sloping. 15. Tail, long and slightly curved. 16. Eyes, dark.

Note—The above in no way alters the "Standard of Excellence," which must in all cases be rigidly adhered to; they simply give the various points in order of merit. If in any case they appear at variance with Standard of Excellence, it is the latter which is correct.

Padraic of Summerhill,
sire or grandsire of many present-day winners.

Paul Paine's Ch. Gillagain of Ambleside, BIS, all breeds, 1946.

Ch. Talgarth of Ambleside, owned by Killybracken Kennels, Mrs. C. G. Ellis. "Hound of the Year" in 1956.

Amplification of the Standard

SOME COMMENTS on the Standard preceded it—here are a few comments to follow it. It is generally conceded that the head is the index of type, for the head often identifies a breed. The Wolfhound head should be long, with plenty in front of the eyes. A Wolfhound is a slasher in battle, an "in and outer," so the muscles are long, not like the Mastiff head (to illustrate a point).

Much is said about Wolfhound ears because there is much to be done. But in seeking the balanced specimen, no one has been able to concentrate on any one point; we move gradually to perfection and we cannot sacrifice what has already been gained, so special points come slowly, though our awareness of what is needed can often help. The greatest assistance lies in personally knowing much about the ancestors we breed from. The Standard says, "ears, small and Greyhound-like in carriage." A Greyhound-like ear is a rose ear—no lengthy explanation is necessary for you can easily look at a Greyhound. The neck should be arched and long and STRONG.

The Standard says nothing of teeth. However, I have always assumed that those who strive to comply with the Standard just took it for granted that anyone and everyone would know a good set of teeth. I am sorry that is not always so in this country. Another thing, until more recent years, excellent mouths were the rule. Now we do see a few that must be considered faulty, and I speak of the undershot mouth or the overshot. The mouth should be level, with just a scissors bite. In the undershot mouth the lower teeth come forward more than is required and in the overshot mouth the upper teeth are too far over the lower teeth. The over-shot mouth often corrects if it is slight in a young puppy; but the undershot one rarely improves. Since these faults can be hereditary, they are something to check in any breed-ing program.

A further study of the bone structure of the "quarters" shows that the great difference between the shoulders and the hindquarters is that there is no joint, in the accepted sense, between the shoulders and the general framework. The body is suspended between the shoulder blades by semi-elastic ligaments. These blades are the "shock-absorbers" which permit us a straight front leg.

The shoulder blade has a three-point performance—*i.e.*, taking the weight, absorbing shock, and lifting the leg. The blades should be set obliquely and should be long, but the greatest importance ought to be attached to the bone known as the humerus, which runs from the point of the shoulder to the elbow. The angle of this bone to the shoulder blade is all important. Despite that fact, the tendency is to over-look too straight fronts. Straight legs, yes—but there must not be a straight line from the neck to the knee. Such struc-ture is unsound. The humerus must lie obliquely backward at a suitable angle from the shoulder to elbow to give the proper leverage and take up shock. If the humerus is overly bent, the legs are too far under and the Hound thrown off balance; if too straight, the legs are too far forward, and the forequarters get a terrific pounding when the dog is gallop-ing.

Too heavy shoulders, or "loaded shoulders," are of exces-sive strength and so are cumbersome. The muscles should taper from the elbows up and in, for when the Hound is gal-loping, the hindquarters must pass the front quarters on the outside. This is why too heavy and bunchy shoulders are a handicap, as is an overly broad front.

The chest houses the heart and lungs, and to afford room for them the ribs must be deep. A good spring or curve of rib is necessary since the acts of expansion and contraction in breathing depend on such formation. But the dog depending on depth of chest for breathing space will be on finer lines (as is the Greyhound family) than one depending on breadth, and although narrower in chest, such a dog does actually possess much greater capacity in the thorax.

Too great width contributes to coarseness, and is a handicap to a coursing Hound, while a too narrow chest could spell lack of room. But the coursing Hounds must never have the breadth of working dogs, and great stress should be laid on depth.

The majority of breeds have as straight a spine as is possible, but the coursing Hounds must have arched loins to give impetus at the gallop (their natural gait); and even in straight-backed dogs, the arch is preferred to the droop. The arched loins on the Wolfhound preclude a straight back, and mean that the correct spine must curve slightly over the loins.

The back should be long. Experience alone can teach one the happy medium between a too long and a too short back. The most important internal organs, including those of reproduction, are housed between the ribs and pelvis, and since these organs need more room, a longer back in a bitch is more acceptable than it is in a male.

The pelvis should be as wide and deep as general conformation permits, and the whole hindquarters must be correct to afford space for the most important muscles of the animal, which have their anchorage in the pelvis. The pelvis is sometimes referred to as "the keystone of the hindquarters." Here lie all the muscles, ligaments, and tendons of the hind legs, the whole framework in which the motive power is produced. Here is the power for the forward thrust. Again, experience must teach the happy medium, but a too broad pelvic structure causes a rolling gait while a too narrow one results in a lack of sufficient muscular development, made obvious by skimpy thighs.

Now the quarters, from the pelvis to the tail, are of major importance, since here is anchored those huge thigh muscles which are the prime requisite of a coursing Hound. If this quarter is too drooping, the muscles are unduly shortened, with evident loss of power; yet neither can the quarter be too square, else the action of the muscles is hindered. A good guide is the set-on of the tail; a badly set-on tail means improper body behind the pelvis.

The thighs should be long and strong, and they will be if the stifle is well bent to give the necessary muscular leverage, which, in our breed, is almost imperative. Movement is imparted to the body by means of the powerful muscles of the hindquarters. The forelegs take little part in propulsion, and for the most part they simply carry the weight of the forward part and steer the dog.

Miss Kearns told me that Captain Graham put great importance on the tail. It needs to be long and is used as a rudder in turning fast. It will be carried even too gaily at the sight of game, but otherwise it is down with a slight curve to one side. A sort of "monkey-tail" that rings too much is objectionable, though a slight ring is common, especially if the dog is running in a field where there is game or where grasses are wet. This type of ring is not usually manifested in shows or at home, but a decided monkey-tail seems to be heritable.

Basically, the show ring seeks type, first and last. Without type, where could we find the uniformity, the nearness to an ideal, which the breed Standard demands? The great need is to make sure soundness is present in the vast majority of specimens. The ideal is *good type* plus *full soundness* —*but*, fundamentally, type must predominate over soundness in the ring, other things being equal. The better type dog that is not entirely sound takes precedence over the less typey but entirely sound dog, inasmuch as soundness is not as a rule hereditary. We breed for type—it does not come from "beefsteak"; and this is where the art of breeding comes in. *All* animals should be sound, and any breeder

98

who takes an unsound dog into the ring is more or less asking for trouble, since *all* understand soundness even if all do *not* know the type. I once asked a well known judge why he put up a certain Hound that was not quite true behind, and he just said, "He has the most magnificent type I have ever seen and I can get all the soundness I want in the dog pound." This is certainly no reason to breed from or to show unsound dogs, but it *does* give pause for thought on the appraisal of "type versus soundness."

The first requisite in the Standard is great size and commanding appearance. This does not mean we breed by the yardstick. There is more to a Hound than inches, but it does mean a tall, sound, rangy Wolfhound can and should be placed over a medium sized one, if type is equal. Nearly everyone wants size; it is what attracted them to the breed, else they would have taken on a shorter, more compact dog. "High on the leg" and "covering a lot of ground" are familiar and true expressions, as is "plenty of daylight under him" (indicating proper length of legs). The Wolfhound must remain the Greyhound in general appearance, rough coated—even the head shows brows over the eyes and "whiskers" under the chin, to give the typical expression. I have used the axiom Mr. Baily gave many times: "To be as powerful as is compatible to the Greyhound conformation and to be as Greyhound-like as is compatible with power." It is a very good balance in appraising.

I do feel strongly that one of the needful things is to understand the gait of an Irish Wolfhound; to "see" it in action. The next chapter describes Wolfhound gait by means of text and drawings by an expert, and the entire Wolfhound fancy will acclaim it.

99

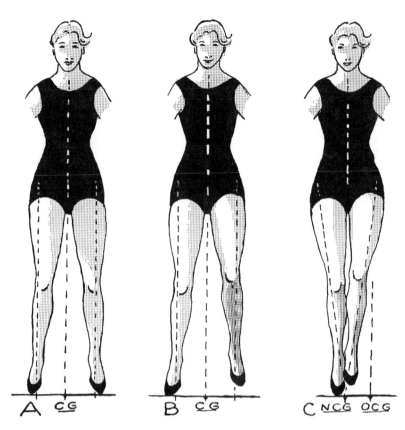

A C̲G̲   B C̲G̲   C N̲C̲G̲ O̲C̲G̲

Stand as in Fig. A, with the balls of your feet as far apart as your hip sockets. Then lift the left foot (Fig. B), without swaying your body to the right, so as to bring the center of gravity over the supporting foot as shown in Fig. C, which creates a new center of gravity.

Wolfhound Gait

By McDowell Lyon

THE GAIT of the Irish Wolfhound is not a single factor like the color of his eyes or type of his coat but is a composite of his entire physical make-up. Except for color and markings, the other twelve sections of the Wolfhound Standard have some influence on gait and movement. The very purpose for which this dog was developed demanded efficient movement in the field and we should maintain this as the foundation on which we continue to breed.

It was his rugged grace that first endeared the Irish Wolfhound to the sportsmen of the past. Grace and efficient movement were wed at his inception and cannot be divorced; they are as much a part of him as his size, coat, and instinct for the chase. We should keep that constantly in mind when evaluating the dogs that we see and breed.

More fallacies have clung to the ideas surrounding movement and the factors which contribute to it than to any other phase of the dog field. This was understandable years ago, for leg action was too fast for the eye to follow it. But today the moving picture camera has given us the answer to those enigmas and, even though with the eye alone we cannot see

101

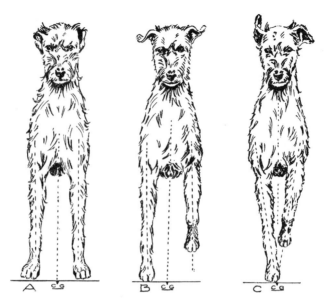

The dog faces you with feet apart, almost under the shoulder sockets, as in Fig. A. When he moves, he cannot do so as in Fig. B, with legs parallel, any more than you could hold the position of "B" in Plate 1. He will place his pad on or near the center-of-gravity line, as in Fig. C, to maintain balance.

Some dogs swing their front legs in an arc to get the pad under the center of gravity, as though doing the Australian Crawl (like the dog in Fig. A), which is a fault. A dog whose pasterns bend inward, as in Fig. B, will move close, for the pastern takes up passing space.

all that takes place, we have learned what happens and can visualize it more clearly.

Leland Stanford's desire to learn exactly what an animal's legs did when he moved, fathered experiments that began in 1872 and were carried out on the farm where the University now stands. A series of twenty-four cameras were tripped in sequence by horses, dogs, deer, and other animals in their various gaits. Thomas Edison and others joined in the work, with the result that the first semblance to our moving pictures was shown at the Chicago World's Fair in 1892. From this and study following, we learned what the eye had never been able to detect before. The importance to us in this is knowing just how the legs of a Wolfhound support his body in movement, and knowing his problems of balance.

He starts his walk by stepping off with one front foot, followed by the opposite back foot, then the other front foot and its opposite back foot. The actual leg sequence here is the same as in the gallop except that it is slower and the steps overlap one another so that his body is always supported partially or wholly by three legs. Therefore, maintaining balance is much easier than in the faster gaits, and can be likened to the tricycle.

The trot is known as a diagonal gait, for the right front and diagonal or opposite rear coordinate, as do the left front and its diagonal rear. This provides two legs, front and back, as support for the body and can be compared to the bicycle, which is more difficult to balance than is the tricycle. Another factor that must be kept in mind when considering this is that these supports are on diagonal corners of the body and, unless the dog does something to prevent it, support would move unsteadily from side to side—wobbling or rolling. The dog can and does correct for this in efficient movement.

The pace is similar to the trot to a certain extent, except that it is a lateral gait where both right legs coordinate and support weight, followed by both left legs. A two-point support results as with the trot. The dog rarely resorts to the pace unless he is very tired and leg weary, over-fat and out

103

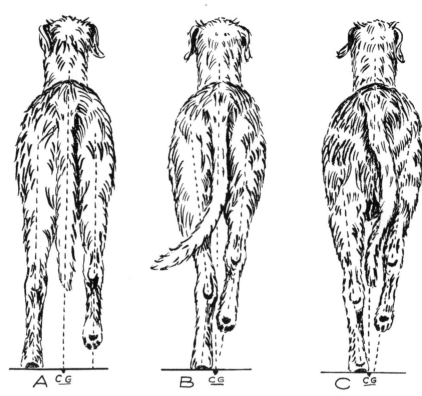

A C̲G̲   B C̲G̲   C C̲G̲

The dog cannot move away efficiently with legs parallel as in Fig. A, where he is "moving wide." The "cow-hocked" dog in Fig. B will move close, often dusting his hocks with the passing foot, and does not have a straight column of bones for body support. The efficient mover keeps the column of bones straight while placing his back pad near or on the center line, as in Fig. C, which will be in line with the front legs unless the dog is "crabbing."

of condition, or has too much or too little age. Consequently, he is not as apt to make sufficient leg correction for support and will generally show a roll as support shifts from side to side.

In the normal or single-suspension gallop, leg sequence follows that of the walk but there is no overlapping and the body at no time is fully supported by more than one leg. A period of suspension, when all legs are off the ground, follows the straightening of the leading front leg. Sometimes two pads will appear to be on the ground but one is leaving and the other arriving and the weight is immediately taken over by the latter. This is used by the horse and by the majority of dogs, but by the Wolfhound only as a slow gallop.

The high speed working gallop of the Wolfhound, as with other gazehounds, antelope, and cheetah, differs from the normal gallop in that there are two periods of suspension. The Wolfhound's second one follows the straightening of the back leg opposite to the leading front leg. This latter period of suspension provides his extra comparative speed. At no time, though, does more than one leg support the body, so both styles of the gallop can be compared to the monocycle, the hardest of all cycles on which to maintain balance.

Visualizing these supports should help us to a clearer understanding of what the Wolfhound's legs have to do and where they should be placed in reference to the body in order to maintain a balanced support with the least muscular effort. Any of us who have ever ridden a bicycle or motorcycle know that, with the exception of turns where centrifugal force is also met, both wheels must be under the center of gravity for efficient progress.

The walk, having more leg support and being more easily followed by the eye, is responsible for some of the misconceptions harbored by some people on the idea of leg action. One of these major delusions is that the legs move perpendicular to the ground and parallel to one another, something like the legs on a table. Some Standards even describe gait relatively in that manner, but fortunately the Wolfhound Standard is not one of these.

In Fig. A the dog is trotting with both front and back feet operating in the same timing, which does not clear the weight-bearing leg out of the way of the over-reaching and approaching back leg. Therefore, the dog must side-step the front leg and will be "crabbing." In Fig. B the dog's front feet are timed slightly ahead of the cooperating back feet. Therefore, the front foot is out of the way of the appoaching back foot and allows travel in a straight line.

A simple check should eliminate this idea from any who might harbor it. Stand with feet as far apart as the hip sockets, legs parallel, then lift one foot off the ground without shifting the body weight over the supporting foot. You will find that you have to sway the body over this base support in order to hold the other foot off the ground.

In efficient movement the dog does not sway his body over this support but places the pad under or near the center line. So, coming toward you, the dog starts his walk with the legs relatively parallel but converges the pads toward the center as speed increases. This is true even before the gait breaks from the walk to the faster styles. One may sometimes be confused on this when watching a dog taking a turn and meeting centrifugal force, which changes the point of balance as the dog must lean into the latter force.

The leg in all these cases should maintain a straight column of bones (when viewed from the front) from shoulder joint to pad. If this is done, the inward angle will not interfere with the passing leg that is sufficiently flexed. It is only when the pastern bends inward or the passing leg is not flexed that the dog tends to brush the supporting leg and "moves close" in front.

It is just as faulty for the pastern to break outward as inward from this straight column of bones. This shows a weakness in the joint itself and the dog tends to run on the outside of his pad. Often this does not show when the dog is standing but is evident even to the eye when moving.

The legs should be carried straight forward from the point of last pad contact to the next one, and the back legs should follow in the same angled plane. Some dogs may swing their legs in an arc, much like a swimmer doing the Australian Crawl. All dogs try to get their support under the center of gravity even in the face of physical handicaps. Two things contribute to this swimming action: insufficient flexing of the leg moving forward, and faulty shoulder placement.

The faulty shoulder is most often placed too far forward so that it is somewhat around the front curve of the rib cage, which provides shoulder action at an angle to the spinal column or line of locomotion. The elbow is then often forced outward, the dog moving "out at the elbow." A dog may even stand true but move in this manner.

A dog has relatively the same bones and muscles as man but he lacks that one muscle which enables man to rotate the forearm. Not taking this into consideration is responsible for another misconception which is prevalent. This is that when the dog is standing, his front feet should face directly forward in a position that is often described as "standing true." Being unable to rotate the forearm as it angles inward, this dog is forced to support his weight and get foot action off one center and one outside toe. The two center and stronger toes are the ones that you want in action, while the smaller toes are used on turns and to counteract side forces.

The pad that is angled outward slightly, so that you see more of the inside than outside, will come into line on the inward swing even as a golf club lines up with the ball on the down stroke. This will enable the dog to move over the two center toes. However, if the pad is angled outward to an extreme, it interferes with sustained movement as much as the one looking straight forward. On a plane surface it is not difficult for the eye to detect this pad action even with the slow trot.

Watching the dog move away from you should also show a straight column of bones—from hip socket to pad. The leg will angle inward toward the center line as speed increases, moving in the same plane as the front leg. Deviations from either of these conditions constitute major faults. If this straight column of bone support is maintained, the passing foot, properly flexed, will have sufficient room to prevent moving close or "dusting" the supporting hock.

The inward angle of the "cowhock" breaks this straight line of bones and takes up the passing space, which forces the dog to "dust" or swing the passing leg in an arc around the supporting leg. Quite often these dogs will move wide behind, sometimes placing the back pads on the outside of both front pads rather than in line with them.

Weak hocks, ones with faulty bone assemblies, tend to

bend outward when weight is applied to the leg. This is another condition that does not always show when the dog is standing at rest or in pose, when the legs are usually placed to favor this weakness.

The major cause in large dogs for "moving close" or "dusting" front and rear is a pendulum rather than a flexed swing of the legs. Some will swing their legs as though the only joints in them are the hip and shoulder sockets. (Where this is pronounced, you can even hear the toes rasp the covering of a show ring.) They will have trouble moving over rough ground and particularly through briars and tight ground covering. The weight-bearing leg reaches its maximum flexion at the mid point of its arc of support, which will be directly under the center of the shoulder blade or hip socket. The passing leg will go by at about this point and should be flexed considerably more. The dog should pick them up and then put them down.

A glaring fault in any dog is "crabbing," or moving with the back legs to one side of the front ones. One back leg may pass to the outside of the front while the other tries to split between them. This rear action is not in line with the front, nor even with the line of progress; thus, we have lost motion and energy. Also, the dog cannot turn quickly into the "crab."

Straight shoulders which shorten the fore-stride as well as over-angulation and a lengthened back stride will create this condition, but the major cause is probably faulty timing of leg sequence.

In the slow walk the dog should step off first with one front foot and then follow with the opposite back one. The front foot should be timed sufficiently ahead of the rear so that it is out of the way when the latter arrives. The eye can observe this in the walk and can check the difference in timing even though the back stride does not reach the vacated front pad mark. In the trot it is even more important that the front action be ahead a split second of its coordinating back leg, or the advancing back leg will have no other choice but to side step.

In the fast gaits, front and back strides overlap. Half the

109

arc of the stride is greater than half the length of the body, which in itself creates an over-stride. Momentum also increases this condition.

Front and rear views of the dog probably show us more action faults than side views, but the latter show us the blending of forehand with rearhand for smooth, graceful passage. The foundation of gait is evident in the two former, and the beauty is revealed by the latter view. Two other im-

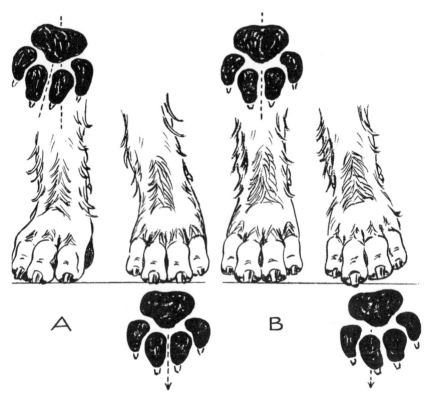

The pad which is angled outward 10 to 15 degrees, as in Fig. A, will, when swung inward under the center of gravity, be placed so that the action is off the two center toes, with the smaller toes used merely for balance on turns.

The pad which is directed straight ahead when the dog is standing as in Fig. B, cannot be rotated when swung inward, so the action must come over one center toe, the smaller, outside toe providing less efficient action.

The outward turn of Fig. A is a rotation of the pastern rather than a bend as in the "French Front," and is not to be confused with the latter.

110

portant factors can be observed better from the side: the flexing of the legs and the supporting action of the pastern under weight, which latter is revealed by the bobbing rather than level movement of the withers.

Even though the trot is not the working gait of the Wolfhound, it is the best by which to judge his movement. All the faults and virtues of his ability to move will be reflected in the trot, and it is not so fast that the eye cannot see some of the virtues and faults. You can see enough to open the door on some of the things which you should look for in posture and to let you understand what to expect of the dog in the field.

Description of gait may sound like an exploration trip in search of faults, though it isn't intended as such. There is nothing more desirable than good movement in an animal and we cite faults for the same reason that traffic signs are posted—taking heed of them gives us a better ride and quicker arrival at our destination.

As pointed out earlier, the Wolfhound's movement tells us a lot more about him than compliance to a simple paragraphic description of this single factor. All parts of his body and their cooperation enter into it. We may love that shaggy head and massive body as it stands majestically on our lawn like a statue sculptured by a great artist, but as the dog moves out across the field with powerful, flowing grace, he is at his best. There is far more beauty in the sweep of a gull over the waves than in his placid perch on the crown of a piling, and so it is with the flash of a Wolfhound in pursuit of game or running just for fun. The more we improve the movement of the Wolfhound, whether we take him afield or not, the better Wolfhound we will have—and that is the end toward which we strive.

THE EMPTY CHAIR

Characteristics of the Breed

YEARS AGO, Joseph A. McAleenan wrote the following, which to me has always typified the Irish Wolfhound character: "No other dog can come so close to the understanding and kindly companionship that exists between humans, as this dog can. A giant in structure, a lamb in disposition, a lion in courage; affectionate and intelligent, thoroughly reliable and dependable at all times, as a companion and as a guard he is perfection."

The Wolfhound is a great griever, as you can "see" by studying the picture of "The Empty Chair" that we reproduce here. Many people experience this grieving by the Hound if anything changes in the family. It is another reason why mature Hounds make slow adjustments. They are family dogs—and that is even true in kennels. Our old Roonagh came to the house a great deal but she preferred the kennel to live in, because there she could see what was happening. The thing I shall never forget was her way of fussing about after a new litter arrived on the place. She was as restless as a lion in a cage. We stumbled onto the cause of her restlessness when we let her out and she came whimpering over to the door that led into the whelping room.

We put the mother out and let Roonagh in just to see if

that was "it." She went over and sniffed each puppy, tail wagging on long, strong waves, then she looked up. Her anxiety was over. We took her out and she never asked to go back in again to that litter. But whenever another arrived, she went through the same thing. We used to call her the "first-nighter," for she liked to be there at the beginning of things. And she is the one that duplicated the situation "The Empty Chair" depicts, after Mr. Starbuck died. She was "his dog," afield and at home. After he was taken from the home she daily stood beside his empty bed and with neck bent and head pressed against the side of the bed, she stood in silent grief. This went on for weeks until she wasted to a mere shadow. Time did not dim her yearning, but the arrival of a new puppy gave her a new purpose for being.

As to character, we continually witness the reliability of our breed. These dogs just naturally "mind their own business" and do not look for trouble, but when called upon to do so, they can simply explode into action. I think the story Alec Scott sent in from Santa Fe, New Mexico, well illustrates this. He writes:

"It happened last winter, while riding with the Hounds, and has to do with a young, eighteen-months-old Hound, Gareth of Rathmullan. There had been two packs of wild dogs roaming around the ranches all winter, killing cattle and running down horses. These wild dogs are abandoned dogs of mixed breeds, which form into packs and become wild.

"When out with the Hounds one morning, I ran into the pack. I called in our Hounds and all came to heel but one; that was Gareth. He started to smell the pack. As he started to leave, two jumped him and then all I could see was the pack of seven on top of him. I had quite a job on my hands keeping the rest of the Hounds from intervening, but in less than two minutes I saw a crossbred Shepherd and police dog go sailing up in the air, then three more in quick succession. The three that were left took to their heels. The four all had their backs broken. He was just a

114

Ch. Sulhamstead Mac of Killybracken, left, with two outstanding sons—
Ch. Caragahoolie O'Killybracken (center), Best in Show winner and BOB
at 1968 Specialty, and Ch. Himself of Killybracken. Owned by Killybracken Kennels, Francestown, N.H.

This is Darragh (picture by Dana Steichen).

young, curious Hound, but when the pack downed him, he came up a 'fightin' fool' for sure.

"You may wonder why I did not let the rest of the Hounds help Gareth out. The reason is, that when out exercising the Hounds, they are broken to not interfere with a strange dog. A strange dog can bark and growl as much as he likes, but it is too bad if he makes a jump at any of them.

"In my experience with the breed, I find them the most gentle and affectionate dogs I've run across yet. This killing fight that Gareth was in has not changed his disposition any. In fact, I turn four dogs and four bitches out together in a small enclosure every evening after they have been fed."

The future dog owner wants "a good watch dog," and the Irish Wolfhound is unrivaled on this point. It is hard to find words to do sufficient justice to the dog in this role. His very size inspires such respect that the tramp or burglar looking for a place to enter will prefer to go elsewhere—where there is less chance of trouble. Like the rest of the world, the prowler will follow the line of least resistance.

But suppose, for argument, that the prowler has entered the guarded premises. The Wolfhound uses his head. He gives warning but is not likely to use his teeth. I know of one case where the dog pushed a prospective chicken thief out of a yard. The man in contact with an animal of such size, respectfully refrained from argument and backed out.

The would-be dog owner wants a dog that "can be trusted with children." Again the Irish dog qualifies. He is loving, and he is patient. He is as good a child guardian as he is a house guardian. Can anyone imagine a ne'er-do-well interfering with a child who is in the company of 150 pounds of loyalty?

"The dog must be intelligent." He is. Thank Heaven, the Irish Wolfhound breeders have never "bred the brains out of him" by inducing a narrow, witless brainpan. He has been allowed to retain his exceptional intelligence, his beautiful forehead and well-set, intelligent eyes. He is a wise dog, whose desire is to find out what his master wants, and then to do it.

He must be "an all-around dog." His intelligence and adaptability make him this. He can be house dog, watch dog, child's playmate, dignified companion for the walk, long-legged companion for the horseback ride, or a hunting dog.

We know dogs at colleges are not uncommon, but Bob Becker, in his "Dog Notes" in the *Chicago Tribune,* some time ago, gave the following account which will interest Irish Wolfhound fanciers:

"A big Irish Wolfhound with a record of killing a 1,100 pound bull, yet as gentle and well mannered a dog around people and other dogs as anyone could ask for, occupies a singular position on the college campus at Beloit, Wisconsin. This Irish Wolfhound is named Patrick Grover Killybracken. Since his battle with an enraged bull he is known as a 'bull-terror.'

"Pat belongs to Tom Lawler, a student at the college. When a year and a half old, Pat was taken to the Lawler country home near Dwyer, Indiana. A bull charged Pat when the latter was trying to make some friendly overtures to the king of the pastures. When the bull came for the Wolfhound, Pat led for the jaw or a little lower down. He got a hold and he hung on. It was the end of the enraged bull, and immediately Pat was branded as a toreador.

"Now Pat is getting culture at Beloit college. Everybody knows him. Children can maul him, because he is friendly and gentle—except to charging bulls! Small dogs dash at him. He turns sideways and they run right under him.

"The tolerance of this dog, Pat, in relation to other dogs and his friendly disposition remind us of the story that Martin Hogan told us the other day. It concerns another Wolfhound, Pat of Barrington, and illustrates how a big Wolfhound puts up with the mauling of smaller dogs.

"This latter Wolfhound will be challenged for a romp by a little Wire-Haired Terrier. The Terrier gets hold of the Wolfhound's neck and hangs on. The big dog will walk

117

around with the little Terrier suspended from its neck. It's all in fun, and the big Irish Hound doesn't mind the fooling of the Terrier, which to a giant Wolfhound is just a handful of dog."

Richard K. Lackey had an experience with his Ch. Killabrick, in Florida. It was late evening. Mr. Lackey had just finished reading, and decided to step out with Killabrick a few moments before retiring, when, as he opened the door, Killabrick sprang off the steps, with a lion's roar, and was off for the back of the place. Almost simultaneously, Mr. Lackey heard the terrified cry of a man calling, "Help! Help!" Then silence.

Mr. Lackey hurried down to find Killabrick standing over the man on the ground. The man was too frightened to speak, and dared not move. At a word from Mr. Lackey, Killabrick stepped aside, and Mr. Lackey took the man down to the house where he found his voice and said: "Your dog's all right, mister. I was stealin' your grapefruit, but I'll never steal another thing as long as I live."

Killabrick had simply knocked him down, and kept him there, rumbling a few threats, until his master arrived to take charge of the situation.

This is just another example of true Irish Wolfhound temperament. Mr. Lackey has traveled a great deal with Killabrick, and the dog is well known for his gentleness of manner, and his dignified response to all extended affection. He has proven many times that "courage dwells with gentleness."

Killabrick knows when to guard and how. He has nothing to fear, so does not find it necessary to sport a belligerent attitude. Many who are naturally afraid of dogs and have approached this huge Hound with a certain amount of caution, have found that his presence melted their distrustfulness and he quickly gained their confidence and admiration. Like all his breed, he is reliable and is a comfort. At home he holds forth merrily with four other canine household members, an English Setter, a German Shepherd, a Boston Terrier, and a Scottish Terrier. They live together in the greatest harmony and seem to crave one another's compan-

118

ionship. Except in hunting, when the English Setter seems to take the lead, they are inclined to look to the Irish Wolfhound as their good-natured "big boss."

And still another character reference was submitted by the late Edward Cooper of Pass-A-Grille, Florida, regarding his eighteen-months-old Irish Wolfhound female. He writes (in part) as follows:

"She is the smartest Hound I ever had. She is whistle broken thoroughly, and comes to the three notes of 'Whip-Poor-Will' with the accent on the 'Will.' She will charge on note of a mourning dove. I hunted her with the horses, at home, in West Virginia, until I came down here, and she was death on rabbits and skunks. Down here, as we are right on the beach, she stays in the water continually, and the children take her out well over her depth in the surf. She knows how to dive through the breakers, and has a big time all by herself at night when it is warm, and she goes in to cool off. She is, as I say, the smartest one I ever had.

"One day, last month, the baby came in from school and, having her bathing suit on under her clothes, undressed on the beach and left her clothes. She came in the house and the tide came in and got the clothes and took them out. Brigit came along the beach and, evidently thinking the child had drowned. swam out and, one at a time, brought every piece of clothing to the house, and piled them up on the steps. Whether from the smell or sight, I don't know, but she recognized the clothing.

"She is slow to make up with strangers, but if you whistle the bird calls to her she will make up readily. She likes to ride in the car, and go with me on the boat, also. She is content either in or out of the house, and sleeps at the foot of my bed. She loves to play, is thoroughly obedient, and an excellent retriever . . . will carry anything she can pick up. She will bring the morning paper in, if she can get out. . . ."

This is just another of the many letters that come in telling what satisfactory family dogs can be found in our breed.

Tralaigh of Boroughbury (Imp.) with Doctor's identical twins.

The Arrival of a New Puppy

THE ARRIVAL age of newly acquired puppies or grown dogs can vary as to months and years, but the average of puppies is in the three-months bracket.

Few new owners realize what a puppy goes through before he reaches his destination. At his natal home he has known only security and implicit trust in humankind. He has known no fear, although puppies do vary in temperament somewhat; some are very bold and hoydenish, while others have an extra amount of caution in their make-up. The average is at a level between these two extremes, but no one can predict how a puppy will react to the experience of shipping. For one thing, it's very likely the first time he has ever been shut up in a crate. He is locked in and he can't get out! He is separated from all he has known and the unknown is now upon him. There is terror in the discovery that he can't get out—even for a grown Hound, if it is the first time. Would that we could explain to the dog that he will be freed shortly.

Soon he is on a train or a plane. The train bounces and bumps (ever ride any distance in an express car?) and this fact, plus the strange noises, the belching and roaring of the engines that pass by him, both in loading and transferring,

121

can turn his crate for the time, into a haven. Then the long ride—the express messenger's voice—and the arrival of food and water. He may or may not eat; even those who have reared him cannot predict what he will do.

Taking off in a plane is different. The roar of the airplane engines before departure is as terrifying as is the noise of the train, but the situation is better after the plane is aloft. Often it is necessary to change from an airplane to a train. This can be troublesome, and some of the boldest, toughest puppies arrive cringing in their crates, confused, be-addled. Fortunately, this is usually a temporary condition.

In contrast, I've also shipped downright cautious puppies that found themselves in transit and arrived on the crest. I recall one instance in particular. This was a very affectionate puppy, not shy, but slightly over-cautious and very bashful. One could see he was destined to be a big fellow. He was three months old and I did hesitate in sending this one out over the two thousand miles I was being asked to ship him. However, the gentleman interested in him was so sure, from his description, that this was HIS puppy, I finally persuaded myself to ship him out.

Express travel is somewhat like sending a package by the U. S. Mail, inasmuch as it is often impossible to give exact time of arrival if there are to be transfers en route. If any train is late or cars are overcrowded, or no messenger is on the express car (a must when livestock is traveling), the express company holds the right to route the dog according to conditions found. For long journeys we can only give approximate arrival time. In this particular case, the new owner acquainted himself with the time of the arrival of trains to his Western Oregon town and on the day the puppy was due, he decided to meet every train. He had read some place that the one who took the puppy out of the crate would be the one the puppy would first accept. He wanted to be that one. He expected a frightened puppy and had conceived the perfect plan for starting him out right.

He met the morning train, but no puppy. The noon train was a fast train stopping only to discharge passengers and carried no express, the station-master told him. So he went home for lunch, expecting to return for the early afternoon express. While lunching, his telephone rang and the express agent at the station said, "We got your puppy down here." Immediately the new owner was excited and his first words were his first thoughts: "How IS he?" "Oh," boomed the agent, "he's fine and he is running around the office here shaking hands with all the fellas." And so he was. They had taken him out of his crate to care for him until his owner showed up, and he was the gayest, happiest puppy in all the world. And on his returned crate was a note to me from one of the express messengers en route out, telling how he had enjoyed that puppy. Most men like dogs and this one had no doubt let the little fellow out in the car during the long, between-station runs. He may even have shared his lunch with the puppy. One thing is certain: he had been let out of his crate, put back in, and let out again. The pup had discovered that if he was put back in, he'd get out again. And I know this has happened with many shipments, especially to those traveling west of Chicago.

We have had a few surprises in shipping our boldest. There was the dark gray Briar Maguire, with the impudent expression that was due, no doubt, to his bewhiskered muzzle. (Some puppies grow whiskers earlier than do others.) Maguire was a "little dickens." As a small puppy, he would climb the stairs in his kennel room and go to sleep on the top step. Relaxed as puppies are in slumber, he fell off one day and came tumbling over the side and a spike nail raked him, cutting through his skin and leaving a straight incision long enough to have constituted the incision for an abdominal operation. I first saw it that day while the pups were out in the snow playing and the sight of it nearly finished me off, even though Maguire was paying no attention to it. Knowing his predilection for top stair sleeping, we investigated and found the nail, quickly figuring out what had happened. Before you decide this was rank carelessness on our part, I want to say these were the only steps in the kennel and they led through a trap door to an attic. Only very young puppies were ever in this room and none had ever before tried to climb up the steps. The steps were open in back and after

123

going up two or three steps, the puppies could see down through and were frightened and slid back or sort of backed down. But not Maguire! He went to the top and he came down with speed. I had seen him do this many times.

He was rushed to the hospital. The vet said, "Let's see how far we can go using a local." So Briar Maguire was strapped to the operating table, his dark, merry eyes roving around, all interested. Believe it or not, he enjoyed it. He was the absolute center of attraction and was commanding the attention of a surgeon, a nurse, his anxious mistress, and a calm but concerned kennel helper. The local anesthetic proved sufficient and we were instructed to keep him quiet until he healed up.

When we arrived back at the kennel, we isolated him from his group (he was about two months old) and put him in the recreation room at the kennel (where hunting equipment, guns, trophies, and fishing tackle were kept). To protect the incision, I put a shirt on him. To make the shirt, I cut off the legs and arms of some woolen underwear of my husband's that the laundry had reduced in size to fit a child of about ten years. Wearing this garment, Maguire was a most unusual looking pup. He made me think of a choir boy and the garment gave him a deceiving air of innocence. But he defeated all our attempts to keep him quiet. I heard a racket as I approached the kennel the next day, so I peered through a window and looked in on him. Here he was, amusing himself by jumping from the day bed into a large rocking chair near by. This would swing and sway and when it slowed up he climbed off, then went back up on the bed and did it all over again. Of course this robust entertainment tore out the stitches, so I just bandaged him up under his "choir jacket" and he came along fine.

We did keep him away from the others. We had to. The others would have made merry with his raiment. But not to leave him alone too much, I kept him with me a great deal and once when he did something he shouldn't have, I stamped my foot and said, "You're baddddd," and he gazed intently up at me and then stamped both his front feet right back at me.

I tell you this to let you picture him and then to try to

124

reconcile yourself to the news that when shipped out somewhat later, he arrived in a very frightened state. He would
accept the women of the household but was afraid of the
men, especially if they had a hat on, though at the kennel he
was more used to men than to women. We never knew what
happened. He was one of the few puppies that was vocal in
his crate as he was put in it at the station. It is possible that
he continued to bark and someone did something to him. He
had never been punished forcibly, but the normal fright of
a first train trip, coupled with some special scare, left a mark
that was some time in leaving. It was overcome, but it took
patient understanding on the part of his new owners for a
few weeks. A less intelligent puppy might not have reacted
so, but often a high degree of intelligence (in both humans
and dogs) travels hand in hand with a certain sensitivity, and
in such cases there is a narrow line between boldness and
shyness.

As I said earlier, one never knows how a puppy will arrive.
I have stated two extreme cases. The *average* experience is
simply that an express trip is frightening and the dog does
not arrive the same puppy he was on leaving. New things
have touched him. It is very rarely too troublesome. Properly handled, the experience is little worse for the puppy
than is the first day of school for an average child.

Usually a young puppy (and sometimes a fairly old one)
has to be practically lifted out of the crate. Remember, he is
in a confused state of mind and nothing should be expected
of him. Instead of coaxing and pulling, just lift the puppy
out and, if possible, carry him to your waiting car. A large
young puppy is most easily carried "calf-fashion."

Plan to call for the new pup at the express depot. It is a
big mistake to have your puppy "delivered to the house," as
the tossing of the crate in a delivery truck makes his trip
that much harder, delays his arrival needlessly, and often
exposes him to weather elements he was protected from in
the express car. For example, to have played in the snow
before leaving is one thing; to ride an hour or so in a delivery truck at the end of a train journey in the coldest weather,
drafty and damp, after having been shut up in a warm place

with no exercise and in a perturbed state—well, humans have been given reason and judgment, and a little can be used at a time like this.

It is wise to take an old blanket to the station. The puppy will probably be crate soiled, but don't bathe him. Just wash the soiled spots and, if needed, then give him a good "dry-cleaning." (We use rubbing alcohol for this purpose, wetting the end of a small bath towel well with alcohol and rubbing the pup vigorously but being *very* careful not to get any in his eyes.)

Arriving a bit frightened or bewildered is a normal thing, but if brought to his future home and quarters without any fuss, the puppy will, in an *unbelievably* short time, be himself and own everyone he meets. It may be almost at once, when he finds he is free and some familiar pats are coming his way. Or it might take a day or two. In very obstinate cases it may be nearly two weeks, especially with a yearling or a grown dog.

Until the dogs have made the adjustment, do not rush them. Let the puppy have a chance to figure things out and start the friendship (or imagine he does). Do not judge him hastily. You have to discover each other *in his way*—the same as we try to understand children on their first day at kindergarten. It is not done at once. A few are difficult. Some are not. All make it.

After the puppy has had a chance to use his legs, and clean himself out—feed him. It is assumed he was given fresh water on arrival. One cannot over-emphasize this water business. Fresh water at all times is essential to this fast-growing breed. The puppy may be too excited to eat, but a good meal to offer is some warm milk toast (just room temperature) and maybe a lean beef (ground) patty, which he can have either raw or lightly cooked, whichever he has been used to, if you have been advised.

After he has eaten, let him be quiet for a time. If the trip has been hard on him he may sleep the better part of the next few days and the older the pup is, the more he seems to need sleep. That is why we like to ship the pups while they are young. And young pups adjust faster and forget the

126

trip sooner. Delivery at three months is very satisfactory. In another month the pups start to cut their second teeth, always a drain on the system for calcium, and they need their energy for growth and should not have it dissipated by the excitement of shipping. We find pups travel well at two and a half months and have had satisfactory results in shipping by plane to both coasts at this age. So we like to send them out from two and a half to three and a half months of age. Puppies are fully immunized at two months, but the new owner should carry out any special instructions forwarded from the kennel.

The young puppy, especially after three months, is a gangling shock to his new owner. He is all huge bones and protuberances and big feet. Yes, even the ears are sometimes ahead of themselves and he will carry them every which way for many months. The feet and joints *have* to grow ahead of the rest to be ready for the weight that is coming. If a puppy looks nice and trim, it is simply a sign that he is more than likely to finish a weedy specimen. The ungainly ones are the "big ones" a-making.

Do not rush your puppy off the first thing to get the opinion of your veterinarian, if all is well. Be patient and carry on with the instructions sent by the breeder, or those contained in this book relative to the rearing of the breed. I hold the veterinary profession in high regard and some of my best friends are members of the profession. But so many veterinarians (and so-called professional dog fanciers as well) have never seen a Wolfhound puppy in the early, tender months, and in such instances I've heard some very shocking statements. If the puppy is not toeing in or out and his elbows are under him, not sticking out sidewise, and if he is reasonably well up on his feet (depending on age here, as many do go down a bit when teething) and not walking way back on his pastern joints, you can know the puppy is all right and that with sensible care he will stay that way and develop out of this loosely built period. He must have a balanced diet and reasonable exercise, which are subjects we will cover elsewhere.

Be glad for big joints and big feet. In a few instances I've seen the forequarters seem to do all the developing one month, and the rear the next, throwing the puppy out of balance for a time. (Colts develop this way, too.) If the puppy has warranted a fine appraisal at three months, you can know that if he is receiving proper care (and barring any debilitating disease), that by eight or nine months, no matter how ungainly he has been, you will see his "goodness" reappearing and a general Wolfhoundy look developing. This will please you, but he is now entering the yearling period, a very discouraging stage, because Wolfhounds seem to finish up so slowly. You hardly perceive it—you only realize a year later what's happened. We have fast finishers, just average, and very slow ones. If your dog is a fast finisher, you escape much of this awkward period. I've seen some lovely females finish up quickly and be very showable by eighteen months, but they rarely hold show form. If they look too good at eighteen months, Wolfhounds (especially the males) are likely to thicken and "miss" some way at full maturity. I'd rather they looked like "a long drink of water," as the saying goes, while yearlings.

Wolfhounds do not reach maximum height under eighteen months to two years of age, and after that they continue to fill out up to age two and one-half, three and one-half, or four years before full maturity and perfection are reached. If they finish slowly, they make better "lasters," and I prefer this. We have had Hounds at seven years of age that had the same elegance and conformation as the two and three year olds. The "added something" is the mental sagacity that the years contribute.

A puppy or grown dog can be kept in the house or out-of-doors all of the time. If in the house, he should have a bed off the floor to be out of drafts. A mattress for a baby's bed is satisfactory and a cover that zips on can be made for it. A divan or a day bed that is "his" can be used, but the puppy must be taught that this alone is his and that he is not to appropriate any other piece of furniture.

If kenneled outside, his house should be interlined and made with two rooms, or with one room and an entrance hall, depending on the climate. The opening for the dog to enter should be thirty-six inches high, to take care of the Wolfhound when grown and not continually rub the hair on his back. Then at the back of the entrance hall a similar opening should be made to enter the other room, or his real bed. It is good to have the hall large enough to use—in fact, it should be the same size as the sleeping room but with no bedding. In hot weather, the Hound will frequently lie in the entrance hall, where he can "see out." If in a cold climate, a flap of canvas can be hung on the inner opening, but a growing puppy often will not leave canvas alone and eventually tears it off. Nevertheless, one can try, and the dog can get along without it in a properly built house that is well bedded. Obviously, in a mild climate the double room is not needed.

Of course, to make a "de luxe" arrangement, you may have two Wolfhounds or a Wolfhound and a dog of another breed "sleep together." And it is a good idea to extend the roof of the house out to make a porch roof, and to add a wooden floor, so the growing puppy or grown Hound will have a place to lie off the ground in damp weather, even in summer. This is a splendid place to feed the dog, out of the rain, or in the shade in hot weather.

"Is he housebroken?" many prospective owners ask. In our case the answer is usually "No," since, as a rule, only a puppy left alone after the others are shipped out, or a single puppy to be reared, is taken to the house to live. Generally, as the dogs develop, they come to the house "to visit," or "to call"; and in these short visits they gradually become accustomed to household things. The periods are lengthened as the puppy develops, but very little house experience is had by those shipped out at an early age. We gradually acquaint them with all things on the place, including the house, and it has been *our* experience that practically all puppies over four months are naturally housebroken. They seem to know that the out-of-doors is the bathroom and quite possibly our method of rearing them in quarters where they always have access to their outside runway may account for some of this.

Obviously, a very young puppy coming to the house to live has to be taught, or watched. Again, it is a case of common

129

sense, or "dog sense," to accomplish the teaching. But how can you have that, you ask, if you've never had a dog before, or been interested in one, and perhaps are being talked into having this one by a lovable wife or a persuasive husband. Truly, I never worry about these last situations, since Wolfhounds are notorious in breaking down all resistance to dog ownership and many who have never wanted a dog find themselves with a Wolfhound and thereafter through the years will never be without one. This Wolfhound-ownership-need, once one has been an owner, is so widespread, it is almost a rule.

In housebreaking, the key is to never let an accident happen! This sounds harder than it is. To begin with, if you are going to keep a puppy in the house, or have one in the house a great deal of the time, do not have him arrive until you have a few days to be with him. Those few days you give up in the beginning will repay beyond measure in starting him off properly in all ways.

When a puppy comes in, he is excited by the house and its furnishings, all strange and new. Excitement causes the puppy to relieve himself; it is a form of nervous activity throughout the system. If he has just arrived, he should be left free to walk about out-of-doors (where he can't run off, if he is old enough to be concerned and decides to look for someone he knows). If he is too excited, he may not relieve himself at once, but after sufficient time has been given, take him in anyway. Leave him inside only about ten minutes, then take him out again. This is particularly necessary for any puppy making his first trip into the house, or if the weather outside is cold, because coming into heated quarters affects the bladder. Leave the pup inside just a short time and *watch,* and carry him right out if he starts to transgress. Then bring him back in and he will probably be good for an hour. But *watch.* A bit of work, maybe, but if he *never does it,* he never will be tempted to do it deliberately! And after a few trips outside, he gets the idea—what the trips outside are for and what is expected of him.

If the puppy is to be housebroken at once, I keep him near by at night. I rarely housebroke very young puppies, but when for some reason I wanted to, and did, I started by sleeping in a room with a door leading outside. This simplified matters for the beginning. The sunroom in my home was convenient and for a few days I kept a warm, handy dressing robe on the emergency day bed on which I slept. The puppy slept on a mattress bed beside me; I often let my arm hang down to touch the puppy with my hand until he settled. Some puppies stay put, others are very restless. In either case, when they get up to move about, I get up and take them out and wait for them. You may do this once the first night. You may do it several times. But each succeeding night is less difficult. When dawn comes, or when *you* get up, he will get up too, *so don't wait to dress—take him out!*

A very few nights of this, plus careful watching daytimes, and nothing will happen. That has been my experience and I'm an average mortal.

Ch. Edain of Ambleside
with three two-week-old puppies (July 1951).

131

Lady Hope of Ambleside,
4½ months old.

Sir Raglan of Ambleside,
6½ months old.

Colleen Bawn of Ambleside with puppies by Ch. Ballyshane of Ambleside.

132

The Irish Wolfhound as a Hunter

COURSING IS THE pursuit of game with dogs that follow by sight instead of by scent. The Irish Wolfhound is noted not only for his keen sight but also for his remarkable powers of scent, and the courage and cleverness that goes to make a great hunter. So I never think of him in terms of coursing but as a mighty hunter. The requirements in these two fields are vastly different and lest we forget, the Wolfhound stands in the front ranks as a great and natural hunter.

Mr. McAleenan started hunting with Wolfhounds years ago and the account of the killing of a grizzly bear by one of his Irish Wolfhounds in the Big Horn Basin in Wyoming, is told on a tablet erected to the Hound's memory.

That the Wolfhound can course, we know. I recall Mrs. Wofford's telling about her ten-months-old Fara, who, to the delight of the family, ran a jack rabbit two miles, caught it and brought it home. And anyone who has coursed jack rabbits knows they are fast. (This same Fara of Rimrock won the Hound of the Year Challenge Trophy in 1942.)

We had two Greyhounds that ran with the Wolfhounds for a time, and as to the dogs' speed I can speak with assurance: the Greyhounds were quicker to get started and had the edge on the Hounds the first three miles, then they were finished; but the Wolfhounds, at that point, were just getting started and would hold up all day.

Wolfhounds are not gun dogs, in the true sense, but like to finish off their own quarry. Mr. Starbuck always felt that dogs, to be at their best, should be reared in the country in which they were to hunt. And the same belief is held by Mr. Monroe, in Australia, and by Warren A. Depuy, who has a fur breeding ranch in Montana. Mr. Depuy says:

"It takes the vast open spaces to bring out the true guise. There he may surmount difficulties and perform feats of strength, speed, grit and fighting that mark him as a superlative expression of the canine species. . . . We were so troubled with wild animals getting our stock, the lynx, coyote and prairie wolf and we had tried nearly every known method to keep this pirate (wolf and coyote) under control, including poison, traps, high-powered rifles, and Hounds of nearly all kinds. Yet he continued to hold his own. . . . Then someone suggested the Irish Wolfhound. It was just an idea and having tried so many other reputedly fast, clever, courageous and strong Hounds, we really did not expect the Irish variety to be much better.

"But from the beginning they were a great success in the killing of wolves and coyotes."

Later the Wolfhounds were used on bear. Mr. Depuy also mentions that it's an advantage for the Hounds to grow up in the country they are to hunt, for their faculties then develop better, they grow sounder, have tougher feet, and better wind and eyesight. Mr. Depuy writes:

"Perhaps I seem too enthusiastic about the Irish Wolfhound, but it would be impossible to live with these dogs and see what they can do without becoming almost rabid on the subject of their excellence. They have speed and fighting ability and SENSE in unstinted degree, but aside from all that they are sturdy, companionable creatures that can stand upon their own feet and do more than their

134

share of the work necessary and which is within the ability of an animal. Their value to us in our business is inestimable."

Mr. Depuy also tells of taking Wolfhounds along on a marvelous pack trip on which pine marten and sable were trapped for use as foundation stock on the ranch.

Our own Martin Hogan wrote, "When farming in Western Canada I saw the Irish Wolfhound at his best. Hunting the fast and wily prairie wolf on the open prairies is great sport. . . . If the Irish Wolfhound grabs on the run, the hold is usually behind the shoulder, the Hound and wolf roll over and over. If the wolf or coyote turns at bay as they often do, the Hound charges right in and bowls him over. In either case the struggle isn't long when a big rangy Hound is used."

The comprehensive picture given by Ronald K. Monroe, of his Australian-born Irish Wolfhound, has a place here (this description originally appeared in one of the English Club books). Mr. Monroe writes:

"Four and a half years ago I was undecided as to which breed of dog to purchase to accompany me on my hunting trips and that would be a real pal for a bachelor who spent a great deal of leisure time away off the beaten tracks. It was not so much a gun dog that I needed as a hunter, and one that would be heavy enough to negotiate rough country. After much reading of doggy books, and talking with breeders and dog lovers generally, I finally decided on the Irish Wolfhound as being the most suitable for my particular requirements. I have never regretted the choice, as Thunder has more than fulfilled my wildest expectations. Now rising five years, he is a perfectly developed, upstanding dog, with a kindly, quiet nature, wonderfully intelligent and obedient, and above all a dashing hunter and a real killer.

"When I brought him home he was just four months old, a loose-limbed, straw-colored pup, very shy and with just his kennel manners. I started in to train him very gently, and rewarded his efforts with a biscuit or two. He quickly

135

became a well-educated dog, obeying my every wish conveyed by word, whistle or sign, every command just being spoken loud enough for him to hear. He was still rather shy in the presence of strangers, so I used to take him out on a lead and walk him among as many as convenient, and in this way he got used to them when in public places, but was still a very good watch-dog at home.

"I started him off hunting rabbits, and he took naturally to the job. He made his first catch at night by the aid of my car headlamps. Now, as he drives along the country roads at night, taking up the whole back seat, he keeps a sharp lookout for game of all kinds, and when let out seldom fails to catch it. He is a splendid jumper and even at night will take five foot wire fences in his stride. His sight at night seems particularly good. In the daytime when I shoot rabbits or hares from the car, I just let him out, and he jumps over the fences and brings them back to me.

"From rabbits I took him out after wallabies with a pack of other mixed dogs. I can well remember the first one that he saw caught. He just peeped into the sprawling dogs, and watched from a safe distance. He was just seven months old then. Now he just picks up the biggest wallaby, and kills it as easily as a terrier does a rat. He soon learnt the idea of wallaby and kangaroo hunting, together with dingoes and foxes. He not only runs by sight, but he has a wonderful nose, and will run a kangaroo for miles on scent until he catches sight of it. Then, he soon has it thrown to earth.

"Early in his career, he was ripped by a 'roo. Now he is very careful, and never rushes in to an old man kangaroo that is balled up and ready to fight for his life. He quickly circles him, then rushing in from behind, grabs him by the butt of the tail and after breaking it, kills by either throat or heart grip, continually pulling away from the terrible and death-dealing blows from the powerful hind legs.

"When Thunder was 3½ years old, I took him into the

136

hills deer hunting. After he had seen one caught and pulled down by a pack of Foxhounds, he soon learnt that the big deer were even better game than the old men kangaroos. The country in which the big Sambhur deer live in Australia is very mountainous and is covered with a dense undergrowth which is almost impossible to penetrate. Foxhounds are used for trailing deer in this class of country. When a moderately clear section is reached such as a river flat, Thunder then joins in the chase, and soon has the huge stag at bay in the river bed or pulled down in some thicket.

"Once, last year, when being led to a likely spot by my brother—Thunder will not leave me to follow anyone else —a big stag broke cover, and Thunder pulled away with six feet of rope tied to his collar. Notwithstanding the handicap this rope must have been in the timber and undergrowth, he pulled the stag down three times and brought him to bay, where he was shot, within five hundred yards of the starting point.

"The stag was found to have broken off one of its huge antlers when either charging at Thunder, or when striking the earth when pulled down by him. So thick was some of the country through which they had run that the antler could not be found, and so a fine trophy was spoilt.

"Thunder is a very good-natured dog and never starts any fights, but when he catches any game, or is with me when I shoot any, he will not allow another dog near his property. He will not let a stranger near me if I am in the bush either sitting or lying down, but as soon as I get to my feet will then let the stranger approach.

"I can honestly say that he is really a wonderful pal, always by my side—he is at my feet as I write this—ready for a game, or serious hunting, or a quiet rest, and understanding all I say to him. He is a thorough gentleman both at home and abroad, and above all a brilliant and natural hunter."

This is a nice place to close this chapter—else the many, many hunting tales I've been told (all of which are true experiences), would tumble out. We know there is little place for the Hound as a hunter in society as we find it today—only a privileged few live where hunting can be found, and the horizon narrows all the time. But these stories help us to understand the Standard for the Irish Wolfhound, which describes a hunting Hound.

At Santa Fe, New Mexico, Alex Scott is off to the hills with a group of the Rathmullan Wolfhounds.

Anyone for Obedience?

INTEREST IN OBEDIENCE classes has swept the country. I have watched the classes on many occasions and once stewarded for Blanche Saunders when she had an entry of 90, for two days' work. I had been slated to steward somewhere and I asked for that assignment because I wanted to know more about obedience. Mr. Dana was very enthusiastic about this branch of activity, and, as I was a bit lukewarm, I felt I should learn more about it. I had watched obedience classes many times, but I felt our breed was not exactly the best type if obedience was the field in which one wanted to go to the top. I did know that dogs that moved with alacrity did better, for I had noticed the Danes were slow to *sit* and that then the ringside would "titter." The dog was performing but not quickly, and I wondered if I wanted anyone laughing at a Wolfhound doing the same work.

Since I've learned more about obedience, I have decided it is exactly like showing in breed classes—some dogs do wonderfully well and get into the spirit of the thing. I *do* know that all young dogs, like children, should be taught restraint. It is the first step in obedience and certainly *no one* can enjoy dogs unless they are controlled. We always,

139

through the years, taught them to lead on a leash, to lie down when told to and to come when called. These were just good manners in our book.

I didn't know if the "drill" of obedience classes would help or hinder the dogs. I found out. There are some Wolfhounds that excel, but the majority do not. They can easily be taught all parts of it, but Wolfhounds do not, as a rule, go through the routine with a spirit of joy as many, many breeds do.

The first thing I advise all people buying a Wolfhound youngster, is, of course, to get him acquainted with the leash and then enroll at an obedience class. Any time after six to eight months of age will do, and in this way, the customers are trained. And that is a vital thing—to have the owner trained. In fact, one of the best books Blanche Saunders wrote was *Training You to Train Your Dog.** Many people do not even know how to put a collar on properly—or how to walk with their dogs. A little instruction in a large class of dogs, from a good instructor, works miracles. The owner will take pride in his dog and his dog will be able to associate with others in the class. It is a very democratic "school."

Originally, I objected to the *sit* every time one stopped. (I mention this since some newcomers may have the same objection.) I did not want my dog to sit every time I stopped. It was suggested that I say "stand" when I stopped, but I decided it was preferable to say nothing when I stopped and then to say "sit" *if* and when I wanted the dog to sit. I have felt that the habit of sitting counts against dogs in the breed ring. I have met judges who were annoyed by the quick sitting of a Hound in the class, when breed competition was going on. But I *still* think obedience training is a necessity for the average American owner starting out with a Hound, for through it he will learn how to handle his dog in a becoming manner. And I especially advise people to have their children enter an obedience class. It should be

* Other books by Blanche Saunders include *The Complete Novice Obedience Course, The Complete Open Obedience Course,* and *The Complete Utility Obedience Course,* all published by Howell Book House Inc., New York.

part of their education for it opens an entirely new field. Actually, children learn about other breeds and develop a "doggy knowledge" the painless way, especially if they come from a family that has never had dogs about.

Various breeds suit various temperaments. The Irish Wolfhound develops into a "knowing" dog and will seek to match your mood. He is not a trick dog and does *not* delight in foolish accomplishments. He will obey his master, but he is indifferent to the commands of "outsiders," and people make a great mistake when they allow more than one in the family to "work" a dog that is being taught the obedience exercises. The dog will know later what "come," "sit," and "lie down" mean, but the training sessions constitute *school*, and a single master at this time is enough—in fact, essential for success for the trainer *and* for the dog!

A good performance comes by much repetition, so that one gets smooth work. And of course that is the first drawback of our breed—they become bored easily. There have been times when I have worked a Hound, having him repeat and repeat, and then have had him suddenly turn and look and refuse, just lie down and look at me as if he wanted to say, "we just *did* that!" And, of course, a Wolfhound won't chase an electric rabbit the second time, so it is not surprising if some just don't see the necessity of repeating the obedience drill. With that kind, after they know the exercises, to go through the entire business once every few days is enough. I mention this to help avoid disappointment, as the Wolfhound can go "sour" easily.

The Wolfhound does not "delight" in showmanship. He often appears a lazy, humiliated Hound—the lion netted— and it sometimes disturbs the owner who has seen the same Hound, with fire and spirit, leap over obstacles, and stand majestically, head up, "seeing" the land before him and searching it with his eyes.

Occasionally we happen on a specimen whose whimsicality is perverted enough so he "plays the game." And that's just what it is and must be to him, if you are to hold his interest and he is to go into the ring with a wagging tail, head up and with a wink for the judge. This one will make

141

a fine Hound for the Group or good timber for the obedience work and he will do the missionary work for the breed, since in showing he will appear the same Hound his owner knows at home.

It is a fact that if your dog is slightly responsive to obedience, you can develop his interest in it by making it seem fun. After he knows the initial work, don't be serious about it unless you want a very dull performance. Give the dog a good hard pat and say something he understands, like "How about it?" You are asking cooperation, so with a heart whistling "Larks in the Morning," swing into the ring as if it is fun. *That,* some dogs will understand, and they will go through their paces with pride.

But how can intelligence be measured? Surely not in the show ring or by the obedience tests. Intelligence is more than the ability to perform certain exercises. All dogs can be taught to do these things, and often the credit goes to an understanding owner. If the Wolfhound performs with lowered head and with distaste, think of the young man whose parents are trying to make a musician out of him with hours of violin practice while he wants to be working on a boat or becoming an engineer. This is a case of misplaced enthusiasm. And we fail our dogs if we do not manage at an early age to create a real spirit of fun in anything we do *with* them—bearing in mind their nature. If they get a grand walk and some real fun afterwards, that helps.

As I said, we do have some dogs that get the spirit of showing—are vain perhaps? But praise can develop the spirit if the dogs have a tendency toward it. If *you* feel happy when you go in the ring, the dog can better catch the idea. If you go in without hoping to win but wondering if the dog will let you down on commands, you might as well stay out. In some unfathomable way the Hound gets it. Dogs are farther advanced than we are in the field of mental telepathy and Wolfhounds are downright psychic to a great degree. On that subject, a separate chapter could be written of actual, factual incidents. The Irish Wolfhound is sensitive to rebuke and if he has failed you when you know he knows, then his failure to adapt himself to your wishes, if rebuked,

142

makes him easy to train. "The pointed finger that I *cannot* bear," of Rudyard Kipling's Scotty, is equally awful to an Irish Wolfhound.

Our Ch. Macushla taught me much. She loved to show. She got into the spirit of it and at times did better than I felt she should. I always went into the ring gaily, and so did she. *That* was important.

I have two other female Wolfhounds that I have been working with so they will give a nice performance in the ring—and as far as I am concerned, if they are with me on the leash, gaily, and will do a *long* stand-stay, they are "in." It is this stand-stay business that keeps a Hound in position so the judge can see him; especially if the judge is looking at a long line of dogs—long enough in a good breed entry—more so in a strong Hound Group with many dogs to be gone over. A dog that "stands-stay" for this will get the attention of the judge, for he is always in a good position when the judge turns quickly for another look, appraising one dog against the other.

Of the two females, one did everything unhappily, though not reluctantly, and I knew I would be able to depend on her; yet she was indifferent, whereas the other one *loved* obedience—she even walked like some of the owners I have seen showing their Hounds in obedience, with that exaggerated look of seriousness on their faces. I discovered this by accident. I had finished with the one, but this other one crowded in and wanted to do the exercises all over again and *that* is not the rule. However, I said nothing, and, not wanting to bother at the moment to put her back in her place, I left her out, and she decided to work right along with the other, with no leash, but doing everything—not gaily, you understand, but seriously, as she is a serious Hound. She loves obedience and just wants to "be in the act."

There is a good report on Rathrahilly Shevauneen by Jack Baird in one of our Club Quarterlies. He said:

"True the thermometer said 95 degrees at the Badger Kennel Club Show in Madison, Wisconsin, where I judged sixty obedience dogs. But it wasn't the heat that made me, or the audience, think we saw the impossible. An Irish Wolfhound gliding through Novice B routine as nicely as a German Shepherd, a Poodle or a Welsh Terrier.

"We really saw it—and on every move beyond this, this judge and his steward's jaws dropped lower and the eyes bugged out. Shevauneen, for that's her name, kept getting better, going through the routine as if she could do it in reverse and not in the usual cumbersome manner of most big dogs.

"The gal, who will not be two years old until a month hence, wound up taking a really hot Novice B Class of 24-entries at a 198 of a possible 200 and long before I announced the scores, everyone knew that the big gal could not be beaten. She is owned by Brandoch Peters and the next time anyone tells you that the Irish Wolfhound isn't smart, that it can't move smoothly and gracefully and fast, that it can't take training, or that it is too awkward to make good in obedience, just show them this story. Tell them that one veteran judge and sizeable audience saw this Shevauneen gal make a monkey out of detractors. I say frankly that Shevauneen's work was one of the highlights of the greatest day of mass obedience work I have seen in 17 years in obedience."

We know the Wolfhounds have no peer in work requiring amazing sight, but not all Wolfhounds have the keen scent. The olfactory nerve is not always well developed. But, again, just as you need a gay Hound for obedience work, you need a naturally keen scent for the U.D.

Our old Roonagh had an unusual scenting ability. She could come out of the kennel in the morning and stand and turn her head this way and that, if a scent was in the air, and in a moment she was off and making a beeline to a group of quail, or flushing up a pheasant. In this scenting ability, Wolfhounds vary. I think since some ability is always there, it can be developed.

144

Obedience Degree Winners

Dog	Degree	Date Awarded	Owner
Algae Acres Gray Elf O'Dublin * H-861458	Companion Dog	November 1959	*
Ard Ri of Ballylyke (D) *	Companion Dog	March 15, 1959	Col. and Mrs. Alfred W. DeQuoy *
Ballindoon of Killybracken (D) HA-71352	Companion Dog	December, 1961	Glenn H. Sheldon
Ballykelly Kate (B) HA-119225	Companion Dog	October 1962	*
Bridgette of Ambleside (B) H-879017	Companion Dog	August 1960	
Brigit of Edgecliff (B) H-78276	Companion Dog	October 14, 1951	Dennis Dunne
Bridgett of Kelligan (B) HA-33006	Companion Dog	December, 1960	John Rugaart, Jr.
Brogan of Hillaway (D) H-519605	Companion Dog	June 15, 1958	Helen Dalton and Catharine Cram
Craig of Shamrock (D) H-158657	Companion Dog	April 26, 1953	Mrs. Wally Dunne
Cuachulain (D) H-637214	Companion Dog	December 1, 1957	W. W. Peters
Feasgar Bruadar of Ballylyke (B) H-604678	Companion Dog Companion Dog Excellent Utility Dog	April 22, 1957 November 30, 1957 March 16, 1958	Col. Alfred W. DeQuoy
Finian of Skyline (D) H-386554	Companion Dog Companion Dog Excellent	May 8, 1955 July 31, 1955	John Scheiner
Grigio of Ballylyke (D) H-847578	Companion Dog	January 15, 1961	Mrs. Dorothy Hillyer
Hillaway's Raegen O'Rory (D) HA-707767	Companion Dog	August, 1961	H. Dalton & C. Cram
Keltic Banshee (B) HA-22480	Companion Dog Companion Dog Excellent Utility Dog	October, 1960 September, 1961 June, 1962	Col. Alfred W. DeQuoy
Kilcreedy of Killybracken (B) H-466431	Companion Dog	September 14, 1957	Brandoch Peters
Kilkelly's Shawn of Skyline (D) H-337307	Companion Dog	June 27, 1954	R. T. Yankie
Lancer of Ambleside (D) H-958088	Companion Dog Companion Dog Excellent	March, 1961 October, 1961	R. T. Yankie
O'Dea of Killybracken (D) H-653392	Companion Dog	May 18, 1958	T. J. Weiler, M.D.
Rathrahilly Magillacuty (D) HA-202471	Companion Dog	December, 1961	Mr. & Mrs. R. Higgins
Rathrahilly Shevauneen (B) H-355672	Companion Dog	August 7, 1955	Brandoch Peters
Ronlae's Ulthan Laidir (D) H-177323	Companion Dog	June 16, 1952	Charles L. Lewis
Sandra of Rathain (B) H-258697	Companion Dog	November 1, 1953	E. V. Kenneally, M.D.
Shamrocks Dark Legend (D) H-269216	Companion Dog Companion Dog Excellent	January 24, 1955 June 29, 1958	Wally Dunne

* not known

Recent Obedience Degree Winners

Dog	Degree	Date Awarded	Owner
Cara Brogaun of Andaki (B) HA-416493	Companion Dog	August, 1964	Mildred Koschara
Gilda of Ballygran (B) Ireland HA-264400	Companion Dog	March, 1963	*
Keltic Phantom II (D) HA-313834	Companion Dog Companion Dog Excellent	June, 1963 December 5, 1964	Col. Alfred W. DeQuoy
Keltic Tara (B) HA-313833	Companion Dog Companion Dog Excellent	April, 1963 March, 1964	Col. Alfred W. DeQuoy
Sulhamstead Samando Patrick (D) Eng. HA-331125	Companion Dog	April, 1963	Col. Alfred W. DeQuoy

TWO SISTERS

Ch. Laith of Kihone in foreground, BOS at 1949 Specialty, and Spag-lainn of Kihone in back. Owned and bred by F. Jeannette McGregor, Kihone Kennels.

Just the Facts

IF YOU OWN an Irish Wolfhound, there is a constant stream of questions coming your way from people unfamiliar with the breed. What do they eat? What are they good for? How much do they weigh? etc.

Wolfhounds eat approximately the same foods as any of the other big breeds, but in lesser amounts, as they have small stomachs for their weight. We feed more minerals, because their frame grows so fast. We know puppies need di-calcium phosphate and also some bone meal. This last we feed all the time. Bone meal is a good organic mineral and we put a tablespoonful in every Hound's meat meal once a day. No matter what the age, bone is always growing, whether it is bone of humans or animals, and proper nutrition is essential. Bodies are constantly rebuilding themselves and where there is a lack of minerals after the animals have matured, many troubles develop in the bones. We buy a very fine bone meal—one that is almost powdery—and it contains all the minerals and the trace minerals.

We also give a vitamin pill or capsule almost every day. This is a safeguard, and any good all-purpose vitamin tablet will do. We also feed a good deal of wheat germ oil—a good grade of cold processed oil. *And* we keep it in the refrigerator. This is the finest source of Vitamin E and its greatest enemy is rancidity, which also causes the destruction of many of our prepared foods. To store such products where they will not turn rancid is a chore at times. Cod-liver oil gets rancid easily, so it, too, should be kept in brown bottles in the refrigerator.

Dogs like fat and should have some. Natural fats are best—natural lard if you can find it, but *no* homogenized fats should be fed. Hence we go to the vegetable oils like corn oil and soybean oil. The homogenization changes the fatty acids which are essential to the dogs' well-being. They can eat some of it, but without fats free from homogenization, dogs can't be properly nourished. Protein owes its diversity to its amino acids, and fat to the fatty acids.

Yeast is an excellent source of essential nutrients and a tablespoonful added to a grown dog's ration will help to keep him in good form. It is brimful of the necessary vitamins, especially those of the B complex. Some experimental work has shown that dogs lacking biotin (one of the B's) in their diet cannot develop properly. And there appears to be a connecting link to the increasing manifestation of monor-chidism. Ultimately, I feel sure, it will be found to be nutri-tional in origin, as much has been proved along this line in experimenting on lower forms of animal life. Since yeast is such a good source of the B complex vitamins, and since it is readily available, it is recommended as a regular supple-ment to the diet. The amount required varies among the different breeds, but lactating bitches need three to five times as much Vitamin B as they do when they are not lactating. Vitamin B is best supplied by natural foods but because such foods cannot be depended upon for a constant supply, additional organic vitamin products should be given.

Liver is an excellent source of Vitamin B. In our own case, the liver was rationed to us at the kennel, but for every so many pounds of horse meat, we were allowed a certain amount of liver. We started feeding it raw. Most dogs learn to like it and bitches in whelp are as eager for it as they are for raw suet. By suet I mean that nice crumbly fat such as that which forms around beef kidneys. *All* dogs

148

like it. We always shave it thin or grind it up and give it raw. Animals store their own vitamins in the fat, so suet is an excellent food to give with the daily rations, but not, of course, to very young puppies. One last word about fats, as I feel strongly about them: many give fats that have become rancid from being kept in warm places, such as on the back of a stove. But rancid fats destroy the vitamins that are in the food you buy and those that you are adding to the food. So it is imperative that rancid fats not be fed.

The dog has a nervous system which exercises great influence on nutrition and so upon growth. Also, the dog has a high mental faculty, the right development and use of which depend largely on proper nourishment of the body.

The best families of our dogs have been raised to their present state of superiority by continued attention to feeding and breeding. Digestion and assimilation, like other functions, are more or less hereditary, and our finest strains have enjoyed the liberal nutrition so necessary to their best development and have thus acquired a digestive system requiring ample food and well balanced feeding. In the wrong hands, a dog can be called a "bad do-er," when he has simply inherited an assimilative system calling for good and plentiful fare. He cannot be expected to thrive on the same foods as do dogs that for generations have become inured to indifferent feeding.

The Wolfhound is a case in point. One has to do well by him during his growth. He comes into the world weighing about one and one-half pounds, and by two months he will be from twenty-five to thirty pounds, and by six months, a hundred and more. By eight months he starts to slow up, but this is the tricky period, as he has outgrown himself and has the least resistance to any disease that might come along. We immunize all our puppies at two months, both for distemper and encephalitis, using a canine distemper vaccine, modified live virus of chick embryo origin, vacuum dried, and avianized. Most of the good drug houses make it. We started about 1949 or 1950 using it, but the vaccine has been improved, inasmuch as we originally had to give one shot intradermally. Now, administering it is simpler and the

149

distemper immunization is combined with the hepatitis vaccine. That is, the two vaccines can be given simultaneously. At eight months, due to the dog's rapid growth, we repeat the immunization with a booster shot. We have shipped from coast to coast and have exhibited widely but have never had a distemper outbreak. We keep check and advise new owners when the second immunization is due.

The Wolfhound, following the period of rapid growth, then goes into a period of slow development. He does *not* reach full height under eighteen months. A lot of males cannot serve under that age and bitches rarely come in season under fifteen to eighteen months (those are average ages). We have had only three instances where bitches came in at a year, and each occurred when the dog was shipped to a warmer climate. We have occasionally had females who did not come in season before two years of age.

Wolfhounds are erratic in the breeding field. They are not easy to manage and this accounts in part for the lack of stock from time to time. Handling a Wolfhound at stud is an art and is best done by experts. Many males will have nothing to do with certain females although they avidly mate with others. And a goodly share of bitches would remain virgins until they died if they weren't muzzled and held for a dog. Usually bitches can be handled, but there is not much to be done for the male if he is not interested.

When people ask what Wolfhounds are good for, I always have to reply, 'The same things most dogs are." The average dog supplements the family life, enriches all departments of it, and if it is a hunting dog, can be used for the hunting season, which grows shorter every year. In society as we find it today, the dog's function is mainly guarding the household and giving companionship.

As a breed, Wolfhounds get along with all dogs, and all animals if they are raised around them, but I am a great believer in fences and agree with Robert Frost that "Good fences make good neighbors." One takes his dog out to walk and run, or wherever he goes, but the dog must not run loose, if for no other reason than that sooner or later the dog that runs loose will be killed by a car.

As to climates, Wolfhounds will get along in any climate a person can stand. In shipping to the hotter climates, it is best that fairly young dogs be sent so they may grow up there. Wolfhound coats help in areas where temperatures are extreme, for they have an outer coarse coat that serves as a shield against sun or cold and an undercoat that insulates against heat or keeps them warm in sub-zero weather. Wolfhounds love cold weather but also can take a lot of heat if properly handled. They have long noses and deep chests, constituting good breathing apparatus for any climate. A tropical climate is hardest on Wolfhounds—in fact on all dogs.

Miss Muller writes from Holland that a Miss Haarman, who lived with her parents in Indonesia before World War II, kept Irish Wolfhounds. She imported a pair from Belgium and bred a few litters. When the Japanese came, the Hounds were put to sleep rather than let them fall into enemy hands. According to Miss Haarman, the Hounds had done well in Indonesia and did not suffer from the heat. They were kenneled in the mountains at Bandung.

Many people ask about Wolfhound longevity. Wolfhounds are much the same as other large breeds, though not so full of years as some smaller breeds such as Terriers. We have sold many that lived from eleven to fourteen years, and a few that lived longer, but they are the exception.

A story of an Irish Wolfhound gone native, was recounted in a letter from Jonathan E. Pierce which was printed in our breed column in the *Gazette* in 1948. Mr. Pierce wrote:

"Several years ago, there was a man in Houston, Texas, who owned an Irish Wolfhound bitch that had been everywhere with him as a hunting dog and companion. She had been in Alaska and also Central America. At the time I first came across her she was around 12 years old.

"The owner lost all of his money and gave the old bitch to an Irish priest. Although old and decrepit in appearance, she was really very active. She was a nice Hound, except that she was dreadfully afraid of thunderstorms. One day soon after the priest took her, a storm came up

151

and he locked her in a shed. As she was by herself, she became frantic and jumped out through a high window and ran away. Although advertised for, she was not found.

"About a year later when I was advertising for an Irish Wolfhound I had lost, someone told me there was an Irish Wolfhound in Freeport, which is a small coastal town about a hundred miles from Houston.

"Imagine my surprise when I got there to find the old Hound looking just about the same as the last time I had seen her. She was running loose on the streets. The week before she had been roped by some cowboys on the plains near there, who at first mistook her for a wolf.

"Apparently she had lived for a year on her own, foraging off the country and none the worse for it. She was taken by some other people who finally had to have her put to sleep when she was hit by a car and run over, at the age of fifteen."

Mr. Pierce, who at that time lived in Houston, remarked, "I have told you this to illustrate the hardiness and fortitude of the breed."

While the Irish Hound undoubtedly benefits from much hard exercise, he only requires a comparatively small amount to keep him in perfect condition. Walking with him is ideal exercise. He has a keen imagination and this mitigates against boredom and creates the feeling of liberty so essential to him.

DEATH OF A HOUND

The great heart cracks; the mighty frame
In chill of death has turned to stone.
With silence in the empty halls
We sit alone,
Too numb to weep, too desolate
For tears or pain-releasing sigh.
A puppy stumbles up to us—
Kings do not die!
—William J. Dammarell

4½-month-old puppy from Rathrahilly Kennels.

Imported Kinsale of Boroughbury with one of her six-week-old puppies and "Dave," long associated with Wolfhounds.

A Feeding Program for Irish Wolfhounds —
From Birth to Maturity:

Note: Because Irish Wolfhounds grow in weight from an approximate one and one-half pounds at birth to 100 pounds or more at six months of age (Page 149), the feeding of puppies develops at a much greater pace than the normal pattern for other breeds outlined in Part II of this book. As a guide for new Irish Wolfhound owners, we offer the feeding program—born of long experience and success with the breed—that is practised at the CU Kennels of Mr. and Mrs. Gordon Graham in St. James, L.I., N.Y.

Depending upon size of the litter, we start with supplementing the dam's milk with Esbilac (a Borden preparation). Mix per instructions, and feed out of an Even Flo bottle (made for infants).

At seven to ten days, feed scraped raw beef (mostly blood), either with a dropper or sucked from finger. Start with once-a-day beef feeding, being sure beef is absolutely fat free, and build up to three feedings a day.

When the eyes are open, at about 12 to 17 days, start feeding a very loose mixture of Primary Diet (a puppy meal prepared by Lifespan) and Esbilac, in small amounts. As with the beef, start once a day and build up to three feedings a day. A demitasse spoon is indispensable in teaching the puppy to lap.

Gradually substitute evaporated milk for the Esbilac, and fine kibble (well-soaked) for the Primary Diet. Trimmed ground steak is added, developing to ground chuck, and then —by age of three to three-and-a-half months, canned dog beef.

If properly managed, when the dam wishes to remain outside of the box, the puppies are satisfied. The dam enjoys regained periods of freedom and exercise. Her liquid intake is reduced, and a gradual drying up of her milk occurs. During this time, she spends night duty with the puppies. By four to five weeks, the puppies are completely weaned. At six to seven weeks, the dam's matronly appearance is gone, and except for an added balanced vitamin supplement—which she is given daily for three months after whelping—her routine is back to normal.

At age of three to six months, the schedule per puppy reads:

Morning: 3 cups kibbled biscuit and 1 can top grade canned beef, moistened with broth or warm water, and tossed together to crumbly consistency.

Mid-day: Boiled egg, or cottage cheese, or yogurt, or cereal—but not too much.

Afternoon: Repeat morning feeding.

Increase kibble as appetite requires, but do not increase meat. Our custom is to add, for each puppy, two tablespoons of *steamed edible* bone meal to morning and afternoon meals, and to feed (as candy) before "breakfast", four cod-liver tablets, each of which is equivalent to a teaspoon.

For young hounds, from six to 24 months (or longer), the schedule reads:

Morning: 4 to 6 cups of kibbled biscuit mixed with ½ to 1 can of top grade canned beef—moistened and mixed.

Afternoon: 6 to 8 cups of kibbled biscuit with 1 can of top grade canned beef, mixed as above.

Reduce bone meal portion by one-half; reduce cod-liver oil portion to two tablets per day from June to September, and to three tablets per day from September through May.

Our guess is that ten breeders would give ten different answers on feeding. There is a wide margin that individual Irish Wolfhounds might vary in food intake, and still prosper. However, on the stress upon ample amounts and finest quality, we feel all will agree. After three years, which is usually the period of full maturity, guard against overweight.

Memorial at Gettysburg

The Irish Hound at Gettysburg

ON THE BATTLEFIELD of Gettysburg is the statue of an Irish Wolfhound reclining in alert repose—watching over the graves of the brave men of the 63rd, 69th, and 88th New York Infantry who fought and died there. "It is altogether fitting and proper" that this breed was chosen, as these units comprised the famed Irish Brigade. The statue was erected by the State of New York as a memorial, and the sculptor was William Rudolf O'Donnovan, born March 28, 1844, in what is now the state of West Virginia. He fought in the Confederate Army during the Civil War.

The memorial is, in general, of stone construction and in form resembles an altar or tomb. The upper part of the altar is sheathed with bronze plates which identify the regiments and the battle. The plates also list the casualties suffered by each unit in battle and depict battle scenes. On top of the altar is the bronze statue of the dog, integral with its bronze base. Surrounding the altar is a Celtic Cross, or Cross of St. Kevin. The cross is of stone and also sheathed with decorated bronze plates.

Two Irish Wolfhounds adorn the original flag of the famous 69th Fighting Irish Regiment and two Wolfhounds head the Color Party of that Regiment in the St. Patrick's

Day Parade in New York City each year and are given special honor when passing the Saluting Base.

RESURGIT

The empty armour stands in silent guard
Along the darkened panels of the Hall
And limp and lifeless as a vanished age
The battle banners hang upon the wall.
The tapestry with faded hunting scene
The pikes which cross behind the crested shield
The leaded windows flecked with coats-of-arms
With brave devices on a tinted field.
All now have lost significance. Ghost things
They haunt this age like spectors in the gloom.
Then in a flash the whole scene leaps to life—
An Irish Wolfhound walks into the room.

       —William J. Dammarell

Greysarge Cristel's Corrigan, 1961 Specialty BOB, with judge, Mrs. Geraldine R. Dodge; breeder-owner-handler, Miss Celeste Winans Hutton; and Miss F. Jeannette McGregor, presenting trophy. Corrigan was whelped October 29, 1958, and is by Int. Ch. Castledawn Tartan ex Ch. Cristel of Ambleside.

Outstanding Breed Wins

The Hound Group Challenge Trophy

THE HOUND GROUP Challenge Trophy is awarded the Irish Wolfhound with the greatest number of points for placing in the Hound Group at AKC licensed shows during the calendar year.

The award is based on the following scale of points:

First Place—6 points
Second Place—4 points
Third Place—2 points
Fourth Place—1 point

In case of a tie, the governing committee decides the winner, and the Hound with the majority of first and second placings is given the greater consideration. Originally, it had to be won three times by the same exhibitor before being won outright.

This is one of our most interesting cups. It has nothing to do with geography, or large entries in the breed. It is a win that can be achieved at *any* AKC show. It was first presented by Miss F. J. McGregor in 1939. It has twice been won outright and each time a new cup has been presented, so it seems to become a sort of perpetual challenge trophy.

It is one of the club's most important ones, and its benefits are felt nation-wide. We hear exhibitors say, "What's the use of showing, there is no competition." But there is always competition as long as the Hound Group Cup is in competition. Following the new AKC ruling about three-time wins, cups now are presented each year for the "Hound of the Year."

Arnold of Edgecliff, owned by Thomas B. Wanamaker, Jr., started his California showing in days when there was practically no breed competition, but by diligent showing, he attracted most rewarding attention. Being an only exhibit in his breed, he naturally got to go into the Hound Group. This caused him to be seen by the ringside and also by the many judges who watch the Group judging at show. His soundness and impressiveness won him many admirers, and judges commenced to take him seriously. Soon he started placing in the Group. Then he started to win Groups, and anyone showing knows the winner is entitled to the same number of points as was made by any breed in that Group. Arnold left for Westminster, New York, without ever having met one of his own in breed competition—yet he was *well* known on the West Coast. He needed but one point, and at New York, with his first breed competition, this he won and had points to spare. Arnold buried forever that old canard, "What's the use, there is no competition."

Record of Hound Group Challenge Trophy Wins

1939—Ch. Chulainn Casey of Kihone (Miss F. J. McGregor)
1940—Ch. Moran of Ouborough (Charles H. Morse, Jr.)
1941—Ch. Molly Killeen of Killybracken (Killybracken Kennels)
1942—Fara of Rimrock (Mrs. John W. Wofford)
1943—Ch. Sulhamstead Flute (Miss F. J. McGregor)
1944—Cragwood Druidh (Mrs. Norwood B. Smith)
1945—(Withdrawn)
1946—Ch. Gillagain of Ambleside (Paul F. Paine)

Edgecliff Kennels' Ch. Arnold of Edgecliff, BIS, all breeds, 1949.

Erin of Edgecliff, Tara of Ouborough, Imp., and Ch. Finn mac Cool of Edgecliff, with owner, Thomas B. Wanamaker, Jr.

1947—Ch. Arnold of Edgecliff (Thomas B. Wanamaker, Jr.)
1948—Ch. Arnold of Edgecliff (T. B. Wanamaker, Jr.)
1949—Ch. Monahan of Tyrone (Laura Lauray Thomas)
1950—Ch. Brian Boru of Edgecliff (Thomas B. Wanamaker, Jr.)
1951—Ch. Roise of Ambleside (Suzanne Bellinger)
1952—Ch. Dian of Ambleside (Killybracken Kennels)
1953—Int. Ch. Sheelagh of Ballytobin (Laura Lauray Thomas)
1954—Ch. Tralee of Ambleside (Charles H. Morse, Jr.)
1955—Ch. Tralee of Ambleside (Charles H. Morse, Jr.)
1956—Ch. Talgarth of Ambleside (Killybracken Kennels)
1957—Ch. Cragwood Ardarragh (Frances Van Brunt)
1958—Ch. Sulhamstead Matador of Killybracken (Killybracken Kennels)
1959—Ch. Sulhamstead Matador of Killybracken (Killybracken Kennels)
1960—Ch. Tyrone of Ballykelly (Miss Barbara O'Neill)
1961—Ch. Riverlawn Barnstorm (Frances Van Brunt)
1962—Ch. Riverlawn Barnstorm (Frances Van Brunt)
1963—Ch. Sulhamstead Mars of Riverlawn (Frances Van Brunt)
1964—Ch. Hillaway's Padraic of Eagle (Samuel Evans Ewing, 3rd)
1965—Ch. Hillaway's Padraic of Eagle (Samuel Evans Ewing, 3rd)
1966—Ch. Ballykelly Colin (Mrs. H. Sheppard Musson)
1967—Ch. Ballykelly Colin (Mrs. H. Sheppard Musson)
1968—Ch. Boroughbury Brona (Samuel Evans Ewing, 3rd)

Ch. Sulhamstead Matador of Killybracken, 1960 Specialty BOB and nine times Best-in-Show-winner.

Irish Wolfhound

Best-in-Show (All Breeds) Winners

1. Shadowhill Felixstowe Magee, at Los Angeles, Calif.— 1921
2. Ch. Felixstowe Kilmorac Halcyon (Imp.), at Tuxedo Park, N. Y.—1930
3. Ch. King Lir of Ambleside, at Syracuse, N. Y.—1931
4. Ch. Balbricken of Ambleside, twice at Denver, Colo.— 1934; at Santa Fe, N. M.—1934; and at Rio Grande, N. M.—1935

5. Ch. Felixstowe Killcully Halcyon (Imp.), at Cambridge, Mass.—1934
6. Ch. Steyning Sorrell Halcyon (Imp.), at Ridgewood, N. J.—1934
7. Shaun of Boyer Ranch, at San Francisco, Calif.—1937
8. Int. Ch. Moran of Ouborough (Imp.), at Syracuse, N. Y. —1940
9. Ch. Gillagain of Ambleside, at Syracuse, N. Y.—1946
10. Int. Ch. Shamus Failinis of Ambleside, at Niagara Falls, N. Y.—1949
11. Ch. Arnold of Edgecliff, at Santa Barbara, Calif.—1949
12. Ch. Barn Hill Dan Malone, at Joliet, Ill.—1950
13. Ch. Brian Boru of Edgecliff, at Pasadena, Calif., and at Odessa, San Angelo, and Wichita, Texas—1950
14. Ch. Finn Mac Cool of Edgecliff, at Meridan, Idaho— 1950
15. Ch. Monahan of Tyrone, at Elyria, Ohio—1951
16. Int. Ch. Sheelagh of Ballytobin (Imp.), at Mansfield, Ohio—1952, and at Columbus and Akron, Ohio—1954
17. Ch. Tralee of Ambleside, at Gates Mills, Ohio (Chagrin Valley K.C.)—1954; at Owensboro, Ky.—1954; and at New Orleans, La.—1955
18. Ch. Timber of Ambleside, at Elizabeth, N. J.—1954
19. Int. Ch. Fuath of Ulaid (Imp.), at Baltimore, Md.—1955
20. Ch. Victoria of Killybracken, at Omaha, Neb.—1957
21. Ch. Sulhamstead Matador of Killybracken, at Greenwood, Miss., at Blue Grass, Iowa, at Rock Island, Ill., at LaCrosse, Wisc., at Scranton, Pa., at Northbrook, Ill., at Shreveport, La., at Gulfport, Miss., and at New Orleans, La.—1958
22. Ch. Tyrone of Ballykelly, at Watertown, N. Y.—1960
23. Ch. Riverlawn Barnstorm, at Charleston, S.C.—1961, and at Lawton, Okla.—1962
24. Ch. Sanctuary Morne of Riverlawn, at Norfolk, Va.— 1964
25. Ch. Ballykelly Colin, at Dayton, Ohio, at Toledo, Ohio, at Kalamazoo, Michigan and at Gambier, Ohio—1967, and at Bradenton, Florida—1968

Ch. Hillaway's Padraic of Eagle, BOB at 1966 IWCA Specialty from Veterans Class; BOS, 1965 Specialty; Hound of the Year, 1964, 1965; sire of 23 champions. Owned by Samuel Evans Ewing, 3rd.

26. Ch. Boroughbury Brona, at Salina, Kansas, at Wichita, Kansas, at Wilmington, North Carolina, and at Painesville, Ohio—1968
27. Ch. Caragahoolie O'Killybracken, at Ludwig's Corner, Pa., at Garden City, N.Y., at Wellesley, Mass., at Wilton, Conn., and at Rochester, N.Y.—1968

Ch. Killybracken Hanna of Cu, winner of 1964 IWCA Specialty. Left to right are Mrs. Marie Meyer, judge; Mrs. C. Groverman Ellis, owner-handler; and Miss F. Jeannette McGregor, IWCA President. Photo by William Brown, courtesy of *Harp and Hound*.

Ch. Deweylimm of Kihone pictured winning Best of Breed at 1965 IWCA Specialty under judge Percy Roberts. "Knotty" was BOS at the '65 Specialty, and paired with her litter sister, Ch. Deweylarn of Kihone, was twice Best Brace. Owned by Miss F. Jeannette McGregor, Kennel Kihone.

Ch. Brogan of Hillaway, BOB at the 1959 Specialty, judged by Mrs. Florence Nagle of England (63 Wolfhounds were present, with 76 entries). Brogan was whelped June 8, 1955, by Ch. Fair Fingal of Ambleside ex Bridie of Ambleside. Bred and owned by Misses Helen Dalton and Catherine Cram.

Irish Wolfhound Club of America
Annual Specialty Winners

(BB-Best of Breed; BOS-Best of Opposite Sex; WD-Winners Dog; WB-Winners Bitch; BW-Best of Winners)

1928

Ch. Cragwood The O'Toole (BB), Mrs. Norwood B. Smith
Ch. Cragwood Macha (BOS), Mrs. Norwood B. Smith

1929
Ch. Felixstowe Kilfree Halcyon (BB), Halcyon Kennels
Ch. Felixstowe Kilgarth (BOS), Halcyon Kennels

167

1930
Ch. Cragwood Ballybilly (BB), Mrs. Norwood B. Smith
— Bournstream Lorna (BOS), Mrs. Victor C. Mather
1931
— Chulainn Rajah Halcyon (BB), Halcyon Kennels
— Dacie II of Ambleside (BOS), Mrs. James Baker
1932
Ch. Halcyon Baronet (BB), Halcyon Kennels
Ch. Halcyon Tamara (BOS), Halcyon Kennels
1933
Ch. Halcyon Baronet (BB), Halcyon Kennels
Ch. Halcyon Tamara (BOS), Halcyon Kennels
1934
Ch. Felixstowe Kilcully Halcyon (BB), Halcyon Kennels
Ch. Roonagh of Ambleside (BOS), Mr. and Mrs. L. O. Starbuck
1935
Ch. Felixstowe Kilcully Halcyon (BB), Halcyon Kennels
Ch. Halcyon Tamara (BOS), Halcyon Kennels
1936
Ch. Croughill of Ouborough (BB), W. D. Roehrs
Ch. Macushla of Ambleside (BOS), Alma J. Starbuck
1937
Ch. Felix of Boyer Ranch (BB), Mrs. J. St. A. Boyer
Ch. Dark Desha of Ambleside (BOS), Whippoorwill Kennels
1938
Ch. Halcyon Alannah of Ambleside (BB), Halcyon Kennels
Ch. Felix of Boyer Ranch (BOS), Mrs. Huhn
1939
Ch. Dark Desha of Ambleside (BB), Whippoorwill Kennels
— Barra of Ambleside (BOS), Miss Susan Bullard
1940
Ch. Shauneen of Chilton (BB), Mrs. Spencer Nauman
Ch. Dark Desha of Ambleside (BOS), Whippoorwill Kennels

1941

Ch. Sulhamstead Flute (BB), Miss F. Jeannette McGregor

Ch. Baine of Kihone (BOS), Miss F. Jeannette McGregor

1942

Ch. Sulhamstead Flute (BB), Miss F. Jeannette McGregor

Ch. Loree Lacroma of Ambleside (BOS), Charles D. Burrage, Jr.

1943–1945 (No Specialty)

1946

Ch. Barn Hill Hilda (BB), Paul F. Paine

— Macha's Mike (BOS), Walter E. Roehrs, Jr.

1947

Ch. Killary of Ambleside (BB), Charles D. Burrage, Jr.

Ch. Mugan Machree of Ambleside (BOS), Margaret L. Fess

1948

Ch. Killary of Ambleside (BB), Charles D. Burrage, Jr.

Ch. Chalet Cam (BOS), Miss F. Jeannette McGregor

1949

Ch. Ballymac of Boroughbury (BB), Joseph A. Coll

Ch. Laith of Kihone (BOS), Miss F. Jeannette McGregor

1950

Ch. Patrick of Ballytobin (BB), Joseph A. Coll

Ch. Roise of Ambleside (BOS), Miss Suzanne Bellinger

1951

Ch. Finn Mac Cool of Edgecliff (BB), Thomas B. Wanamaker, Jr.

— Kinsale of Boroughbury (BOS), Thomas B. Wanamaker, Jr.

1952

Ch. Cragwood Barney O'Shea (BB), Mrs. Peter Van Brunt

Ch. Ambleside Edain of Edgecliff (BOS), Ambleside Kennels

1953

Ch. Cragwood Barney O'Shea (BB), Mrs. Peter Van Brunt

Ch. Windale Killala (BOS), Miss Celeste W. Hutton

1954

Ch. Tralee of Ambleside (BB), Charles H. Morse, Jr.

Ch. Timber of Ambleside (BOS), Mrs. Thomas F. Madigan

1955

Ch. Tralee of Ambleside (BB), Charles H. Morse, Jr.

Ch. The McGillacudy (BOS), Clyde B. Smith

1956

Ch. Tralee of Ambleside (BB), Charles H. Morse, Jr.

Ch. Sullivan of Boroughbury (BOS), Comdr. and Mrs. Peter Hopkinson

1957

Ch. Sweet Kathy of Kilrain (BB), Mrs. Mary E. Britcher

Ch. Owen of Killybracken (BOS), Miss Suzanne Bellinger

1958

Ch. Sweet Kathy of Kilrain (BB), Mrs. Mary E. Britcher

Ch. Sulhamstead Matador of Killybracken (Imp.) (BOS), Killybracken Kennels

1959

Ch. Brogan of Hillaway, C.D. (BB), Misses Helen Dalton and Catharine Cram

Ch. Brickeen of Hillaway (BOS), Misses Helen Dalton and Catharine Cram

1960

Ch. Sulhamstead Matador of Killybracken (BB), Killybracken Kennels

Ch. Derry's Molly Maguire (BOS), Mrs. Lionel White

1961

— Greysarge Cristel's Corrigan (BB), Miss Celeste W. Hutton

Ch. Feasgar Bruadar of Ballylyke, U.D. (BOS), Col. Alfred W. DeQuoy

1962

Ch. Greysarge Cristel's Corrigan (BB), Miss Celeste W. Hutton

Ch. Victoria of Killybracken (BOS), Killybracken Kennels

1963
— Sulhamstead Mars of Riverlawn (BB), Mrs. Peter Van
 Brunt
Ch. Keltic Ghost of Ballylyke (BOS), Mr. Henry B. Weaver,
 Jr.

1964
— Killybracken Hanna of Cu (BB), Mrs. C. Groverman
 Ellis
— Sanctuary Morne of Riverlawn (BOS), Mrs. Peter Van
 Brunt

1965
Ch. Deweylimm of Kihone (BB), Kennel Kihone
Ch. Hillaway's Padraic of Eagle (BOS), Samuel Evans
 Ewing, 3rd
— Iona of Dunamaise (WB and BW), Mrs. Robert J. Fox
 2nd
— Sulhamstead Mac of Killybracken (WD), Killybrack-
 en Kennels
Ch. Deweylimm of Kihone (Best Moving Hound)

1966
Ch. Hillaway's Padraic of Eagle (BB), Samuel Evans
 Ewing, 3rd
Ch. Deweylimm of Kihone, Kennel Kihone
— Polaris Artel (WD and BW), Mrs. Robert J. Fox 2nd
— Sulhamstead Marlene (WB), Mrs. Grant Messinger
Ch. Riverlawn Linda II (Best Moving Hound), Mrs. Basil
 Stetson

1967
Ch. Ballykelly Colin (BB), Mrs. H. Sheppard Musson
Ch. Aisling of St. Doulagh's (BOS), Mrs. Winifred L. Heck-
 mann
— Annalea of Nendrum (WB and BW), Miss Celeste W.
 Hutton
— Sionnach Cam's Mickey (WD), Mrs. D. L. Garland, Jr.
Ch. Tralee of Cu (Best Moving Hound), Mrs. Gordon F.
 Graham

1968

Ch. Caragahoolie O'Killybracken (BB), Killybracken Kennels

Ch. Boroughbury Brona (BOS), Samuel Evans Ewing, 3rd

— Deric of Kihone (WD and BW), Kennel Kihone

— Fleetwind Raglan of Eagle (WB), Samuel Evans Ewing, 3rd

Ch. Caragahoolie O'Killybracken (Best Moving Hound)

1969

Ch. Annalea of Nendrum (BB), Miss Celeste W. Hutton

Ch. Timothy of Edgecliff (BOS), Edgecliff Kennels

— Maela of Mistimourne (WB and BW), Richard S. Staudt

— Catch the Wind's Timothy (WD), Maud Alexander

Brace Class at IWCA Specialty, June 1968, judge Percy Roberts. Left to right: G. W. DeQuoy's Ch. Keltic Phantom II, C.D.X. and Ch. Keltic Tara, C.D.X., litter brother and sister; Edgecliff Kennels' Ch. Coolaney of Ambleside and Ch. Timothy of Edgecliff, dam and son; and Kennel Kihone's Ch. Deweylimm of Kihone and Ch. Deweylarn of Kihone, litter sisters.

172

Ch. The McGillacudy pictured in the third of three straight Best of Breed wins at Westminster, 1953, 1954, and 1955. Judge, Percy Roberts. Owned by Clyde B. Smith.

Westminster Kennel Club Wins

(BB—Best of Breed; WD—Winners Dog; BOS—Best Opposite Sex; WB—Winners Bitch)

1928
Ch. Mona of Ambleside (BB), Mr. and Mrs. L. O. Starbuck
Ch. Cragwood The O'Toole (WD), Mrs. Norwood B. Smith
Ch. Felixstowe Kilbagie (WB), Halcyon Kennels

1929
Ch. Cragwood The O'Toole (BB), Mrs. Norwood B. Smith
Ch. Killabrick (WD), Richard K. Lackey
Ch. Kathleen of Ambleside (WB), Mr. and Mrs. L. O. Starbuck

1930
Ch. Felixstowe Kilmorac Halcyon (BB), Halcyon Kennels
Ch. Cragwood Ballybilly (WD), Mrs. Norwood B. Smith
Ch. Felixstowe Kilfree Halcyon (WB), Halcyon Kennels

1931
Ch. King Lir of Ambleside (BB), Mrs. Northrup T. Bellinger
Ch. Mallyree of Ambleside (WB), Mr. and Mrs. L. O. Starbuck

1932
Ch. Garragh of Ambleside (BB & WD), Mrs. Junius S. Morgan
— Ficra of Ambleside (WB), B. C. Cobb

173

1933

Ch. Brannish of Ambleside (BB & WD), Thomas N. Howell

Ch. Roonagh of Ambleside (WB), Mr. and Mrs. L. O. Starbuck

1934

Void

1935

Ch. Dan Riley (BB & WD), Marjorie Arms Roberts

Ch. Roonagh of Ambleside (WB), Mr. and Mrs. L. O. Starbuck

1936

Ch. Roonagh of Ambleside (BB), Mrs. Alma Starbuck

Ch. Ambleside Duke of Raglan (WD), Mr. and Mrs. J. Gordon Ridsdale

Ch. Halcyon Dana (WB), Halcyon Kennels

1937

Ch. Dan Riley (BB), Dr. Chester Reynolds

Ch. Sulhamstead Gala (WD), Mr. and Mrs. Huhn

Ch. Taffy of Ambleside (WB), Mrs. Alma Starbuck

1938

Ch. Halcyon Allannah of Ambleside (BB & WB), Halcyon Kennels

— Petersham of Ambleside (WD), Mrs. Alma Starbuck

1939

Ch. Halcyon Alannah of Ambleside (BB), Halcyon Kennels

Ch. Felix of Boyer Ranch (WD), Mrs. Huhn

Ch. Killesandra of Ambleside (WB), Mrs. Alma Starbuck

1940

Ch. Moran of Ouborough (BB & WD), Charles H. Morse, Jr.

— Brickeen of Ambleside (WB), Mrs. Alma Starbuck

1941

Ch. Shauneen of Chilton (BB & WD), Mrs. Spencer Nauman

Ch. Molly Killeen of Killybracken (WB), Killybracken Kennels

1942

Ch. Nene Riley (BB), Henry S. Jeanes, Jr.
— Barra of Ambleside (WD), Miss Susan Bullard
— July of Whippoorwill (WB), Whippoorwill Kennels

1943

No Entry

1944

Ch. Barn Hill Daisy (BB & WB), Barn Hill Kennels
— Tim O'Brian of Whippoorwill (WD), Whippoorwill Kennels

1945

Ch. Jerry (BB & WD), Barn Hill Kennels
Ch. Barn Hill Daisy (WB), Barn Hill Kennels

1946

— Cragwood Druidh (BB & WD)
Ch. Barn Hill Hilda (WB), Barn Hill Kennels

1947

Ch. Arnold of Edgecliff (BB & WD), Thomas B. Wanamaker, Jr.
— Irish Mary (WB)

1948

Ch. Killary of Ambleside (BB & WD), Charles D. Burrage, Jr.
Ch. Chalet Armagh (WB), Killybracken Kennels

1949

No Wolfhounds

1950

Ch. Monahan of Tyrone (BB), Mrs. Laura Lauray Thomas
— Ballymac of Boroughbury (WD), Joseph A. Coll
(No Bitches entered)

1951

Ch. Brian Boru of Edgecliff (BB & WD), Thomas B. Wanamaker, Jr.
— Corinna of Enfelcarne (WB), Joseph Coll

1952

Ch. Ambleside Edain of Edgecliff (BB), Mrs. Alma Star-buck

— Rathain Lorna of Ambleside (WB), Robert Ewing

— Bartel of Sommerton (WD), David Jaffee

1953

Ch. The McGillacudy (BB), Clyde B. Smith

Int. Ch. Sheelagh of Ballytobin (WB & BOS), Mrs. L. L. Thomas

1954

Ch. The McGillacudy (BB), Clyde B. Smith

— Ardarragh of Ambleside (WD), Lee O. Gunson

— Windale Barley Sugar (WB), Henry F. Wegner

1955

Ch. The McGillacudy (BB), Clyde B. Smith

Ch. Sheelagh of Ballytobin (BOS), Mrs. Laura L. Thomas

Ch. Fuath of Ulaid (WD), Celeste W. Hutton

— Rathain Miss Erin (WB), Rose Sterzinger

1956

Ch. Tralee of Ambleside (BB), Charles W. Morse, Jr.

— Derry's Barney O'Dea (WD), Mr. and Mrs. John F. Dunnigan

— Dearg of Killybracken (WB), Mrs. Gordon F. Graham

1957

Ch. Belcrest Harp of Ambleside (BB), Miss Suzanne Bel-linger

Ch. Sir Gelert of Ambleside (BOS), Miss Barbara O'Neill

1958

Ch. Sir Gelert of Ambleside (BB), Miss Barbara O'Neill

Ch. Cristel of Ambleside (BOS), Miss Celeste W. Hutton

Sgurra Dubh of Ballylyke (WB), Miss Celeste W. Hutton

1959

Ch. Holly Lawn Kevin McGillacudy (BB), Mr. and Mrs. Arthur R. Bentzig

— Moiragh of Ballykelly (BOS)

176

1960
Ch. Castledawn Tartan (BB), Miss Celeste W. Hutton
Ch. Feasgar Bruadar of Ballylyke, U.D. (BOS), Col. Alfred
W. DeQuoy

1961
Ch. Castledawn Tartan (BB), Miss Celeste W. Hutton
Ch. Sweet Kathy of Kilrain (BOS), Mrs. Henry E. Britcher

1962
Ch. Keltic Banshee UD (BB), A. W. DeQuoy
— Greysarge Cristels Corrigan (BOS), Celeste W. Hutton

1963
Ch. Greysarge Cristel's Corrigan (BB), Celeste W. Hutton
Ch. Keltic Banshee UD (BOS), A. W. DeQuoy
— Barter of Glimmer (WD), Mrs. Joseph L. Roberts

1964
Ch. Hillaway's Padraic of Eagle (BB), Samuel Evans
Ewing, 3rd
Ch. Keltic Banshee UD (BOS), A. W. DeQuoy
— Sulhamstead Samando Patrick (WD), A. W. DeQuoy
— Riverlawn Linda II (WB), Elizabeth McC. Stetson

1965
Ch. Hillaway's Padraic of Eagle (BB), Samuel Evans
Ewing, 3rd
Ch. Keltic Banshee UD (BOS), Col. Alfred W. DeQuoy
— Greysarge Tartan's Tipperary (WD and BW), Celeste
W. Hutton
— Ballykelly Urtagh (WB), Elizabeth D. Clarke

1966
Ch. Ballykelly Colin (BB), Mrs. H. Sheppard Musson
Ch. Keltic Tara, C.D.X., (BOS), Alfred W. DeQuoy
— The Uliath of Cu (WD and BW), J. Mark Grigsby
— Boru's Kelly of Andaki (WB), Lawrence Bloom

1967
Ch. Ballykelly Colin (BB), Mrs. H. Sheppard Musson
Ch. Keltic Tara, C.D.X. (BOS), Alfred W. DeQuoy
— Branwen Luath (WD and BW), Branwen Kennels
— Oighe Dubh of Eagle (WB), Samuel Evans Ewing, 3rd

1968

Ch. Boroughbury Brona (BB), Samuel Evans Ewing, 3rd

Ch. Caragahoolie O'Killybracken (BOS), Killybracken
Kennels

— Ballykelly Charlie Girl (WB and BW), Alfred W. De-
Quoy

— Sanctuary Shamus Again (WD), Mrs. S. O. Schneider

1969

Ch. Armore of Nendrum (BB), Samuel Evans Ewing, 3rd

— Ch. Sulhamstead Marda of Killybracken (BOS), Killybracken Kennels

— Ballykelly Powerscourt Thomas (WD), Dr. and Mrs.
Thomas F. Powers

The quizzical youngster whose head appears at left grew up to be one of
the breed's immortals. He is Hillaway's Padraic of Eagle (p. 165), here
pictured with Ch. Carraig's Burke. Both owned by Samuel Evans Ewing, 3rd.

178

Irish Wolfhound Champions of AKC Record *

Dog	Date of Title	Owner
Achris of Ambleside (D) H-290783	June 19, 1957	Miss Louise Schwennesen
Ambleside Duke of Raglan (D) A-6555	July 9, 1937	Mr. and Mrs. J. Gordon Ridsdale
Ambleside Edain of Edgecliff (B) H-70204	June 26, 1949	Ambleside Kennels
Ambleside Maida of Kincora (B) A-348138	July 5, 1944	C. D. Burrage, Jr.
Ardarragh of Ambleside (D) H-229641	April 4, 1954	Leo J. Gunson, Jr.
Arnold of Edgecliff (D) A-822913	March 10, 1947	Thomas B. Wanamaker, Jr.
Baccara of Spean (B) (Eng.) H-79702	February 22, 1953	Mrs. John W. Wofford
Baine of Kihone (B) A-337531	November 9, 1940	Miss F. J. McGregor
Ballymacad of Ambleside (D) H-404163	October 12, 1957	Samuel Evans Ewing, III
Ballymac of Boroughbury (D) (Eng.) H-68151	June 2, 1951	Mrs. Winifred L. Heckman
Ballyshane of Ambleside (D) 784744	November 9, 1935	Philip A. Bennett
Balricken of Ambleside (D) 865481	October 12, 1957	Rathmullan Kennels
Barn Hill Daisy (B) A-519680	August 10, 1944	Paul F. Paine
Barn Hill Dan Malone (D) A-909281	June 17, 1950	Killybracken Kennels
Barn Hill Hilda (B) A-702889	August 10, 1946	Paul F. Paine
Belcrest Harp of Ambleside (B) H-241519	June 19, 1955	Miss Suzanne Bellinger
Belcrest's Piper (B) H-578997	May 16, 1959	Robert J. Fox
Beowulf of Rathain (D) 980641	October 10, 1936	C. D. Burrage, Jr.
Bhalgair of Ballylyke (B) H-604680	August 3, 1958	Henry B. Weaver
Booyan of Bremore (D) (Eng.) H-100050	October 30, 1949	Mrs. Peter Van Brunt
Bran of Rathmullan (B) 995976	August 20, 1937	Rathmullan Kennels
Brannish of Ambleside (D) 747365	April 20, 1933	Thomas M. Howell
Branwen Clooty of Cu (B) H-743880	May 23, 1959	Miss Rosalie Graham
Brian Boru of Edgecliff (D) H-69468	March 26, 1950	Thomas B. Wanamaker, Jr.
Brickeen of Boroughbury (B) (Eng.) H-78001	September 11, 1949	Ambleside Kennels
Brickeen of Hillaway (B) H-519608	January 14, 1957	Helen Dalton and C. Cram
Bricken of Killybracken (D) H-338033	October 2, 1955	Clifford P. Garvey, Jr.
Brogan of Hillaway (D) H-519605	June 16, 1957	H. Dalton and C. Cram

*A supplemental list of champions finished since 1961 begins on page 185.

Dog	Date of Title	Owner
Carraig's Burke (D) H-792208	September 6, 1959	Samuel Evans Ewing, III
Irish Ch. Castledawn Tartan (D) H-796923	September 28, 1957	Celeste W. Hutton
Chalet Armagh (B) H-2162	May 15, 1948	Killybracken Kennels
Cheevers of Ambleside (D) H-93555	June 13, 1952	Charles D. Burrage, Jr.
Chulainn Casey of Kihone (D) (Eng.) A-356384	December 20, 1939	Miss F. J. McGregor
Clontarf Cormac (D) H-47168	September 10, 1950	William J. Williams
Cragwood Ardarragh (D) H-518489	June 8, 1957	Mrs. P. Van Brunt
Cragwood Ballybilly (D) 694433	October 20, 1930	Jesse A. Howland
Cragwood Barney O'Shea (D) H-107086	September 30, 1951	Mrs. Frances R. Van Brunt
Cragwood Gaelic Gift (B) A-206443	August 20, 1951	Rathbunwood Kennels
Cragwood Gold Rush (B) H-160306	May 24, 1953	Jonathan E. Pierce
Cragwood Macha (B) 557314	June 10, 1931	Mrs. Norwood B. Smith
Cragwood Muldoon (D) 757227	February 20, 1934	Mrs. Norwood B. Smith
Cragwood The O'Toole (D) 465760	October 29, 1928	Mrs. Norwood Browning Smith
Cragwood Victoria (B) A-858138	May 30, 1949	Mrs. Peter Van Brunt
Cristel of Ambleside (B) H-290784	March 3, 1955	Killybracken Kennels
Croughil of Ouborough (D) (Eng.) 870704	July 20, 1936	Walter E. Roehrs, Jr.
Cullykilty of Ambleside (D) H-93558	August 26, 1951	Jack McKenna
Cumeala of Ambleside (D) H-88667	March 2, 1952	Ambleside Kennels
Dan Riley (D) 896776	March 20, 1935	Dr. Chester Lee Reynolds
Dark Desha of Ambleside (B) A-25265	August 10, 1939	Whippoorwill Kennels
Dereen of Killybracken (B) H-422183	July 10, 1958	F. Jeannette McGregor
Derry's Molly Maguire (B) 431808	June 17, 1956	Mrs. Helaine White
Derry's Barney O'Dea (D) H-431805	August 5, 1956	Mr. and Mrs. John F. Dunnigan
Dearg of Killybracken (B) H-338038	October 21, 1956	Mrs. Gordon F. Graham
Dian of Ambleside (D) H-93561	October 12, 1952	Killybracken Kennels
Dromore Gweebarra (*) Not Reg.	April 12, 1915	Miss V. Moore
Edain of Ambleside (B) 734319	April 20, 1932	Rathmullan Kennels
Erin II (D) A-400194	January 10, 1947	Mrs. F. R. Van Brunt

Dog	Date of Title	Owner
Fair Fingal of Ambleside (D) H-117991	April 18, 1954	Misses Helen Dalton and Catherine Cram
Feasgar Bruadar of Ballylyke, U.D. (B) H-604678	*	Col. Alfred W. DeQuoy
Felix of Boyer Ranch (D) A-117411	July 20, 1938	Mr. and Mrs. Clark Foote Huhn
Felixstone Kilbagie (B) (Eng.) 620526	December 30, 1929	Halcyon Kennels
Felixstone Kilgarth (B) (Eng.) A-595356	October 10, 1929	Halcyon Kennels
Felixstowe Killcully Halcyon (D) (Eng.) 923029	August 20, 1934	Halcyon Kennels
Felixstowe Kilmorac Halcyon (D) (Eng.) 710706	March 20, 1930	Halcyon Kennels
Felixstowe Navan (D) (Eng.) 223096	October 27, 1917	Mrs. Paul Courtney
Felixstowe's Kilfree Halcyon (B) (Eng.) 710707	March 20, 1930	Halcyon Kennels
Finn Mac Cool of Edgecliff (D) H-69470	June 25, 1950	Thomas B. Wanamaker, Jr.
Finn-mac-Cumaill of Ambleside (D) H-42249	October 22, 1950	Ambleside Kennels
Finn of Rathmullan (D) 995973	December 19, 1936	Rathmullan Kennels
Flynn of Ballygran (D) H-666851	September 20, 1959	Robert and Maureen Fox
Fuath of Ulaid (D) (Ire.) H-413785	February 15, 1955	Miss Celeste Winans Hutton
Gael of Rathain (B) H-258693	October 11, 1953	Charles D. Burrage, Jr.
Gareth of Rathmullan (D) 815986	December 10, 1934	Rathmullan Kennels
Garragh of Ambleside (D) 760830	April 20, 1932	Mr. and Mrs. L. O. Starbuck
Gartha of Ambleside (B) A-714225	December 2, 1946	Paul F. Paine
Gillagain of Ambleside (D) A-699260	September 10, 1946	Paul F. Paine
Gilmichael of Ambleside (D) H-229644	August 15, 1953	Mrs. Richard Ayer
Halcyon Alannah of Ambleside (B) A-203019	July 20, 1938	Halcyon Kennels
Halcyon Baronet (D) 785270	November 2, 1931	Halcyon Kennels
Halcyon Dana (B) 938664	December 10, 1934	Halcyon Kennels
Halcyon Tamara (B) 770757	November 2, 1931	Halcyon Kennels
Hillaway's Annora O'Dea (B) H-584655	March 30, 1958	Helen Dalton and Catharine Cram
Hillaway's Craigan (D) H-584653	November 9, 1958	H. Dalton and C. Cram
Holly Lawn Kevin McGillacudy (D) H-593490	June 7, 1958	Arthur R. Bentzig
Inverdale Dawn (B) A-78823	October 1, 1937	Charles D. Burrage, Jr.
Inverdale Trouble (B) 793259	November 20, 1934	Charles D. Burrage, Jr.

Dog	Date of Title	Owner
Jericho's Ballaghboy (D) (Eng.) 229015	January 25, 1918	Jericho Kennels
Jerry (D) (Can.) A-760819	May 10, 1946	Paul F. Paine
Kathleen of Ambleside (B) 471340	November 20, 1929	Mr. and Mrs. L. O. Starbuck
Keelta of Killybracken (B) H-705704	October 1, 1960	Mr. and Mrs. G. Graham
Killabrick (D) 629676	December 10, 1929	R. K. Lackey
Killary of Ambleside (D) A-714226	October 10, 1946	Charles D. Burrage, Jr.
Killesandra of Ambleside (B) A-198770	December 10, 1938	Mrs. Alma J. Starbuck
Killfree Kilmorac of Halcyon (B) 760453	October 20, 1933	Rathmullan Kennels
King Lir of Ambleside (D) 608532	March 10, 1931	Mrs. N. T. Bellinger
King Shane of Brabyns (D) (Eng.) 587323	July 20, 1931	Whippoorwill Kennels
Kinvara (D) (Ire.) 164600	June 4, 1915	Michael Creighton
Lacey of Ambleside (B) H-404166	July 30, 1957	Alma J. Starbuck
Laith of Kihone (B) A-968583	October 2, 1949	Miss F. J. McGregor
Lance of Ambleside (D) H-167999	April 27, 1952	Ambleside Kennels
Lansdowne Bloom (B) (Eng.) 145639	June 3, 1912	Mr. and Mrs. T. D. Robinson
Lansdowne Watch (D) (Eng.) 145638	February 26, 1912	T. D. Robinson
Loree Lacroma of Ambleside (B) A-436151	July 10, 1942	Charles D. Burrage, Jr.
Macushla of Ambleside (B) 967309	May 20, 1936	Mrs. Alma J. Starbuck
Mallyree of Ambleside (B) 761333	July 20, 1931	Mr. and Mrs. L. O. Starbuck
Marchmoor Brigitte (B) HA-32632	April 9, 1961	Dr. and Mrs. W. Moir
Maureen of Tyrone (B) H-36382	May 29, 1949	Jonathan E. Pierce
Merry of Rathain (B) H-2160	September 16, 1947	Charles D. Burrage, Jr.
Moiragh of Ballykelly (B) H-84747	April 11, 1959	Mrs. W. Heckmann
Molly Craig of Ambleside (B) H-177582	September 28, 1952	Miss Suzanne V. Bellinger
Molly Killeen of Killybracken (B) A-386160	November 20, 1940	Killybracken Kennels
Molly of Killybracken (B) A-221874	April 1, 1941	Killybracken Kennels
Mona Craig of Ambleside (B) H-177581	June 13, 1953	Ambleside Kennels
Mona of Ambleside (B) 471345	June 21, 1927	Mr. and Mrs. L. O. Starbuck
Monahan of Tyrone (D) H-36383	August 21, 1949	Mrs. Laura Lauray Thomas
Moran of Ouborough (D) (Eng.) A-374271	August 19, 1940	Mrs. Elizabeth Morse
Mugan Machree of Ambleside (B) A-968558	April 9, 1948	LeRoy E. and Margaret L. Fess

Dog	Date of Title	Owner
My Sheila (B) 617319	December 3, 1928	Mr. and Mrs. A. T. Pettey
Nene Riley (B) A-232611	January 10, 1942	Henry S. Jeanes, Jr.
O'Dermody of Killybracken (D) H-653395	August 16, 1959	F. Jeannette McGregor
Owen of Killybracken (D) H-237267	November 14, 1954	Miss Suzanne V. Bellinger
Patrick of Ballytobin (D) (Ire.) H-157002	December 3, 1950	Joseph A. Coll
Rathain Deirdre of Edgecliff (B) H-70756	May 30, 1953	Charles D. Burrage, Jr.
Rathain Derek of Ambleside (D) H-65604	July 31, 1949	Ambleside Kennels
Rathain Gaelic Chieftain (D) H-452476	August 3, 1958	Charles D. Burrage, Jr.
Rathrahilly Ardarragh (B) H-578867	September 29, 1957	Mrs. John W. Wofford
Rathrahilly Clagon (D) H-333018	May 29, 1955	Mrs. John W. Wofford
Rathrahilly Shevauneen, C.D. (B) H-353672	December 9, 1956	Brandoch Peters
Riverlawn Brukk (D) H-187508	July 17, 1954	Mrs. Frances R. Van Brunt
Riverlawn Sandorleigh Paddy (D) H-642902	May 16, 1960	Basil W. and Elizabeth Stetson
Roise of Ambleside (B) H-88665	October 15, 1950	Miss Suzanne V. Bellinger
Roonagh of Ambleside (B) 784743	April 2, 1934	Mr. and Mrs. L. O. Starbuck
Rooney II (D) Not Reg.	June 18, 1917	Parker Conning
Rory O'Moore (D) Not. Reg.	August 1928	Mrs. A. Butler Duncan
Saill of Kihone (D) A-968458	September 25, 1948	Miss F. Jeannette McGregor
Sandra of Rathain, C.D. (B) H-258697	September 12, 1954	Dr. E. V. Kenneally
Satan of Boyer Ranch (D) A-117412	December 1, 1937	Mr. and Mrs. Clark Foote Huhn
Sean Craig of Ambleside (D) H-441886	January 31, 1960	Kennett and Dorothy Patrick
Shadowhill Felixstowe Magee (B) Not. Reg.	(Not Given)	Capt. S. M. Spalding
Shamus Failinis of Ambleside (D) A-968554	August 21, 1948	Mr. and Mrs. LeRoy Fess
Shauneen of Chilton (D) A-361957	June 20, 1941	Mrs. Spencer G. Nauman
Shaun of Kilrain (D) H-521030	June 15, 1958	Dr. and Mrs. E. V. Kenneally
Sheelagh of Ballytobin (B) (Ire.) H-296176	February 10, 1953	Mrs. Laura Lauray Thomas
Sir Gelert of Ambleside (D) H-404162	September 3, 1956	Miss Barbara O'Neill
Steyning Sorrell Halcyon (B) (Eng.) 874932	July 10, 1934	Halcyon Kennels
Sulhamstead Fame (D) (Eng.) A-339142	June 10, 1941	Robert H. Button

Dog	Date of Title	Owner
Sulhamstead Fara of Cragwood (B) (Eng.) A-283504	August 20, 1941	Cragwood Kennels
Sulhamstead Felrose (B) (Eng.) H-544896	August 16, 1956	Mrs. Frances R. Van Brunt
Sulhamstead Flute (D) (Eng.) A-409102	November 9, 1940	Constance R. Winant
Sulhamstead Gala (D) (Eng.) 885768	July 20, 1934	Fredson Thayer Bowers
Sulhamstead Kiora (B) (Eng.) 928950	May 20, 1936	Miss F. Jeannette McGregor
Sulhamstead Marion of Riverlawn (B) H-754729	August 6, 1960	Katherine A. O'Connell
Sulhamstead Matador of Killybracken (D) H-816992	May 22, 1958	Killybracken Kennels
Sulhamstead Rebecca (B) (Eng.) A-339143	June 1, 1942	Robert H. Button
Sullivan of Boroughbury (D) (Eng.) H-281975	October 11, 1953	Comdr. and Mrs. Peter Hopkinson
Surfside Donegal Ain (B) H-89513	July 8, 1951	Herve A. Holly
Sterncrest's Hillaway (B) H-519614	September 30, 1956	Dr. R. L. Huggins
Sweet Kathy of Kilrain (B) H-521034	September 9, 1956	Mrs. Mary E. Britcher
Taffy of Ambleside (B) 920112	April 10, 1937	Mrs. Alma J. Starbuck
Talgarth of Ambleside (D) H-290779	September 23, 1956	Killybracken Kennels
Taraledge Toram (D) H-115328	June 12, 1955	Taraledge Kennels
The McGillacudy (D) H-215340	May 23, 1953	Clyde B. Smith
Timber of Ambleside (D) H-150354	September 20, 1952	Mrs. Thomas F. Madigan
Top Lady of Ambleside (B) 822632	September 1, 1936	Mrs. Clark Foote Huhn
Toyan Diana (B) 307006	September 22, 1924	Mrs. Norwood B. Smith
Trailmoor Lady Colleen (B) A-206874	September 1, 1942	Paul F. Paine
Tralee of Ambleside (B) H-203192	June 7, 1952	Ambleside Kennels
Tullagh of Killybracken (B) H-305328	June 2, 1955	Killybracken Kennels
Tyrone of Ballykelly (B) H-647574	March 20, 1960	Miss Barbara O'Neill
Vivid of Grevel (D) (Eng.) 747173	June 20, 1934	Mrs. J. G. Ridsdale
Victoria of Killybracken (B) H-459699	June 2, 1957	Killybracken Kennels
War Buckler of Ambleside (D) A-201779	August 18, 1939	Ambleside Kennels
Windale Barley Sugar (B) H-227481	April 25, 1954	Henry F. Wegner
Windale Killala (B) H-157615	April 19, 1953	Miss Celeste W. Hutton

Irish Wolfhound Champions Since 1961

Dog	Date of Title	Owner
Kaoc's Macushla Ardarragh (B) H-865130	March 19, 1961	Mrs. Winifred L. Heckmann
Liath Cailin of Ballylyke (B) H-847580	April 9, 1961	Henry B. Weaver
Riverlawn Barnstorm (D) H-862643	May 27, 1961	Riverlawn Kennels
Ambleside Coppersmith II (D) H-933630	July 16, 1961	Mrs. Alma J. Starbuck
Keltic Banshee CDX (B) HA-22480	September 10, 1961	Alfred W. DeQuoy
Keltic Ghost of Ballylyke (B) HA-22483	September 9, 1961	Henry B. Weaver
Cheelainn of Roreen (B) H-976357	September 24, 1961	Robert J. Fox
Hillaway's Cumaela (B) H-584657	November 5, 1961	Mrs. Alma J. Starbuck
Cragwood Lovely Mary (B) H-632245	January 14, 1962	Mrs. Peter Van Vrunt
Hillaway's Padraic of Eagle (D) HA-63233	March 11, 1962	Samuel Evans Ewing, 3rd
Greysarge Cristel's Corrigan (D) H-889664	April 22, 1962	Miss Celeste W. Hutton
Hillaway's Fagan (D) H-68600	May 26, 1962	C. Cram and H. Dalton
Sionnach Cam (B) HA-87402	April 29, 1962	Mrs. Elizabeth Stetson
Blarna of Killybracken (B) HA-71353	June 3, 1962	Killybracken Kennels
Branwen Dana (B) H-880436	June 9, 1962	Mrs. Cynthia B. Madigan
Laggan of Arraghglen (D) (not reg.)	June 3, 1962	Christian Schulz
Ballykelly Shannagh (Ireland) (B) HA-171448	July 13, 1962	Mrs. L. H. Tillman
Sulhamstead Mirza of Kihone (England) (D) HA-267675	July 10, 1962	Kennel Kihone
Ballykelly Kate (Ireland) (B) HA-119225	August 11, 1962	Mrs. L. H. Tillman
Rathain Glory Be of Cu (B) H-903295	September 29, 1962	Mrs. Rosalie D. Graham
Fleetwind Glentara (B) HA-119718	October 21, 1962	Mr. and Mrs. Douglas N. Huntley
Taraledge Teanhra of Roreen (B) H-976356	November 11, 1962	Erinbrook Kennels
Fleetwind Finn MacCool (D) H-877418	November 28, 1962	Lois J. and Norman Hall
Sulhamstead Mars of Riverlawn (D) HA-242671	March 23, 1963	Riverlawn kennels
Sulhamstead Martha of Riverlawn (B) HA-242672	April 19, 1963	Riverlawn Kennels
Deweylarn of Kihone (B) HA-204832	June 15, 1963	Kennel Kihone
Lovat of Arraghglen (D) HA-186523	June 9, 1963	Henry B. Weaver

Dog	Date of Title	Owner
McGavin of Ambleside (D) HA-211216	June 23, 1963	John J. Donohue
Deweylimm of Kihone (B) HA-204831	August 18, 1963	Kennel Kihone
Barter of Glimmer (D) HA-55088	September 21, 1963	Mrs. Helen S. Roberts
Timber's Gaelert O'Laggan (D) HA-395916	September 7, 1963	Mrs. Christian Schulz
Fleetwind Roonagh (B) HA-166220	November 3, 1963	Lois J. and Norman Hall
Fleetwind Chellis (B) HA-119719	November 10, 1963	Lois J. and Norman Hall
Ballykelly Thady (D) HA-261649	March 10, 1964	Mrs. Frances B. Messigner
Riverlawn Linda, II (B) HA-325938	April 11, 1964	Mrs. Elizabeth McC. Stetson
Sanctuary Morne of Riverlawn (D) HA-242669	April 17, 1964	Riverlawn Kennels
Gort of Dunamaise (D) HA-380000	May 10, 1964	Mrs. Harold Correll
Linarra Loree of Cu (B) HA-96807	May 16, 1964	Miss Rosalie R. Graham
Haneen of Cu (B) HA-298484	June 7, 1964	Roberta Tener
Arract of Ballylyke (D) HA-259637	June 7, 1964	Henry B. Weaver
Balbrigan of Balingary (D) HA-291458	June 20, 1964	Mr. and Mrs. Douglas N. Huntley
Killybracken Hanna of Cu (B) HA-299181	July 7, 1964	Killybracken Kennels
Hillaway's O'Keeffe Sean (D) HA-197810	July 26, 1964	Mr. and Mrs. Paul O'Keeffe, Jr.
Sionnach Paddy's Liagin (D) HA-256679	1964	Wayne L.' Larrick
Denmar's Deirdriu of Andaki (B) HA-416491	September 27, 1964	Joseph A. Gilleaudeau, Jr.
Carna's Colleen of Andaki (B) HA-416495	1964	Doris D. Kalish
Glentara Grania of Eagle (B) HA-425163	November 7, 1964	Samuel Evans Ewing, 3rd
Feena of Glimmer Glen (B) HA-227858	January 17, 1965	Lewis Devlin
Sulhamstead Samando Patrick (D) HA-331125	April 25, 1965	Alfred W. DeQuoy
Aislinn of Ballylyke (B) HA-259633	April 25, 1965	Mari E. Kennedy
Ambleside Edain of Eagle (B) HA-341832	May 8, 1965	Samuel Evans Ewing, 3rd
Keltic Phantom II (D) HA-313834	June 5, 1965	Alfred W. DeQuoy
Keltic Tara (B) HA-313833	June 5, 1965	Alfred W. DeQuoy
Timber's Gaelorna O'Laggan (B) HA-395917	May 23, 1965	Mrs. Christian Schulz
Sulhamstead Mac of Killybracken (D) HA-494401	June 20, 1965	Killybracken Kennel
Jocopa's Juleva of Eagle (B) HA-425162	June 20, 1965	J. C. Parker
Fleetwind Balshavna (B) HA-449892	August 1, 1965	Mr. and Mrs. Douglas Huntley

Dog	Date of Title	Owner
Greysarge Tartan's Tipperary (D) HA-271811	September 12, 1965	Miss C. W. Hutton
Ballykelly Urtagh (B) HA-389249	September 12, 1965	Elizabeth D. Clark
Timothy of Edgecliff (D) HA-389249	September 25, 1965	R. Douglass Montgomery
Houlihan of Cu (D) HA-310976	October 9, 1965	Gordon F. Graham
Ballykelly Colin (D) HA-590450	October 16, 1965	Mrs. H. Sheppard Musson
Oisin Dhu of Ambleside (D) HA-341838	October 24, 1965	Agnes Liris
Fleetwind Fingal (D) HA-460838	November 21, 1965	Andrew B. and Phyllis Talbot
Fleetwind Tralaigh of Eagle (D) HA-534789	December 9, 1965	Samuel Evans Ewing, 3rd
Windale Whiddy of Eagle (B) HA-546253	December 10, 1965	Samuel Evans Ewing, 3rd
Belle's Amorak (D) HA-592112	March 19, 1966	Winston W. McCauley
Bard of Glen Tara (D) HA-421923	March 27, 1966	Lewis Devlin
Eirin of Ambleside (D) HA-357978	April 2, 1966	Dr. D. M. Blatchley
Fleetwind Sheila of Dublin (B) HA-260447	April 17, 1966	Catherine Schickle
Fleetwind Tracy (B) HA-291459	April 3, 1966	Mr. and Mrs. H. M. Strecker
Ballykelly Rosie O'Grady (B) HA-413027	May 7, 1966	Don Rogers
Belle's Trojan Gentleheart (D) HA-551095	June 4, 1966	Lucille M. McCauley
Sulhamstead Marlene (B) HA-529576	May 21, 1966	Frances B. Messinger
Branwen Tara (B) HA-265384	June 19, 1966	Bethany Carman
Fleetwind Bregon (D) HA-291462	June 5, 1966	Fleetwind Kennels
Iona of Dunamaise (B) HA-618803	June 19, 1966	Maureen A. Fox
Polaris Artel (D) HA-531624	June 18, 1966	Maureen A. Fox
Tralee of Cu (B) HA-413020	June 11, 1966	Rosalie D. Graham
Dermid of Kihone (D) HA-205072	July 9, 1966	Kennel Kihone
Ailish of Ballinaboy (B) HA-765652	July 17, 1966	Mrs. Christian Schulz
Fleetwind Derek (D) HA-449896	July 31, 1966	Richard L. Rogers and B. A. Riley Jr.
Eohey of Eagle (D) HA-671117	August 28, 1966	Samuel Evans Ewing, 3rd
The Uliath of Cu (D) HA-453422	August 21, 1966	J. Mark Grigsby
Kilkristoir of Killybracken (B) HA-602318	August 28, 1966	Mrs. Christian M. Lauritzen II
Owvane of Eagle (D) HA-514696	September 24, 1966	A. E. Bennett, Jr.
Glimmer Gealain of Eagle (B) HA-624866	September 25, 1966	Samuel Evans Ewing, 3rd

187

Dog	Date of Title	Owner
Millwood Heavenly Days (B) HA-505160	September 24, 1966	Mrs. Everett Sherwood
Irish Laddy of Ulaid (D) HA-706276	September 11, 1966	Paul J. and Irene Burczycki
Fleetwind Kinsale (B) HA-495208	October 2, 1966	Lois J. and Norman Hall
Blarney of Ballinaboy (B) HA-603125	October 1, 1966	Milton B. Simpson
Fleetwind Macushla (B) HA-362846	September 18, 1966	Mr. and Mrs. Eugene F. Pilz
Ailbhe of Ballinaboy (B) HA-609150	October 15, 1966	Charles Musson
Caragahoolie O'Killybracken (D) HA-627925	October 8, 1966	Killybracken Kennel
Sullane of Eagle (B) HA-514691	October 23, 1966	Patricia A. Galloway
Timber of Whitespeak (D) HA-643025	October 23, 1966	Jack and Laurel Seltsam
O'Sullivan of Ballinaboy (D) HA-650674	October 1, 1966	Stephen M. Murray
Clancy of Tara Heights (D) HA-642664	November 27, 1966	John and Agnes Tara
Padraic's Kim of Glimmer (B) HA-636237	December 17, 1966	Shirley McFarland
Tivoli's Buinne of Eagle (B) HA-671113	December 3, 1966	A. B. and Roxanne Bleecker
Garda Siocana Amram (D) HA-528360	January 8, 1967	Mari Thomas
Imperial Amy of Barter (B) HA-481522	January 22, 1967	Paul J. and Irene Burczycki
Bellaire of Kingarrow (B) HA-638425	January 15, 1967	Gordon E. and Evelyn D. Turnage
Bane Tara's Morna of Ambleside (B) HA-605324	March 5, 1967	Dr. and Mrs. Paul A. Williams
Branwen Luath (D) HA-258403	February 18, 1967	Branwen Kennels
Aisling of St. Doulaghs (B) HA-559800	March 18, 1967	Mrs. Winifred L. Heckmann
Aefe of Eagle (B) HA-671114	May 6, 1967	Samuel Evans Ewing, 3rd
Oighe Dubh of Eagle (B) HA-657928	May 6, 1967	Samuel Evans Ewing, 3rd
Fergus of Ballinaboy (D) HA-480100	April 30, 1967	Eugene B. Kavanaugh
Ballykelly Ailbhe (D) HA-714226	May 21, 1967	Dr. and Mrs. Thomas F. Powers
Ballykelly Carrigan (D) HA-546699	June 4, 1967	Primrose Allen Barry
Millwood The Highwayman (D) HA-505157	June 4, 1967	Judith E. and Michael C. Polen
Sionnach Cam's Mickey (D) HA-732931	June 3, 1967	Mrs. P. L. Garland, Jr.
Sulhamstead Minita (B) HA-649575	June 17, 1967	Richard S. Staudt
Torin of Ambleside (D) HA-778766	July 24, 1967	Kennel Kihone
Windale Ridire Dubh of Eagle (D) HA-845750	August 26, 1967	Samuel Evans Ewing, 3rd and J. C. Parker
Fleetwind Maria Brogaun (B) HA-736508	August 27, 1967	Mrs. Mildred H. Koschara

Dog	Date of Title	Owner
Finn McCool of Emone (D) HA-439843	September 17, 1967	Charles R. and Julia M. Williams
Kingarrow's Melissa (B) HA-649374	September 17, 1967	Harold and Mary Major
Fleetwind Edain (B) HA-587636	September 24, 1967	Fleetwind Kennels
Sanctuary Fiannoula (B) HA-717625	September 16, 1967	Vernon I. Smith, M.D.
Maghera Glass Colleen (B) HA-766902	October 1, 1967	Charles Musson
Boroughbury Brona (B) HA-930976	October 21, 1967	Samuel Evans Ewing, 3rd
Castleborn Ard-Mallen of Eagle (B) HA-874700	October 15, 1967	Samuel Evans Ewing, 3rd
Jocopa's Dorcha Clay of Eagle (D) HA-845749	October 22, 1967	J. C. Parker and Samuel Evans Ewing, 3rd
Banshee of Balingary (B) HA-719695	October 22, 1967	Mr. and Mrs. Douglas N. Huntley
Kilmoira of Killybracken (B) HA-602317	August 20, 1967	Elsa C. Richardson
Sconnach Cam's Sheena (B) HA-727541	August 20, 1967	Paul and Irene Burczycki
Ambleside Chellis (B) HA-367453	October 29, 1967	Helen Dalton and Catharine Cram
Belle's Golden Boy (D) HA-729789	November 11, 1967	Richard Ernest Davids
Hercules of Ardarra (D) HA-606999	November 18, 1967	Stephen Schaefer
Kilsioban of Killybracken (B) HA-602314	November 11, 1967	Mrs. Joseph Rowe
Mary of Eaglescrag (B) HA-305650	November 26, 1967	Robert Hunter
Ballykelly Biddy Flanagan (B) HA-907603	February 4, 1968	Harold and Mary Major
Robin Kelly of Kingarrow (D) HA-767811	February 4, 1968	Mr. and Mrs. Carl Batten
Befinn of Eagle (B) HA-760949	March 17, 1968	Samuel Evans Ewing, 3rd
Killykeen Micky Finn (D) HA-847202	March 9, 1968	Mr. and Mrs. H. Sheppard Musson
Maghera Glass Sean (D) HA-766903	February 25, 1968	Mrs. Elise Quigley
Fleetwind Raglan of Eagle (B) HA-911252	April 7, 1968	Samuel Evans Ewing, 3rd
Sean Shillelagh of Killarney (D) HA-723027	April 7, 1968	Cynthia L. Foresman and Stanley G. Foresman
Annalea of Nendrum (B) HA-740440	April 22, 1968	Miss C. W. Hutton
Kilfineen of Killybracken (B) HA-949293	April 27, 1968	Dr. and Mrs. Thomas F. Powers
Rathrahilly Cassandra (B) HA-639695	April 28, 1968	Mrs. Donald MacWillie
Deric of Kihone (D) HA-861849	June 1, 1968	Kennel Kihone
Garda Siocana Astoir (B) HA-528367	May 19, 1968	Jack Tielrooy
Sanctuary Shamus Again (D) HA-674726	May 12, 1968	Mrs. Gwen Schneider
Sulhamstead Marda (B) HA-782250	June 2, 1968	Alfred W. DeQuoy

189

Dog	Date of Title	Owner
Argideen of Eagle (B) HA-514690	June 15, 1968	Elizabeth C. Clark
Ben Bane of Glen Tara (D) HA-449663	June 9, 1968	Dr. Paul A. Williams
Beowulf of Crooked Billet (D) HA-909704	June 15, 1968	Linda Dugan Reiff
Bidelia of Killybracken (B) HA-737443	June 16, 1968	Killybracken Kennel
Garda Siocana Serendipity (D) HA-861860	June 22, 1968	Mari E. Thomas
Kilkara Boroughbury Peggy (B) HA-904940	June 8, 1968	Kelly Fox
Mapleton Breda (B) HA-852969	June 9, 1968	D. D. Dahl
Myown Michael McManus (D) HA-825647	June 9, 1968	Frances B. Messinger
Rory Carragh of Andaki (D) HA-416496	June 9, 1968	Antoinette B. Crawford
Rory of Red Rock (D) HA-799766	June 9, 1968	Dr. E. Michael and Margaret C. Henry
Slattery of Ballinaboy (D) HA-873525	July 6, 1968	Stephanie Myles
Cilwych Dragon (D) HA-976801	July 8, 1968	Mr. and Mrs. Norman C. Poston
Eabh (B) HA-623400	August 17, 1968	Dorothy L. Woodbury
Fleetwind Frona (B) HA-889879	August 17, 1968	Fleetwind Kennels
Himself of Killybracken (D) HA-602320	July 14, 1968	Killybracken Kennel
Imperial Aleita (B) HA-887404	August 17, 1968	Paul J. and Irene Burczycki
Shannon of Keystone (B) HA-962085	July 28, 1968	Murray Ehrenburg
Sionnach Smuitean of Eagle (D) HA-647707	July 28, 1968	David B. Owen
Sulhamstead Marta of Killybracken (B) HA-874875	August 10, 1968	Killybracken Kennel
Applearbor Peggy of Tralee (B) HA-930176	August 18, 1968	Mr. and Mrs. Norman C. Poston
Blawcliah Bob of Sherua HB-70251	September 1, 1968	R. P. O'Neill
Imperial Paddy of Kilkenny (B) GA-903949	August 18, 1968	P. and J. O'Flanagan
Kelso (D) HA-892714	1968	Donna Turman
Kevin of Ballinaboy (D) HA-637075	1968	Round Table Kennels
Sable Kathy of Shanid (B) HA-915961	1968	Paul Pilat
Shaun of Roreen (D) HA-509099	1968	Belcrest Kennels
Sionnach Sigill of Eagle (B) HA-647709	May 25, 1968	Samuel Evans Ewing, 3rd
Ardmore of Nendrum (D) HA-701025	November 9, 1968	Samuel Evans Ewing, 3rd
Cordelia of Denmar (B) HA-757932	October 20, 1968	Dorcas R. Sparr
Fleetwind Rusheen (D) HA-738510	November 3, 1968	Richard and Eleanor Riley

190

Ch. Victoria of Killybracken, BOS and Brood Bitch winner 1963 Specialty; twice BIS at all-breed shows. Owner: Mrs. C. Groverman Ellis, Killybracken Kennels, Francestown, New Hampshire.

BIBLIOGRAPHY

ALL OWNERS of pure-bred dogs will benefit themselves and their dogs by enriching their knowledge of breeds and of canine care, training, breeding, psychology and other important aspects of dog management. The following list of books covers further reading recommended by judges, veterinarians, breeders, trainers and other authorities. Books may be obtained at the finer book stores and pet shops, or through Howell Book House Inc., publishers, New York.

Breed Books

AFGHAN HOUND, Complete	Miller & Gilbert
AIREDALE, New Complete	Edwards
AKITA, Complete	Linderman & Funk
ALASKAN MALAMUTE, Complete	Riddle & Seeley
BASSET HOUND, Complete	Braun
BEAGLE, New Complete	Noted Authorities
BLOODHOUND, Complete	Brey & Reed
BORZOI, Complete	Groshans
BOXER, Complete	Denlinger
BRITTANY SPANIEL, Complete	Riddle
BULLDOG, New Complete	Hanes
BULL TERRIER, New Complete	Eberhard
CAIRN TERRIER, Complete	Marvin
CHESAPEAKE BAY RETRIEVER, Complete	Cherry
CHIHUAHUA, Complete	Noted Authorities
COCKER SPANIEL, New	Kraeuchi
COLLIE, New	Official Publication of the Collie Club of America
DACHSHUND, The New	Meistrell
DALMATIAN, The	Treen
DOBERMAN PINSCHER, New	Walker
ENGLISH SETTER, New Complete	Tuck, Howell & Graef
ENGLISH SPRINGER SPANIEL, New	Goodall & Gasow
FOX TERRIER, New Complete	Silvernail
GERMAN SHEPHERD DOG, New Complete	Bennett
GERMAN SHORTHAIRED POINTER, New	Maxwell
GOLDEN RETRIEVER, Complete	Fischer
GREAT DANE, New	Noted Authorities
GREAT DANE, The—Dogdom's Apollo	Draper
GREAT PYRENEES, Complete	Strang & Giffin
IRISH SETTER, New	Thompson
IRISH WOLFHOUND, Complete	Starbuck
KEESHOND, Complete	Peterson
LABRADOR RETRIEVER, Complete	Warwick
LHASA APSO, Complete	Herbel
MINIATURE SCHNAUZER, Complete	Eskrigge
NEWFOUNDLAND, New Complete	Chern
NORWEGIAN ELKHOUND, New Complete	Wallo
OLD ENGLISH SHEEPDOG, Complete	Mandeville
PEKINGESE, Quigley Book of	Quigley
PEMBROKE WELSH CORGI, Complete	Sargent & Harper
POODLE, New Complete	Hopkins & Irick
POODLE CLIPPING AND GROOMING BOOK, Complete	Kalstone
PULI; Complete	Owen
SAMOYED, Complete	Ward
SCHIPPERKE, Official Book of	Root, Martin, Kent
SCOTTISH TERRIER, New Complete	Marvin
SHETLAND SHEEPDOG, The New	Riddle
SHIH TZU, Joy of Owning	Seranne
SHIH TZU, The (English)	Dadds
SIBERIAN HUSKY, Complete	Demidoff
TERRIERS, The Book of All	Marvin
WEST HIGHLAND WHITE TERRIER, Complete	Marvin
WHIPPET, Complete	Pegram
YORKSHIRE TERRIER, Complete	Gordon & Bennett

Breeding

ART OF BREEDING BETTER DOGS, New	Onstott
BREEDING YOUR OWN SHOW DOG	Seranne
HOW TO BREED DOGS	Whitney
HOW PUPPIES ARE BORN	Prine
INHERITANCE OF COAT COLOR IN DOGS	Little

Care and Training

DOG OBEDIENCE, Complete Book of	Saunders
NOVICE, OPEN AND UTILITY COURSES	Saunders
DOG CARE AND TRAINING FOR BOYS AND GIRLS	Saunders
DOG NUTRITION, Collins Guide to	Collins
DOG TRAINING FOR KIDS	Benjamin
DOG TRAINING, Koehler Method of	Koehler
DOG TRAINING, Step by Step Manual	Volhard & Fisher
GO FIND! Training Your Dog to Track	Davis
GUARD DOG TRAINING, Koehler Method of	Koehler
OPEN OBEDIENCE FOR RING, HOME AND FIELD, Koehler Method of	Koehler
STONE GUIDE TO DOG GROOMING FOR ALL BREEDS	Stone
SUCCESSFUL DOG TRAINING, The Pearsall Guide to	Pearsall
TOY DOGS, Kalstone Guide to Grooming All	Kalstone
TRAINING THE RETRIEVER	Kersley
TRAINING YOUR DOG TO WIN OBEDIENCE TITLES	Morsell
TRAIN YOUR OWN GUN DOG, How to	Goodall
UTILITY DOG TRAINING, Koehler Method of	Koehler
VETERINARY HANDBOOK, Dog Owner's Home	Carlson & Giffin

General

CANINE TERMINOLOGY	Spira
COMPLETE DOG BOOK, The	Official Publication of American Kennel Club
DOG IN ACTION, The	Lyon
DOG BEHAVIOR, New Knowledge of	Pfaffenberger
DOG JUDGE'S HANDBOOK	Tietjen
DOG JUDGING, Nicholas Guide to	Nicholas
DOG PEOPLE ARE CRAZY	Riddle
DOG PSYCHOLOGY	Whitney
DOGSTEPS, Illustrated Gait at a Glance	Elliott
DOG TRICKS	Haggerty & Benjamin
ENCYCLOPEDIA OF DOGS, International	Dangerfield, Howell & Riddle
FROM RICHES TO BITCHES	Shattuck
IN STITCHES OVER BITCHES	Shattuck
JUNIOR SHOWMANSHIP HANDBOOK	Brown & Mason
MY TIMES WITH DOGS	Fletcher
OUR PUPPY'S BABY BOOK (blue or pink)	
SUCCESSFUL DOG SHOWING, Forsyth Guide to	Forsyth
TRIM, GROOM AND SHOW YOUR DOG, How to	Saunders
WHY DOES YOUR DOG DO THAT?	Bergman
WILD DOGS in Life and Legend	Riddle
WORLD OF SLED DOGS, From Siberia to Sport Racing	Coppinger

Part II

GENERAL CARE AND TRAINING
OF YOUR DOG

by
Elsworth S. Howell
Milo G. Denlinger
A. C. Merrick, D.V.M.

Introduction

THE normal care and training of dogs involve
no great mysteries. The application of common sense and good
judgment is required, however. The pages that follow distill the
combined experience and knowledge of three authorities who have
devoted most of their lives to dogs.

Milo Denlinger wrote many books out of his rich and varied
experience as a breeder, exhibitor and owner of a commercial
kennel. Elsworth Howell has been a fancier since young boyhood
and claims intimate knowledge of 25 different breeds; he is an American Kennel Club delegate and judge of the sporting breeds. Dr.
A. C. Merrick is a leading veterinarian with a wide practice.

The chapter on "Training and Simple Obedience" covers the
basic behavior and performance every dog should have to be accepted by your friends, relatives, neighbors and strangers. The good
manners and exercises described will avoid costly bills for damage
to the owner's or neighbor's property and will prevent heartbreak-
ing accidents to the dog and to the people he meets. The instructions are given in simple, clear language so that a child may easily
follow them.

"The Exhibition of Dogs" describes the kinds of dog shows, their
classes and how an owner may enter his dog and show it. If one
practices good sportsmanship, shows can be enjoyable.

The chapter on feeding offers sound advice on feeding puppies,

3

adult dogs, the stud dog and the brood bitch. The values of proteins, carbohydrates, fats, minerals and vitamins in the dog's diet are thoroughly covered. Specific diets and quantities are not given because of the many variations among dogs, even of the same breed or size, in their individual needs, likes, dislikes, allergies, etc.

"The Breeding of Dogs" contains the fundamental precepts everyone who wishes to raise puppies should know. Suggestions for choosing a stud dog are given. The differences among outcrossing, inbreeding and line breeding are clearly explained. Care tips for the pregnant and whelping bitch will be found most helpful.

The material on "External Vermin and Parasites" gives specific treatments for removing and preventing fleas, lice, ticks and flies. With today's wonder insecticides and with proper management there is no excuse for a dog to be infested with any of these pests which often cause secondary problems.

"Intestinal Parasites and Their Control" supplies the knowledge dog owners must have of the kinds of worms that invade dogs and the symptoms they cause. While drugs used for the removal of these debilitating dog enemies are discussed, dosages are not given because it is the authors' and publisher's belief that such treatment is best left in the hands of the veterinarian. These drugs are powerful and dangerous in inexperienced hands.

The chapter on "Skin Troubles" supplies the information and treatments needed to recognize and cure these diseases. The hints appearing on coat care will do much to prevent skin problems.

One of the most valuable sections in this book is the "instant" advice on "FIRST AID" appearing on pages 95-98. The publisher strongly urges the reader to commit this section to memory. It may save a pet's life.

The information on diseases will help the dog owner to diagnose symptoms. Some dog owners rush their dogs to the veterinarian for the slightest, transitory upsets.

Finally, the chapters on "Housing for Dogs" and "Care of the Old Dog" round out this highly useful guide for all dog lovers.

Training and
Simple Obedience

E VERY DOG that is mentally and physically sound can be taught good manners and simple obedience by any normal man, woman, or child over eight years old.

Certain requirements must be met by the dog, trainer and the environment if the training is to be enjoyable and effective. The dog must be rested and calm. The trainer must be rested, calm, gentle, firm, patient and persistent. The training site should be dry, comfortable and, except for certain exercises, devoid of distractions.

Proper techniques can achieve quick and sure results. Always use short, strong words for commands and always use the *same* word or words for the same command. Speak with authority; never scream or yell. Teach one command or exercise at a time and make sure the dog understands it and performs it perfectly before you proceed to the next step. Demand the dog's undivided attention; if he wavers or wanders, speak his name or pat him smartly or jerk his leash. Use pats and praise plentifully; avoid tidbit training if at all possible because tidbits may not always be available in an emergency and the dog will learn better without them. Keep lessons short; when the dog begins to show boredom, stop and do not resume in less than two hours. One or two ten-minute lessons a day should be ample, especially for a young puppy. Dogs have their good and bad days; if your well dog seems unduly lazy, tired, bored or off-color, put off the lesson until tomorrow. Try to make lessons a joy, a happy time both for you and the dog, but do demand and get the desired action. Whenever correction or punishment is needed, use ways and devices that the dog does not connect with you; some of these means are given in the following instructions. Use painful punishment only as a last resort.

"NO!"

The most useful and easily understood command is "NO!" spoken in a sharp, disapproving tone and accompanied with a shaking finger. At first, speak the dog's name following with "NO!" until the meaning of the word—your displeasure—is clear.

"COME!"

Indoors or out, let the dog go ten or more feet away from you. Speak his name following at once with "COME!" Crouch, clap your hands, pick up a stick, throw a ball up and catch it, or create any other diversion which will lure the dog to you. When he comes, praise and pat effusively. As with all commands and exercises repeat the lesson, until the dog *always* comes to you.

THE FIRST NIGHTS

Puppies left alone will bark, moan and whine. If your dog is not to have the run of the house, put him in a room where he can do the least damage. Give him a Nylabone and a strip of beef hide (both available in supermarkets or pet shops and excellent as teething pacifiers). A very young puppy may appreciate a loud-ticking clock which, some dog trainers say, simulates the heart-beat of his former litter mates. Beyond providing these diversions, grit your teeth and steel your heart. If in pity you go to the howling puppy, he will howl every time you leave him. Suffer one night, two nights or possibly three, and you'll have it made.

The greatest boon to dog training and management is the wooden or wire crate. Any two-handed man can make a ⅜" plywood crate. It needs only four sides, a top, a bottom, a door on hinges and

6

with a strong hasp, and a fitting burlap bag stuffed with shredded newspaper, cedar shavings or 2″ foam rubber. Feed dealers or seed stores should give you burlap bags; be sure to wash them thoroughly to remove any chemical or allergy-causing material. The crate should be as long, as high and three times as wide as the dog will be full grown. The crate will become as much a sanctuary to your dog as a cave was to his prehistoric ancestor; it will also help immeasurably in housebreaking.

HOUSEBREAKING

The secret to housebreaking a healthy normal dog is simple: take him out every hour if he is from two to six months old when you get him; or the first thing in the morning, immediately after every meal, and the last thing at night if he is over six months.

For very young puppies, the paper break is indicated. Lay eight or ten layers of newspapers in a room corner most remote from the puppy's bed. By four months of age or after two weeks in a new home if older, a healthy puppy should not need the paper *IF* it is exercised outdoors often and *IF* no liquid (including milk) is given after 5 P.M. and *IF* it is taken out not earlier than 10 P.M. at night and not later than 7 A.M. the next morning.

When the dog does what it should when and where it should, praise, praise and praise some more. Be patient outdoors: keep the dog out until action occurs. Take the dog to the same general area always; its own traces and those of other dogs thus drawn to the spot will help to inspire the desired action.

In extreme cases where frequent exercising outdoors fails, try to catch the dog in the act and throw a chain or a closed tin can with pebbles in it near the dog but not on him; say "NO!" loudly as the chain or can lands. In the most extreme case, a full 30-second spanking with a light strap may be indicated but be sure you catch the miscreant *in the act*. Dog memories are short.

Remember the crate discussed under "THE FIRST NIGHTS." If you give the dog a fair chance, he will NOT soil his crate.

Do not rub his nose in "it." Dogs have dignity and pride. It is permissible to lead him to his error as soon as he commits it and to remonstrate forcefully with "NO!"

7

COLLAR AND LEASH TRAINING

Put on a collar tight enough not to slip over the head. Leave it on for lengthening periods from a few minutes to a few hours over several days. A flat collar for shorthaired breeds; a round or rolled collar for longhairs. For collar breaking, do NOT use a choke collar; it may catch on a branch or other jutting object and strangle the dog.

After a few days' lessons with the collar, attach a heavy cord or rope to it without a loop or knot at the end (to avoid snagging or catching on a stump or other object). Allow the dog to run free with collar and cord attached a few moments at a time for several days. Do not allow dog to chew cord!

When the dog appears to be accustomed to the free-riding cord, pick up end of the cord, loop it around your hand and take your dog for a walk (not the other way around!). DON'T STOP WALK-ING if the dog pulls, balks or screams bloody murder. Keep going and make encouraging noises. If dog leaps ahead of you, turn sharply left or right whichever is *away* from dog's direction— AND KEEP MOVING! The biggest mistake in leash training is stopping when the dog stops, or going the way the dog goes when the dog goes wrong. You're the leader; make the dog aware of it. This is one lesson you should continue until the dog realizes who is boss. If the dog gets the upper leg now, you will find it difficult to resume your rightful position as master. Brutality, no; firm-ness, yes!

If the dog pulls ahead, jerk the cord—or by now, the leash— backward. Do not pull. Jerk or snap the leash only!

JUMPING ON PEOPLE

Nip this annoying habit at once by bumping the dog with your knee on his chest or stepping with authority on his rear feet. A sharp "NO!" at the same time helps. Don't permit this action when you're in your work clothes and ban it only when dressed in glad rags. The dog is not Beau Brummel, and it is cruel to expect him to distinguish between denim and silk.

8

THE "PROBLEM" DOG

The following corrections are indicated when softer methods fail. Remember that it's better to rehabilitate than to destroy.

Biting. For the puppy habit of mouthing or teething on the owner's hand, a sharp rap with a folded newspaper on the nose, or snapping the middle finger off the thumb against the dog's nose, will usually discourage nibbling tactics. For the biter that means it, truly drastic corrections may be preferable to destroying the dog. If your dog is approaching one year of age and is biting in earnest, take him to a professional dog trainer and don't quibble with his methods unless you would rather see the dog dead.

Chewing. For teething puppies, provide a Nylabone (trade mark) and beef hide strips (see "THE FIRST NIGHTS" above). Every time the puppy attacks a chair, a rug, your hand, or any other chewable object, snap your finger or rap a newspaper on his nose, or throw the chain or a covered pebble-laden tin can near him, say "NO!" and hand him the bone or beef hide. If he persists, put him in his crate with the bone and hide. For incorrigible chewers, check diet for deficiencies first. William Koehler, trainer of many movie dogs including *The Thin Man's* Asta, recommends in his book, *The Koehler Method of Dog Training,* that the chewed object or part of it be taped crosswise in the dog's mouth until he develops a hearty distaste for it.

Digging. While he is in the act, throw the chain or noisy tin can and call out "NO!" For the real delinquent Koehler recommends filling the dug hole with water, forcing the dog's nose into it until the dog thinks he's drowning—and he'll never dig again. Drastic perhaps, but better than the bullet from an angry neighbor's gun, or a surreptitious poisoning.

The Runaway. If your dog wanders while walking with you, throw the chain or tin can and call "COME!" to him. If he persists, have a friend or neighbor cooperate in chasing him home. A very long line, perhaps 25 feet or more, can be effective if you permit the dog to run its length and then snap it sharply to remind him not to get too far from you.

Car Chasing. Your dog will certainly live longer if you make him car-wise; in fact, deathly afraid of anything on wheels. Ask a friend or neighbor to drive you in *his* car. Lie below the windows and as your dog chases the car throw the chain or tin can while your neighbor or friend says "GO HOME!" sharply. Another method is to shoot a water pistol filled with highly diluted ammonia at the dog. If your dog runs after children on bicycles, the latter device is especially effective but may turn the dog against children.

The Possessive Dog. If a dog displays overly protective habits, berate him in no uncertain terms. The chain, the noisy can, the rolled newspaper, or light strap sharply applied, may convince him that, while he loves you, there's no percentage in overdoing it.

The Cat Chaser. Again, the chain, the can, the newspaper, the strap—or the cat's claws if all else fails, but only as the last resort.

The Defiant, or Revengeful, Wetter. Some dogs seem to resent being left alone. Some are jealous when their owners play with another dog or animal. Get a friend or neighbor in this case to heave the chain or noisy tin can when the dog relieves himself in sheer spite.

For other canine delinquencies, you will find *The Koehler Method of Dog Training* effective. William Koehler's techniques have been certified as extremely successful by directors of motion pictures featuring dogs and by officers of dog obedience clubs.

OBEDIENCE EXERCISES

A well-mannered dog saves its owner money, embarrassment and possible heartbreak. The destruction of property by canine delinquents, avoidable accidents to dogs and children, and other unnecessary disadvantages to dog ownership can be eliminated by simple obedience training. The elementary exercises of heeling, sitting, staying and lying down can keep the dog out of trouble in most situations.

The only tools needed for basic obedience training are a slip collar made of chain link, leather or nylon and a strong six-foot leather leash with a good spring snap. Reviewing the requirements and basic techniques given earlier, let's proceed with the dog's schooling.

Heeling.   Keep your dog on your left side, with the leash in your left hand. Start straight ahead in a brisk walk. If your dog pulls ahead, jerk (do not pull) the leash and say "Heel" firmly. If the dog persists in pulling ahead, stop, turn right or left and go on for several yards, saying "Heel" each time you change direction.

If your dog balks, fix leash *under* his throat and coax him forward by repeating his name and tapping your hip.

Whatever you do, don't stop walking! If the dog jumps up or "fights" the leash, just keep moving briskly. Sooner than later he will catch on and with the repetition of "Heel" on every correction, you will have him trotting by your side with style and respect.

Sit.   Keeping your dog on leash, hold his neck up and push his rump down while repeating "Sit." If he resists, "spank" him lightly several times on his rump. Be firm, but not cruel. Repeat this lesson often until it is learned perfectly. When the dog knows the command, test him at a distance without the leash. Return to him every time he fails to sit and repeat the exercise.

Stay.   If you have properly trained your dog to "Sit," the "Stay" is simple. Take his leash off and repeat "Stay" holding your hand up, palm toward dog, and move away. If dog moves toward you, you must repeat the "sit" lesson until properly learned. After your

11

dog "stays" while you are in sight, move out of his sight and keep repeating "Stay." Once he has learned to "stay" even while you are out of his sight, you can test him under various conditions, such as when another dog is near, a child is playing close to him, or a car appears on the road. (Warning: do not tax your dog's patience on the "stay" until he has learned the performance perfectly.)

Down. For this lesson, keep your dog on leash. First tell him to "sit." When he has sat for a minute, place your shoe over his leash between the heel and sole. Slowly pull on the leash and repeat "Down" while you push his head down with your other hand. Do this exercise very quietly so that dog does not become excited and uncontrollable. In fact, this performance is best trained when the dog is rather quiet. Later, after the dog has learned the voice signal perfectly, you can command the "Down" with a hand signal, sweeping your hand from an upright position to a downward motion with your palm toward the dog. Be sure to say "Down" with the hand signal.

For more advanced obedience the following guides by Blanche Saunders are recommended:

The Complete Novice Obedience Course
The Complete Open Obedience Course
The Complete Utility Obedience Course (with Tracking)
Dog Training for Boys and Girls (includes simple tricks.)
All are published by Howell Book House at $3.00 each.

OBEDIENCE TRIALS

Booklets covering the rules and regulations of Obedience Trials may be obtained from The American Kennel Club, 51 Madison Avenue, New York, N.Y. 10010. In Canada, write The Canadian Kennel Club, 667 Yonge Street, Toronto, Ontario.

Both these national clubs can give you the names and locations of local and regional dog clubs that conduct training classes in obedience and run Obedience Trials in which trained dogs compete for degrees as follow: CD (Companion Dog), CDX (Companion Dog Excellent), UD (Utility Dog), TD (Tracking Dog) and UDT (Utility Dog, Tracking.)

The Exhibition
of Dogs

NOBODY should exhibit a dog in the shows unless he can win without gloating and can lose without rancor. The showing of dogs is first of all a sport, and it is to be approached in a sportsmanlike spirit. It is not always so approached. That there are so many wretched losers and so many supercilious winners among the exhibitors in dog shows is the reason for this warning.

The confidence that one's dog is of exhibition excellence is all that prompts one to enter him in the show, but, if he fails in comparison with his competitors, nobody is harmed. It is no personal disgrace to have a dog beaten. It may be due to the dog's fundamental faults, to its condition, or to inexpert handling. One way to avoid such hazards is to turn the dog over to a good professional handler. Such a man with a flourishing established business will not accept an inferior dog, one that is not worth exhibiting. He will put the dog in the best possible condition before he goes into the ring with him, and he knows all the tricks of getting out of a dog all he has to give. Good handlers come high, however. Fees for taking a dog into the ring will range from ten to twenty-five dollars, plus any cash prizes the dog may win, and plus a bonus for wins made in the group.

Handlers do not win all the prizes, despite the gossip that they do, but good handlers choose only good dogs and they usually finish at or near the top of their classes. It is a mistake to assume that this is due to any favoritism or any connivance with the judges; the handlers have simply chosen the best dogs, conditioned them well, and so maneuvered them in the ring as to bring out their best points.

The services of a professional handler are not essential, however. Many an amateur shows his dogs as well, but the exhibitor without previous experience is ordinarily at something of a disadvantage. If the dog is good enough, he may be expected to win.

The premium list of the show, setting forth the prizes to be offered, giving the names of the judges, containing the entry form, and describing the conditions under which the show is to be held, are usually mailed out to prospective exhibitors about a month before the show is scheduled to be held. Any show superintendent is glad to add names of interested persons to the mailing list.

Entries for a Licensed show close at a stated date, usually about two weeks before the show opens, and under the rules no entry may be accepted after the advertised date of closing. It behooves the exhibitor to make his entries promptly. The exhibitor is responsible for all errors he may make on the entry form of his dog; such errors cannot be rectified and may result in the disqualification of the exhibit. It therefore is wise for the owner to double check all data submitted with an entry. The cost of making an entry, which is stated in the premium list, is usually from six to eight dollars. An unregistered dog may be shown at three shows, after which he must be registered or a statement must be made to the American Kennel Club that he is ineligible for registry and why, with a request for permission to continue to exhibit the dog. Such permission is seldom denied. The listing fee for an unregistered dog is twenty-five cents, which must be added to the entry fee.

Match or Sanctioned shows are excellent training and experience for regular bench shows. Entry fees are low, usually ranging from fifty cents to a dollar, and are made at the show instead of in advance. Sanctioned shows are unbenched, informal affairs where the puppy may follow his owner about on the leash and become accustomed to strange dogs, to behaving himself in the ring, and to being handled by a judge. For the novice exhibitor, too, Sanctioned shows will provide valuable experience, for ring procedure is similar to that at regular bench shows.

14

The classes open at most shows and usually divided by sex are as follows: Puppy Class (often Junior Puppy for dogs 6 to 9 months old, and Senior Puppy for dogs 9 to 12 months); Novice Class, for dogs that have never won first in any except the Puppy Class; Bred-by-Exhibitor Class, for dogs of which the breeder and owner are the same person or persons; the American-bred Class, for dogs whose parents were mated in America; and the Open Class, which is open to all comers. The respective first prize winners of these various classes compete in what is known as the Winners Class for points toward championship. No entry can be made in the Winners Class, which is open without additional charge to the winners of the earlier classes, all of which are obligated to compete.

A dog eligible to more than one class can be entered in each of them, but it is usually wiser to enter him in only one. A puppy should, unless unusually precocious and mature, be placed in the Puppy Class, and it is unfair to so young a dog to expect him to defeat older dogs, although an exceptional puppy may receive an award in the Winners Class. The exhibitor who is satisfied merely that his dog may win the class in which he is entered is advised to place him in the lowest class to which he is eligible, but the exhibitor with confidence in his dog and shooting for high honors should enter the dog in the Open Class, where the competition is usually the toughest. The winner of the Open Class usually (but by no means always) is also the top of the Winners Class; the runner-up to this dog is named Reserve Winners.

The winner of the Winners Class for dogs competes with the Winners Bitch for Best of Winners, after competing for Best of Breed or Best of Variety with any Champions of Record which may be entered for Specials Only. In the closing hours of the show, the Best of Breed or Best of Variety is eligible to compete in the respective Variety Group to which his breed belongs. And if, perchance, he should win his Variety Group, he is obligated to compete for Best Dog in Show. This is a major honor which few inexperienced exhibitors attain and to which they seldom aspire.

Duly entered, the dog should be brought into the best possible condition for his exhibition in the show and taught to move and to pose at his best. He should be equipped with a neat, strong collar without ornaments or spikes, a show lead of the proper length, width and material for his size and coat, and a nickel bench chain of strong links with which to fasten him to his bench. Food such as the dog is used to, a bottle of the water he is accustomed to drink, and all grooming equipment should be assembled in a bag the night before departure for the show. The exhibitor's pass, on which the dog is assigned a stall number, is sent by mail by the show superintendent and should not be left behind, since it is difficult to have the pass duplicated and it enables the dog's caretaker to leave and return to the show at will.

The time of the opening of the show is stated in the premium list, and it is wise to have one's dog at the show promptly. Late arrivals are subject to disqualification if they are protested.

Sometimes examination is made by the veterinarian at the entrance of the show, and healthy dogs are quickly passed along. Once admitted to the show, if it is a "benched" show, it is wise to find one's bench, the number of which is on the exhibitor's ticket, to affix one's dog to the bench, and not to remove him from it except for exercising or until he is to be taken into the ring to be judged. A familiar blanket or cushion for the bench makes a dog feel at home there. It is contrary to the rules to remove dogs from their benches and to keep them in crates during show hours, and these rules are strictly enforced. Many outdoor shows are not "benched," and you provide your own crate or place for your dog.

At bench shows some exhibitors choose to sit by their dog's bench, but if he is securely chained he is likely to be safe in his owner's absence. Dogs have been stolen from their benches and others allegedly poisoned in the shows, but such incidents are rare indeed. The greater danger is that the dog may grow nervous and insecure, and it is best that the owner return now and again to the bench to reassure the dog of his security.

The advertised program of the show permits exhibitors to know the approximate hour of the judging of their respective breeds. Although that time may be somewhat delayed, it may be depended upon that judging will not begin before the stated hour. The dog should have been groomed and made ready for his appearance in the show ring. When his class is called the dog should be taken unhurriedly to the entrance of the ring, where the handler will receive an arm band with the dog's number.

When the class is assembled and the judge asks that the dogs be paraded before him, the handler should fall into the counter-clock-

16

wise line and walk his dog until the signal to stop is given. In moving in a circle, the dog should be kept on the inside so that he may be readily seen by the judge, who stands in the center of the ring. In stopping the line, there is no advantage to be gained in maneuvering one's dog to the premier position, since the judge will change the position of the dogs as he sees fit.

Keep the dog alert and facing toward the judge at all times. When summoned to the center of the ring for examination, go briskly but not brashly. It is unwise to enter into conversation with the judge, except briefly to reply to any questions he may ask. Do not call his attention to any excellences the dog may possess or excuse any shortcomings; the judge is presumed to evaluate the exhibit's merits as he sees them.

If asked to move the dog, he should be led directly away from the judge and again toward the judge. A brisk but not too rapid trot is the gait the judge wishes to see, unless he declares otherwise. He may ask that the movement be repeated, with which request the handler should respond with alacrity. It is best not to choke a dog in moving him, but rather to move him on a loose lead. The judge will assign or signal a dog to his position, which should be assumed without quibble.

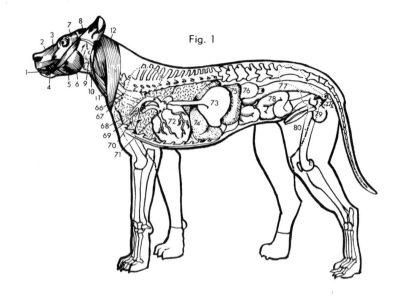

Fig. 1

Fig. 2

Fig. 1

1 Orbicularis oris.
2 Levator nasolabialis.
3 Levator labii superioris proprius (levator of upper lip).
4 Dilator naris lateralis.
5 Zygomaticus.
6 Masseter (large and well developed in the dog).
7 Scutularis.
8 Parotid Gland.
9 Submaxillary Gland.
10 Parotido-auricularis.
11 Sterno-hyoideus.
12 Brachio-cephalicus.

(Between figures 8 and 12 on top the Elevator and Depressor muscles of the ear are to be seen.)

66 Œsophagus (gullet).
67 Trachea (wind pipe).
68 Left Carotid Artery.
69 Anterior Aorta.
70 Lungs.
71 Posterior Aorta.
72 Heart.
73 Stomach.

74 Liver. (The line in front of Liver shows the Diaphragm separating Thoracic from Abdominal cavity.)
75 Spleen.
76 Kidney (left).
77 Rectum.
77A Anal Glands (position) just inside rectum.
78 Intestine.
79 Testicle.
80 Penis.
   (Midway between 76 and 79 is the seat of the Bladder and behind this the seat of the Prostate gland in males, uterus in females.)

Fig. 2

Section of Head and Neck.
1 Nasal septum.
2 Tongue.
3 Cerebrum.
4 Cerebellum.
5 Medulla oblongata.
6 Spinal Cord.
7 Œsophagus (gullet).
8 Trachea (wind pipe).
9 Hard palate.
10 Soft palate.
11 Larynx, containing vocal cords.

18

The Feeding of Dogs, Constitutional Vigor

I N selecting a new dog, it is quite as essential that he shall be of sound constitution as that he shall be of the correct type of his own particular breed. The animal that is thoroughly typical of his breed is likely to be vigorous, with a will and a body to surmount diseases and ill treatment, but the converse of this statement is not always true. A dog may have constitutional vigor without breed type. We want both.

Half of the care and effort of rearing a dog is saved by choosing at the outset a puppy of sound constitution, one with a will and an ability to survive and flourish in spite of such adversity and neglect as he may encounter in life. This does not mean that the reader has any intention of obtaining a healthy dog and ill treating it, trusting its good constitution to bring it through whatever crises may beset it. It only means that he will save himself work, expense, and disappointment if only he will exercise care in the first place to obtain a healthy dog, one bred from sound and vigorous parents and one which has received adequate care and good food.

The first warning is not to economize too much in buying a dog. Never accept a cull of the litter at any price. The difference in first cost between a fragile, ill nourished, weedy, and unhealthy puppy and a sound, vigorous one, with adequate substance and the will to survive, may be ten dollars or it may be fifty dollars. But whatever it may be, it is worthwhile. A dog is an investment and it

19

is not the cost but the upkeep that makes the difference. We may save fifty dollars on the first price of a dog, only to lay out twice or five times that sum for veterinary fees over and above what it would cost to rear a dog of sound fundamental constitution and structure.

The vital, desirable dog, the one that is easy to rear and worth the care bestowed upon him, is active, inquisitive, and happy. He is sleek, his eyes free from pus or tears, his coat shining and alive, his flesh adequate and firm. He is not necessarily fat, but a small amount of surplus flesh, especially in puppyhood, is not undesirable. He is free from rachitic knobs on his joints or from crooked bones resultant from rickets. His teeth are firm and white and even. His breath is sweet to the smell. Above all, he is playful and responsive. Puppies, like babies, are much given to sleep, but when they are awake the sturdy ones do not mope lethargically around.

An adult dog that is too thin may often be fattened; if he is too fat he may be reduced. But it is essential that he shall be sound and healthy with a good normal appetite and that he be active and full of the joy of being alive. He must have had the benefit of a good heredity and a good start in life.

A dog without a fundamental inheritance of good vitality, or one that has been neglected throughout his growing period is seldom worth his feed. We must face these facts at the very beginning. Buy only from an owner who is willing to guarantee the soundness of his stock, and before consummating the purchase, have the dog, whether puppy or adult, examined by a veterinarian in order to determine the state of the dog's health.

If the dog to be cared for has been already acquired, there is nothing to do but to make the best of whatever weaknesses or frailties he may possess. But, when it is decided to replace him with another, let us make sure that he has constitutional vigor.

THE FEEDING AND NUTRITION OF
THE ADULT DOG

The dog is a carnivore, an eater of meat. This is a truism that cannot be repeated too often. Dog keepers know it but are prone to disregard it, although they do so at their peril and the peril of their dogs. Despite all the old-wives' tales to the contrary, meat does not cause a dog to be vicious, it does not give him worms nor cause him to have fits. It is his food. This is by no means all that is needed to know about food for the dog, but it is the essential knowledge. Give a dog enough sound meat and he will not be ill fed.

The dog is believed to have been the first of the animals that was brought under domestication. In his feral state he was almost exclusively an eater of meat. In his long association with man, however, his metabolism has adjusted itself somewhat to the consumption of human diet until he now can eat, even if he cannot flourish upon, whatever his master chooses to share with him, be it caviar or corn pone. It is not to be denied that a mature dog can survive without ill effects upon an exclusive diet of rice for a considerable period, but it is not to be recommended that he should be forced to do so.

Even if we had no empirical evidence that dogs thrive best upon foods of animal origin, and we possess conclusive proof of that fact, the anatomy and physiology of the dog would convince us of it. An observation of the structure of the dog's alimentary canal, superimposed upon many trial and error methods of feeding, leads us to the conclusion that a diet with meat predominating is the best food we can give a dog.

To begin with, the dental formation of the dog is typical of the carnivores. His teeth are designed for tearing rather than for mastication. He bolts his food and swallows it with a minimum of chewing. It is harmless that he should do this. No digestion takes place in the dog's mouth.

The capacity of the dog's stomach is great in comparison with the size of his body and with the capacity of his intestines. The amounts of carbohydrates and of fats digested in the stomach are minimal. The chief function of the dog's stomach is the digestion of proteins. In the dog as in the other carnivores, carbohydrates

21

and fats are digested for the most part in the small intestine, and absorption of food materials is largely from the small intestine. The enzymes necessary for the completion of the digestion of proteins which have not been fully digested in the stomach and for the digestion of sugars, starches, and fats are present in the pancreatic and intestinal juices. The capacity of the small intestine in the dog is not great and for that reason digestion that takes place there must be rapid.

The so-called large intestine (although in the dog it is really not "large" at all) is short and of small capacity in comparison with that of animals adapted by nature to subsist wholly or largely upon plant foods. In the dog, the large gut is designed to serve chiefly for storage of a limited and compact bulk of waste materials, which are later to be discharged as feces. Some absorption of water occurs there, but there is little if any absorption there of the products of digestion.

It will be readily seen that the short digestive tract of the dog is best adapted to a concentrated diet, which can be quickly digested and which leaves a small residue. Foods of animal origin (flesh, fish, milk, and eggs) are therefore suited to the digestive physiology of the dog because of the ease and completeness with which they are digested as compared with plant foods, which contain considerable amounts of indigestible structural material. The dog is best fed with a concentrated diet with a minimum of roughage.

This means meat. Flesh, milk, and eggs are, in effect, vegetation partly predigested. The steer or horse eats grain and herbage, from which its long digestive tract enables it to extract the food value and eliminate the indigestible material. The carnivore eats the flesh of the herbivore, thus obtaining his grain and grass in a concentrated form suitable for digestion in his short alimentary tract. Thus it is seen that meat is the ideal as a chief ingredient of the dog's ration.

Like that of all other animals, the dog's diet must be made up of proteins, carbohydrates, fats, minerals, vitamins, and water. None of these substances may be excluded if the dog is to survive. If he fails to obtain any of them from one source, it must come from another. It may be argued that before minerals were artificially supplied in the dog's diet and before we were aware of the existence of the various vitamins, we had dogs and they (some of them)

22

appeared to thrive. However, they obtained such substances in their foods, although we were not aware of it. It is very likely that few dogs obtained much more than their very minimum of requirements of the minerals and vitamins. It is known that rickets were more prevalent before we learned to supply our dogs with ample calcium, and black tongue, now almost unknown, was a common canine disease before we supplied in the dog's diet that fraction of the vitamin B complex known as nicotinic acid. There is no way for us to know how large a portion of our dogs died for want of some particular food element before we learned to supply all the necessary ones. The dogs that survived received somewhere in their diet some of all of these compounds.

PROTEIN

The various proteins are the nitrogenous part of the food. They are composed of the amino acids, singly or in combination. There are at least twenty-two of these amino acids known to the nutritional scientists, ten of which are regarded as dietary essentials, the others of which, if not supplied in the diet, can be compounded in the body, which requires an adequate supply of all twenty-two. When any one of the essential ten amino acids is withdrawn from the diet of any animal, growth ceases or is greatly retarded. Thus, a high protein content in any food is not an assurance of its food value if taken alone; it may be lacking in one or more of the essential ten amino acids. When the absent essential amino acids are added to it in sufficient quantities or included separately in the diet, the protein may be complete and fully assimilated.

Proteins, as such, are ingested and in the digestive tract are broken down into the separate amino acids of which they are composed. These amino acids have been likened to building stones, since they are taken up by the blood stream and conveyed to the various parts of the animal as they may be required, where they are deposited and re-united with other complementary amino acids again to form bone and muscles in the resumed form of protein.

To correct amino acid deficiencies in the diet, it is not necessary to add the required units in pure form. The same object may be accomplished more efficiently by employing proteins which contain the required amino acids.

Foods of animal origin—meat, fish, eggs, and milk—supply proteins of high nutritive value, both from the standpoint of digestibility and amino acid content. Gelatin is an exception to that statement, since gelatin is very incomplete.

Even foods of animal origin vary among themselves in their protein content and amino acid balance. The protein of muscle meat does not rank quite as high as that of eggs or milk. The glandular tissues—such as liver, kidneys, sweetbreads or pancreas—contain proteins of exceptionally high nutritive value, and these organs should be added to the dog's diet whenever it is possible to do so. Each pint of milk contains two-thirds of an ounce (dry weight) of particularly high class protein, in addition to minerals, vitamins, carbohydrates, and fats. (The only dietary necessity absent

24

from milk is iron.) Animal proteins have a high content of dietary-essential amino acids, which makes them very effective in supplementing many proteins of vegetable origin. The whites of eggs, while somewhat inferior to the yolks, contain excellent proteins. The lysine of milk can be destroyed by excessive heat and the growth promoting value of its protein so destroyed. Evaporated tinned milk has not been subjected to enough heat to injure its proteins.

Thus we can readily see why meat with its concentrated, balanced, and easily assimilated proteins should form the major part of dry weight of a dog's ration.

It has never been determined how much protein the dog requires in his diet. It may be assumed to vary as to the size, age, and breed of the dog under consideration; as to the individual dog, some assimilating protein better, or utilizing more of it than others; as to the activity or inactivity of the subject; and as to the amino acid content of the protein employed. When wheat protein gliadin is fed as the sole protein, three times as much of it is required as of the milk protein, lactalbumin. It has been estimated that approximately twenty to twenty-five percent of animal protein (dry weight) in a dog's diet is adequate for maintenance in good health, although no final conclusion has been reached and probably never can be.

Our purpose, however, is not to feed the dog the minimum ration with which he can survive or even the minimum ration with which he can flourish. It is rather to give him the maximum food in quantity and balance which he can digest and enjoy without developing a paunch. Who wants to live on the minimum diet necessary for adequate sustenance? We all enjoy a full belly of good food, and so do our dogs.

Roy G. Daggs found from experimentation that milk production in the dog was influenced by the different kinds of proteins fed to it. He has pointed out that relatively high protein diets stimulate lactation and that, in the bitch, animal proteins are better suited to the synthesis of milk than plant proteins. He concluded that liver was a better source of protein for lactation than eggs or round steak.

THE CARBOHYDRATES

The carbohydrates include all the starches, the sugars, and the cellulose and hemicellulose, which last two, known as fiber, are the chief constituents of wood, of the stalks and leaves of plants, and of the coverings of seeds. There remains considerable controversy as to the amount of carbohydrates required or desirable in canine nutrition. It has been shown experimentally that the dog is able to digest large quantities of cornstarch, either raw or cooked. Rice fed to mature dogs in amounts sufficient to satisfy total energy requirements has been found to be 95 percent digested. We know that the various commercial biscuits and meals which are marketed as food for dogs are well tolerated, especially if they are supplemented by the addition of fresh meat. There seems to be no reason why they should not be included in the dog's ration.

Carbohydrates are a cheap source of energy for the dog, both in their initial cost and in the work required of the organism for their metabolism. Since there exists ample evidence that the dog has no difficulty in digesting and utilizing considerable amounts of starches and sugars for the production of energy, there is no reason why they should be excluded from his diet. Some carbohydrate is necessary for the metabolism of fats. The only danger from the employment of carbohydrates is that, being cheap, they may be employed to the exclusion of proteins and other essential elements of the dog's diet. It should be noted that meat and milk contain a measure of carbohydrates as well as of proteins.

Thoroughly cooked rice or oatmeal in moderate quantities may well be used to supplement and cheapen a meat diet for a dog without harm to him, as may crushed dog biscuit or shredded wheat waste or the waste from manufacture of other cereal foods. They are not required but may be used without harm.

Sugar and candy, of which dogs are inordinately fond, used also to be *verboten.* They are an excellent source of energy—and harmless. They should be fed in only moderate quantities.

26

FATS

In the dog as in man, body fat is found in largest amounts under the skin, between the muscles and around the internal organs. The fat so stored serves as a reserve source of heat and energy when the caloric value of the food is insufficient, or for temporary periods when no food is eaten. The accumulation of a certain amount of fat around vital organs provides considerable protection against cold and injury.

Before fats can be carried to the body cells by means of the circulating blood, it is necessary for them to be digested in the intestines with the aid of enzymes. Fats require a longer time for digestion than carbohydrates or proteins. For this reason, they are of special importance in delaying the sensations of hunger. This property of fats is frequently referred to as "staying power."

It is easily possible for some dogs to accumulate too much fat, making them unattractive, ungainly, and vaguely uncomfortable. This should be avoided by withholding an excess of fats and carbohydrates from the diets of such dogs whenever obesity threatens them. There is greater danger, however, that dogs may through inadequacy of their diets be permitted to become too thin.

Carbohydrates can in part be transformed to fats within the animal body. The ratio between fats and carbohydrates can therefore be varied within wide limits in the dog's ration so long as the requirements for proteins, vitamins, and minerals are adequately met. Some dogs have been known to tolerate as much as forty percent of fat in their diets over prolonged periods, but so much is not to be recommended as a general practice. Perhaps fifteen to twenty percent of fat is adequate without being too much.

Fat is a heat producing food, and the amount given a dog should be stepped up in the colder parts of the year and reduced in the summer months. In a ration low in fat it is particularly important that a good source of the fat-soluble vitamins be included or that such vitamins be artificially supplied. Weight for weight, fat has more than twice the food value of the other organic food groups— carbohydrates and proteins. The use of fat tends to decrease the amount of food required to supply caloric needs. The fats offer a means of increasing or decreasing the total sum of energy in the diet with the least change in the volume of food intake.

It is far less important that the dog receive more than a minimum amount of fats, however, than that his ration contain an adequate amount and quality balance of proteins. Lean meat in adequate quantities will provide him with such proteins, and fats may be added to it in the form of fat meat, suet, or lard. Small quantities of dog biscuits, cooked rice, or other cereals in the diet will supply the needed carbohydrates. However, cellulose or other roughage is not required in the diet of the carnivore. It serves only to engorge the dog's colon, which is not capacious, and to increase the volume of feces, which is supererogatory.

MINERALS

At least eleven minerals are present in the normal dog, and there are probably others occurring in quantities so minute that they have not as yet been discovered. The eleven are as follows: Calcium (lime), sodium chloride (table salt), copper, iron, magnesium, manganese, phosphorus, zinc, potassium, and iodine.

Of many of these only a trace in the daily ration is required and that trace is adequately found in meat or in almost any other normal diet. There are a few that we should be at pains to add to the diet. The others we shall ignore.

Sodium chloride (salt) is present in sufficient quantities in most meats, although, more to improve the flavor of the food than to contribute to the animal's nutrition, a small amount of salt may be added to the ration. The exact amount makes no material difference, since the unutilized portions are eliminated, largely in the urine. If the brand of salt used is iodized, it will meet the iodine requirements, which are very small. Iodine deficiency in dogs is rare, but food crops and meats grown in certain areas contain little or no iodine, and it is well to be safe by using iodized salt.

Sufficient iron is usually found in meat and milk, but if the dog appears anemic or listless the trace of iron needed can be supplied with one of the iron salts—ferric sulphate, or oxide, or ferrous gluconate. Iron is utilized in the bone marrow in the synthesis of hemoglobin in the blood corpuscles. It is used over and over; when a corpuscle is worn out and is to be replaced, it surrenders its iron before being eliminated.

When more iron is ingested than can be utilized, some is stored in the liver, after which further surplus is excreted. The liver of the newborn puppy contains enough iron to supply the organism up until weaning time. No iron is present in milk, which otherwise provides a completely balanced ration.

A diet with a reasonable content of red meat, especially of liver or kidney, is likely to be adequate in respect to its iron. However, bitches in whelp require more iron than a dog on mere maintenance. It is recommended that the liver content of bitches' diets be increased for the duration of pregnancy.

Iron requires the presence of a minute trace of copper for its utilization, but there is enough copper in well nigh any diet to supply the requirements.

Calcium and phosphorous are the only minerals of which an insufficiency is a warranted source of anxiety. This statement may not be true of adult dogs not employed for breeding purposes, but it does apply to brood bitches and to growing puppies. The entire skeleton and teeth are made largely from calcium and phosphorus, and it is essential that the organism have enough of those minerals.

If additional calcium is not supplied to a bitch in her diet, her own bone structure is depleted to provide her puppies with their share of calcium. Moreover, in giving birth to her puppies or shortly afterward she is likely to go into eclampsia as a result of calcium depletion.

The situation, however, is easily avoided. The addition of a small amount of calcium phosphate diabasic to the ration precludes any possible calcium deficiency. Calcium phosphate diabasic is an inexpensive substance and quite tasteless. It may be sprinkled in or over the food, especially that given to brood bitches and puppies. It is the source of strong bones and vigorous teeth of ivory whiteness.

But it must be mentioned that calcium cannot be assimilated into the bone structure, no matter how much of it is fed or otherwise administered, except in the presence of vitamin D. That is D's function, to facilitate the absorption of calcium and phosphorus. This will be elaborated upon in the following discussion of the vitamins and their functions.

VITAMINS

Vitamins have in the past been largely described by diseases resulting from their absence. It is recognized more and more that many of the subacute symptoms of general unfitness of dogs may be attributable to an inadequate supply in the diet of one or more of these essential food factors. It is to be emphasized that vitamins are to be considered a part of the dog's food, essential to his health and well being. They are not to be considered as medication. Often the morbid conditions resultant from their absence in the diet may be remedied by the addition of the particular needed vitamin.

The requirements of vitamins, as food, not as medication, in the diet cannot be too strongly emphasized. These vitamins may be in the food itself, or they may better be added to it as a supplement to insure an adequate supply. Except for vitamin D, of which it is remotely possible (though unlikely) to supply too much, a surplus of the vitamin substances in the ration is harmless. They are somewhat expensive and we have no disposition to waste them, but if too much of them are fed they are simply eliminated with no subsequent ill effect.

It must be realized that vitamins are various substances, each of which has a separate function. It is definitely not safe to add to a dog's (or a child's) diet something out of a bottle or box indefinitely labeled "Vitamins," as is the practice of so many persons. We must know which vitamins we are giving, what purpose each is designed to serve, and the potency of the preparation of the brand of each one we are using.

Any one of the "shotgun" vitamin preparations is probably adequate if administered in large enough dosages. Such a method may be wasteful, however; to be sure of enough of one substance, the surplus of the others is wasted. It is much better to buy a product that contains an adequate amount of each of the needed vitamins and a wasteful surplus of none. Such a procedure is cheaper in the long run.

There follows a brief description of each of the various vitamins so far discovered and a statement of what purpose in the diet they are respectively intended to serve:

Vitamin A—This vitamin in some form is an absolute requisite for good health, even for enduring life itself. Symptoms of advanced deficiency of vitamin A in dogs are an eye disease with resulting impaired vision, inflammation of the conjunctiva or mucous membranes which line the eyelid, and injury to the mucous membranes of the body. Less easily recognized symptoms are an apparent lowered resistance to bacterial infection, especially of the upper respiratory tract, retarded growth, and loss of weight. Diseases due to vitamin A deficiency may be well established while the dog is still gaining in weight. Lack of muscular coordination and paralysis have been observed in dogs and degeneration of the nervous system. Some young dogs deprived of vitamin A become wholly or partially deaf.

The potency of vitamin A is usually calculated in International Units, of which it has been estimated that the dog requires about 35 per day for each pound of his body weight. Such parts as are not utilized are not lost, but are stored in the liver for future use in time of shortage. A dog well fortified with this particular vitamin can well go a month or more without harm with none of it in his diet. At such times he draws upon his liver for its surplus.

It is for its content of vitamins A and D that cod-liver oil (and the oils from the livers of other fish) is fed to puppies and growing children. Fish liver oils are an excellent source of vitamin A, and if a small amount of them is included in the diet no anxiety about deficiency of vitamin A need be entertained. In buying cod-liver oil, it pays to obtain the best grade. The number of International Units it contains per teaspoonful is stated on most labels. The vitamin content of cod-liver oil is impaired by exposure to heat, light, and air. It should be kept in a dark, cool place and the bottle should be firmly stopped.

Another source of vitamin A is found in carrots but it is almost impossible to get enough carrots in a dog to do him any good. It is better and easier to use a preparation known as carotene, three drops of which contains almost the vitamin A in a bushel of carrots.

Other natural sources of vitamin A are liver, kidney, heart, cheese, egg yolks, butter and milk. If these foods, or any one of them, are generously included in the adult dog's maintenance ration, all other sources of vitamin A may be dispensed with. The ration for all puppies, however, and for pregnant and lactating bitches should be copiously fortified either with fish liver oil or with tablets containing vitamin A.

32

Vitamin B. What was formerly known as a single vitamin B has now been found to be a complex of many different factors. Some of them are, in minute quantities, very important parts of the diets of any kind of animals. The various factors of this complex, each a separate vitamin, are designated by the letter B followed by an inferior number, as B_1, B_2, or B_6.

The absence or insufficiency in the diet of Vitamin B_1, otherwise known as thiamin, has been blamed for retarded growth, loss of weight, decreased fertility, loss of appetite, and impaired digestion. A prolonged shortage of B_1 may result in paralysis, the accumulation of fluid in the tissues, and finally in death, apparently from heart failure.

It is not easy to estimate just how much B_1 a dog requires per pound of body weight, since dogs as individuals vary in their needs, and the activity of an animal rapidly depletes the thiamin in his body. The feeding of 50 International Units per day per pound of body weight is probably wasteful but harmless. That is at least enough.

Thiamin is not stored in the system for any length of time and requires a daily dosage. It is destroyed in part by heat above the boiling point. It is found in yeast (especially in brewer's yeast), liver, wheat germ, milk, eggs, and in the coloring matter of vegetables. However, few dogs or persons obtain an optimum supply of B_1 from their daily diet, and it is recommended that it be supplied to the dog daily.

Brewer's yeast, either in powdered or tablet form affords a cheap and rather efficient way to supply the average daily requirements. An overdose of yeast is likely to cause gas in the dog's stomach.

Another factor of the vitamin B complex, riboflavin, affects particularly the skin and hair. Animals fed a diet in which it is deficient are prone to develop a scruffy dryness of the skin, especially about the eyes and mouth, and the hair becomes dull and dry, finally falling out, leaving the skin rough and dry. In experiments with rats deprived of riboflavin the toes have fallen off.

Riboflavin is present in minute quantities in so many foods that a serious shortage in any well balanced diet is unlikely. It is especially to be found in whey, which is the explanation of the smooth skin and lively hair of so many dogs whose ration contains cottage cheese.

33

While few dogs manifest any positive shortage of riboflavin, experiments on various animals have shown that successively more liberal amounts of it in their diets, up to about four times as much as is needed to prevent the first signs of deficiency, result in increased positive health.

Riboflavin deteriorates with exposure to heat and light. Most vitamin products contain it in ample measure.

Dogs were immediately responsible for the discovery of the existence of vitamin B_2, or nicotinic acid, formerly known as vitamin G. The canine disease of black tongue is analogous with the human disease called pellagra, both of which are prevented and cured by sufficient amounts of nicotinic acid in the diet. Black tongue is not a threat for any dog that eats a diet which contains even a reasonable quantity of lean meat, but it used to be prevalent among dogs fed exclusively upon corn bread or corn-meal mush, as many were.

No definite optimum dosage has been established. However, many cases of vaguely irritated skin, deadness of coat, and soft, spongy, or bleeding gums have been reported to be remedied by administration of nicotinic acid.

It has been demonstrated that niacin is essential if a good sound healthy appetite is to be maintained. Pantothenic acid is essential to good nerve health. Pyridoxin influences proper gastro-intestinal functions. Vitamin B_{12}, the "animal protein factor," is essential for proper growth and health in early life. And the water soluble B factor affects the production of milk.

Vitamin C, the so-called anti-scorbutic vitamin, is presumed to be synthesized by the dog in his own body. The dog is believed not to be subject to true scurvy. Vitamin C, then, can well be ignored as pertains to the dog. It is the most expensive of the vitamins, and, its presence in the vitamin mixture for the dog will probably do no good.

Vitamin D, the anti-rachitic vitamin, is necessary to promote the assimilation of calcium and phosphorus into the skeletal structure. One may feed all of those minerals one will, but without vitamin D they will pass out of the system unused. It is impossible to develop sound bones and teeth without its presence. Exposure to sunshine unimpeded by glass enables the animal to manufacture vitamin D in his system, but sunshine is not to be depended upon for an entire supply.

Vitamin D is abundant in cod-liver oil and in the liver oils of some other fish, or it may be obtained in a dry form in combination with other vitamins. One International Unit per pound of body weight per day is sufficient to protect a dog from rickets. From a teaspoonful to a tablespoonful of cod-liver oil a day will serve well instead for any dog.

This is the only one of the vitamins with which overdosage is possible and harmful. While a dog will not suffer from several times the amount stated and an excess dosage is unlikely, it is only fair to warn the reader that it is at least theoretically possible.

Vitamin E is the so-called fertility vitamin. Whether it is required for dogs has not as yet been determined. Rats fed upon a ration from which vitamin E was wholly excluded became permanently sterile, but the finding is not believed to pertain to all animals. Some dog keepers, however, declare that the feeding of wheat germ oil, the most abundant source of vitamin E, has prevented early abortions of their bitches, has resulted in larger and more vigorous litters of puppies, has increased the fertility of stud dogs, has improved the coats of their dogs and furthered the betterment of their general health. Whether vitamin E or some other factor or factors in the wheat germ oil is responsible for these alleged benefits is impossible to say.

Vitamin E is so widely found in small quantities in well nigh all foods that the hazard of its omission from any normal diet is small.

Numerous other vitamins have been discovered and isolated in recent years, and there are suspected to be still others as yet unknown. The ones here discussed are the only ones that warrant the use of care to include them in the dog's daily ration. It is well to reiterate that vitamins are not medicine, but are food, a required part of the diet. Any person interested in the complete nutrition of his dog will not neglect them.

It should go without saying that a dog should have access to clean, fresh, pure drinking water at all times, of which he should be permitted to drink as much or as little as he chooses. The demands of his system for drinking water will depend in part upon the moisture content of his food. Fed upon dry dog biscuits, he will probably drink considerable water to moisten it; with a diet which contains much milk or soup, he will need little additional water.

That he chooses to drink water immediately after a meal is harmless. The only times his water should be limited (but not entirely withheld from him) is after violent exercise or excitement, at which times his thirst should be satisfied only gradually.

The quantities of food required daily by dogs are influenced and determined by a number of factors: the age, size, individuality, and physical condition of the animal; the kind, quality, character, and proportions of the various foods in the ration; the climate, environment and methods of management; and the type and amount of work done, or the degree of exercise. Of these considerations, the age and size of the dog and the kind and amount of work are particularly important in determining food requirements. During early puppyhood a dog may require two or three (or even more) times as much food per pound of body weight as the same dog will require at maturity.

Any statement we should make here about the food requirements of a dog as to weight or volume would be subject to modification. Dogs vary in their metabolism. One dog might stay fat and sleek on a given amount of a given ration, whereas his litter brother in an adjoining kennel might require twice or only half as much of the same ration to maintain him in the same state of flesh.

The only sound determiners of how much to feed a dog are his appetite and his condition. As a general rule, a dog should have as much food for maintenance as he will readily clean up in five or ten minutes, unless he tends to lay on unwanted fat, in which case his intake of food should be reduced, especially its content of fats and carbohydrates. A thin dog should have his ration increased and be urged to eat it. The fats in his ration should be increased, and he may be fattened with a dessert of candy, sugar, or sweet cake following his main meal. These should never be used before a meal, lest they impair the appetite, and they should not be given to a fat dog at all. Rightly employed, they are useful and harmless, contrary to the prevalent belief.

Growing puppies require frequent meals, as will be discussed later. Pregnant and lactating bitches and frequently used stud dogs should have at least two meals, and better three, each day. For the mere maintenance of healthy adult dogs, one large meal a day appears to suffice as well as more smaller ones. Many tenderhearted dog keepers choose to divide the ration into two parts

36

and to feed their dogs twice each day. There can be no objection offered to such a program except that it involves additional work for the keeper. Whether one meal or two, they should be given at regular hours, to which dogs soon adjust and expect their dinner at a given time.

It is better to determine upon an adequate ration, with plenty of meat in it, and feed it day after day, than to vary the diet in the assumption that a dog tires of eating the same thing. There is no evidence that he does, and it is a burden upon his carnivorous digestion to be making constant adjustments and readjustments to a new diet.

Today there are available for dogs many brands of canned foods, some good and others not so good. But it is safe to feed your dog exclusively—if you do not object to the cost—a canned dog food which has been produced by a reliable concern. Many of the producers of canned dog foods are subject to Federal inspection because they also process meat and meat products for human consumption. The Federal regulations prohibit the use of diseased or unsuitable by-products in the preparation of dog food. Some of the canned dog foods on the market are mostly cereal. A glance at the analysis chart on the label will tell you whether a particular product is a good food for your dog.

If fish is fed, it should be boned—thoroughly. The same is true of fowl and rabbit meats. Small bones may be caught in the dog's throat or may puncture the stomach or intestines. Large, raw shank bones of beef may be given to the dog with impunity, but they should be renewed at frequent intervals before they spoil. A dog obtains much amusement from gnawing a raw bone, and some nutrition. Harm does not accrue from his swallowing of bone fragments, which are dissolved by the hydrochloric acid in his stomach. If the dog is fed an excessive amount of bones, constipation may result. When this occurs, the best way to relieve the condition is by the use of the enema bag. Medicinal purges of laxatives given at this time may cause irreparable damage.

Meat for dogs may be fed raw, or may be roasted, broiled, or boiled. It is not advisable to feed fried foods to dogs. All soups, gravies and juices from cooked meat must be conserved and included in the food, since they contain some of the minerals and vitamins extracted from the meat.

37

A well-known German physician selected a medium sized, strong, healthy bitch, and after she had been mated, he fed her on chopped horse meat from which the salts were to a large extent extracted by boiling for two hours in distilled water. In addition to this she was given each day a certain quantity of fried fat. As drink she had only distilled water. She gave birth to six healthy puppies, one of which was killed immediately, and its bones found to be strong and well built and free from abnormalities. The other puppies did not thrive, but remained weak, and could scarcely walk at the end of a month, when four died from excessive feebleness. And the sixth was killed two weeks· later. The mother in the meantime had become very lean but was tolerably lively and had a fair appetite. She was killed one hundred and twenty-six days after the beginning of the experiment, and it was then found that the bones of her spine and pelvis were softened—a condition known to physicians as osteomalacia.

The results of this experiment are highly interesting and instructive, showing clearly as they do that the nursing mother sends out to her young, in her milk, a part of her store of lime, which is absolutely essential to their welfare. They show also that if proper food is denied her, when in whelp and when nursing, not only her puppies but she as well must suffer greatly in consequence. And in the light of these facts is uncovered one of the most potential causes of rickets, so common among large breeds.

It may therefore be accepted that bitches in whelp must have goodly quantities of meat; moreover, that while cooking may be the rule if the broth is utilized, it is a wise plan to give the food occasionally in the raw state.

There is little choice among the varieties of meat, except that pork is seldom relished by dogs, usually contains too much fat, and should be cooked to improve its digestibility when it is used at all. Beef, mutton, lamb, goat, and horse flesh are equally valuable. The choice should be made upon the basis of their comparative cost and their availability in the particular community. A dog suddenly changed from another diet to horse flesh may develop a harmless and temporary diarrhea, which can be ignored. Horse flesh is likely to be deficient in fats, which may be added in the form of suet, lard or pure corn oil.

The particular cuts of whatever meat is used is of little consequence. Liver and kidney are especially valuable and when it is possible they should be included as part of the meat used. As the only meat in the ration, liver and kidney tend to loosen the bowels. It is better to include them as a part of each day's ration than to permit them to serve as the sole meat content one or two days a week.

It makes no difference whether meat is ground or is fed to the dog in large or medium sized pieces. He is able to digest pieces of meat as large as he can swallow. The advantage of grinding meat is that it can be better mixed with whatever else it is wished to include in the ration, the dog being unable to pick out the meat and reject the rest. There is little harm in his doing so, except for the waste, since it is the meat upon which we must depend for the most part for his nutrition.

Fresh ground meat can be kept four or five days under ordinary refrigeration without spoiling. It may be kept indefinitely if solidly frozen. Frozen ground horse meat for dogs is available in many markets, is low in price, and is entirely satisfactory for the purpose intended.

A suggested ration is made as follows: Two-thirds to three-quarters by weight of ground meat including ten to twenty percent of fat and a portion of liver or kidney, with the remainder thoroughly cooked rice or oatmeal, or shredded wheat, or dog biscuit, or wheat germ, with a sprinkling of calcium phosphate diabasic. Vitamins may be added, or given separately.

If it is desired to offer the dog a second meal, it may be of shredded wheat or other breakfast cereal with plenty of milk, with or without one or more soft boiled eggs. Evaporated canned milk or powdered milk is just as good food for the dog as fresh milk. Cottage cheese is excellent for this second meal.

These are not the only possible rations for the dog, but they will prove adequate. Leavings from the owner's table can be added to either ration, but can hardly be depended upon for the entire nourishment of the dog.

The dog's food should be at approximately body heat, tepid but never hot.

Little consideration is here given to the costs of the various foods. Economies in rations and feeding practices are admittedly desirable, but not if they are made at the expense of the dog's health.

39

SOME BRIEF PRECEPTS ABOUT FEEDING

Many dogs are overfed. Others do not receive adequate rations. Both extremes should be avoided, but particularly overfeeding of grown dogs. Coupled with lack of exercise, overfeeding usually produces excessive body weight and laziness, and it may result in illness and sterility. Prolonged undernourishment causes loss of weight, listlessness, dull coats, sickness, and death.

An adequate ration will keep most mature dogs at a uniform body weight and in a thrifty, moderately lean condition. Observation of condition is the best guide in determining the correct amount of food.

The axiom, "One man's meat is another man's poison," is applicable to dogs also. Foods that are not tolerated by the dog or those that cause digestive and other disturbances should be discontinued. The use of moldy, spoiled, or rotten food is never good practice. Food should be protected from fouling by rats or mice, especially because rats are vectors of leptospirosis. The excessive use of food of low energy content and low biological values will often result in poor condition and may cause loss of weight and paunchiness.

All feeding and drinking utensils must be kept scrupulously clean. They should be washed after each using.

It is usually desirable to reduce the food allotment somewhat during hot weather. Dogs should be fed at regular intervals, and the best results may be expected when regular feeding is accompanied by regular, but not exhausting, exercise.

Most dogs do not thrive on a ration containing large amounts of sloppy foods, and excessive bulk is to be avoided especially for hardworking dogs, puppies, and pregnant or lactating bitches. If the ration is known to be adequate and the dog is losing weight or is not in good condition, the presence of intestinal parasites is to be suspected. However, dogs sometimes go "off feed" for a day or two. This is cause for no immediate anxiety, but if it lasts more than two or three days, a veterinarian should be consulted.

FOOD FOR THE STUD DOG

The stud dog that is used for breeding only at infrequent intervals requires only the food needed for his maintenance in good health, as set forth in the foregoing pages. He should be well fed with ample meat in his diet, moderately exercised to keep his flesh firm and hard, and not permitted to become too thin or too fat.

More care is required for the adequate nutrition of the dog offered at public stud and frequently employed for breeding. A vigorous stud dog may very handily serve two bitches a week over a long period without a serious tax upon his health and strength if he is fully nourished and adequately but not excessively exercised. Such a dog should have at least two meals a day, and they should consist of even more meat, milk (canned is as good as fresh), eggs, cottage cheese, and other foods of animal origin than is used in most maintenance rations. Liver and some fat should be included, and the vitamins especially are not to be forgotten. In volume this will be only a little more than the basic maintenance diet, the difference being in its richness and concentration.

An interval of an hour or two should intervene between a dog's meal and his employment for breeding. He may be fed, but only lightly, immediately after he has been used for breeding.

The immediate reason that a stud dog should be adequately fed and exercised is the maintenance of his strength and virility. The secondary reason is that a popular stud dog is on exhibition at all times, between the shows as well as at the shows. Clients with bitches to be bred appear without notice to examine a dog at public stud, and the dog should be presented to them in the best possible condition—clean, hard, in exactly the most becoming state of flesh, and with a gleaming, lively coat. These all depend largely upon the highly nutritious diet the dog receives.

FOOD FOR THE BROOD BITCH

Often a well fed bitch comes through the ordeal of rearing a large litter of puppies without any impairment of her vitality and flesh. In such case she may be returned to a good maintenance ration until she is ready to be bred again. About the time she weans her puppies her coat will be dead and ready to drop out, but if she is healthy and well fed a new and vigorous coat will grow in, and she will be no worse off for her maternal ordeal. Some bitches, either from a deficient nutrition or a constitutional disposition to contribute too much of their own strength and substance to the nutrition of the puppies, are thin and exhausted at the time of weaning. Such a bitch needs the continuance of at least two good and especially nutritious meals a day for a month or more until her flesh and strength are restored before she is returned to her routine maintenance ration, upon which she may be kept until time comes to breed her again.

At breeding time a bitch's flesh should be hard, and she should be on the lean side rather than too fat. No change in her regular maintenance diet need be made until about the fourth or fifth week of her pregnancy. The growth of the fetus is small up until the middle of the pregnancy, after which it becomes rapid.

The bitch usually begins to "show in whelp" in four to six weeks after breeding, and her food consumption should be then gradually stepped up. If she has been having only one meal a day, she should be given two; if she has had two, both should be larger. Henceforth until her puppies are weaned, she must eat not merely for two, as is said of the pregnant woman, but for four or five, possibly for ten or twelve. She is not to be encouraged to grow fat. Especial emphasis should be laid upon her ration's content of meat, including liver, milk, calcium phosphate, and vitamins A and D, both of which are found in cod-liver oil.

Some breeders destroy all but a limited number of puppies in a litter in the belief that a bitch will be unable adequately to nourish all the puppies she has whelped. In some extreme cases it may be necessary to do this or to obtain a foster mother or wet nurse to share the burden of rearing the puppies. However, the healthy bitch with normal metabolism can usually generate enough milk to feed adequately all the puppies she has produced, pro-

42

vided she is well enough fed and provided the puppies are fed additionally as soon as they are able to eat.

After whelping until the puppies are weaned, throughout the lactating period, the bitch should have all the nourishing food she can be induced to eat—up to four or five meals a day. These should consist largely of meat and liver, some fat, a small amount of cereals, milk, eggs, cottage cheese, calcium phosphate, and vitamins, with especial reference to vitamins A and D. At that time it is hardly possible to feed a bitch too much or to keep her too fat. The growth of the puppies is much more rapid after they are born than was their growth in the dam's uterus, and the large amount of food needed to maintain that rapid growth must pass through the bitch and be transformed to milk, while at the same time she must maintain her own body.

THE FEEDING OF PUPPIES

If the number of puppies in a litter is small, if the mother is vigorous, healthy, and a good milker, the youngsters up until their weaning time may require no additional food over and above the milk they suck from their dam's breasts. If the puppies are numerous or if the dam's milk is deficient in quality or quantity, it is wise to begin feeding the puppies artificially as soon as they are able and willing to accept food. This is earlier than used to be realized.

It is for the sake of the puppies' vigor rather than for the sake of their ultimate size that their growth is to be promoted as rapidly as possible. Vigorous and healthy puppies attain early maturity if they are given the right amounts of the right quality of food. The ultimate size of the dog at maturity is laid down in his germ plasm, and he can be stunted or dwarfed, if at all, only at the expense of his type. If one tries to prevent the full growth of a dog by withholding from him the food he needs, one will wind up with a rachitic, cowhocked dog, one with a delicate digestive apparatus, a sterile one, one with all of these shortcomings combined, or even a dead dog.

Growth may be slowed with improper food, sometimes without serious harm, but the dog is in all ways better off if he is forced along with the best food and encouraged to attain his full size at an early age. Dogs of the smaller breeds usually reach their full maturity several months earlier than those of the larger breeds. A well grown dog reaches his sexual maturity and can be safely used for limited breeding at one year of age.

As soon as teeth can be felt with the finger in a puppy's mouth, which is usually at about seventeen or eighteen days of age, it is safe to begin to feed him. His first food (except for his mother's milk) should be of scraped raw beef at body temperature. The first day he may have $1/4$ to 2 teaspoonfuls, according to size. He will not need to learn to eat this meat; he will seize upon it avidly and lick his chops for more. The second day he may have $1/3$ to 3 teaspoonfuls, according to size, with two feedings 12 hours apart. Thereafter, the amount and frequency of this feeding may be rapidly increased. By the twenty-fifth day the meat need not be scraped, but only finely ground. This process of the early feeding of raw meat to puppies not only gives them a good start in life, but

44

it also relieves their mother of a part of her burden of providing milk for them.

At about the fourth week, some cereal (thoroughly cooked oatmeal, shredded wheat, or dried bread) may be either moistened and mixed with the meat or be served to the puppies with milk, fresh or canned. It may be necessary to immerse their noses into such a mixture to teach them to eat it. Calcium phosphate and a small amount of cod-liver oil should be added to such a mixture, both of which substances the puppies should have every day until their maturity. At the fourth week, while they are still at the dam's breast, they may be fed three or four times a day upon this extra ration, or something similar, such as cottage cheese or soft boiled egg. By the sixth week their dam will be trying to wean them, and they may have four or five meals daily. One of these may be finely broken dog biscuit thoroughly soaked in milk. One or two of the meals should consist largely or entirely of meat with liver.

The old advice about feeding puppies "little and often" should be altered to "much and often." Each puppy at each meal should have all the food he will readily clean up. Food should not be left in front of the puppies. They should be fed and after two or three minutes the receptacle should be taken away. Young puppies should be roly-poly fat, and kept so up to at least five or six months of age. Thereafter they should be slightly on the fat side, but not pudgy, until maturity.

The varied diet of six-week-old puppies may be continued, but at eight or nine weeks the number of meals may be reduced to four, and at three months, to three large rations per day. After six months the meals may be safely reduced again to two a day, but they must be generous meals with meat, liver, milk, cod-liver oil, and calcium phosphate. At full maturity, one meal a day suffices, or two may be continued.

The secret of turning good puppies into fine, vigorous dogs is to keep them growing through the entire period of their maturation. The most important item in the rearing of puppies is adequate and frequent meals of highly nourishing foods. Growth requires two or three times as much food as maintenance. Time between meals should be allowed for digestion, but puppies should never be permitted to become really hungry. Water in a shallow dish should be available to puppies at all times after they are able to walk.

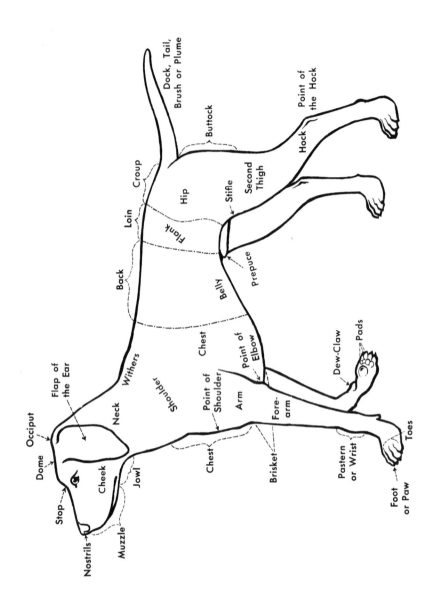

The Breeding
of Dogs

HERE, if anywhere in the entire process of the care
and management of dogs, the exercise of good judgment is involved.
Upon the choice of the two dogs, male and female, to be mated
together depends the future success or failure of one's dogs. If the
two to be mated are ill chosen, either individually or as pertains
to their fitness as mates, one to the other, all the painstaking care
to feed and rear the resultant puppies correctly is wasted. The
mating together of two dogs is the drafting of the blueprints and
the writing of the specifications of what the puppies are to be
like. The plans, it is true, require to be executed; the puppies,
when they arrive, must be adequately fed and cared for in order
to develop them into the kinds of dogs they are in their germ plasm
designed to become. However, if the plans as determined in the
mating are defective, just so will the puppies that result from them
be defective, in spite of all the good raising one can give them.

The element of luck in the breeding of dogs cannot be discounted,
for it exists. The mating which on paper appears to be the best
possible may result in puppies that are poor and untypical of
their breed. Even less frequently, a good puppy may result from
a chance mating together of two ill chosen parents. These results
are fortuitous and unusual, however. The best dogs as a lot come
from parents carefully chosen as to their individual excellences and
as to their suitability as mates for each other. It is as unwise as

it is unnecessary to trust to luck in the breeding of dogs. Careful planning pays off in the long run, and few truly excellent dogs are produced without it.

Some breeders without any knowledge of genetics have been successful, without knowing exactly why they succeeded. Some of them have adhered to beliefs in old wives' tales and to traditional concepts that science has long since exploded and abandoned. Such as have succeeded have done so in spite of their lack of knowledge and not because of it.

There is insufficient space at our disposal in this book to discuss in detail the science of genetics and the application of that science to the breeding of dogs. Whole books have been written about the subject. One of the best, clearest, and easiest for the layman to understand is *The New Art of Breeding Better Dogs,* by Philip Onstott, which may be obtained from Howell Book House, the publisher. In it and in other books upon the subject of genetics will be found more data about the practical application of science to the breeding of livestock than can be included here.

The most that can be done here is to offer some advice soundly based upon the genetic laws. Every feature a dog may or can possess is determined by the genes carried in the two reproductive cells, one from each parent, from the union of which he was developed. There are thousands of pairs of these determiners in the life plan of every puppy, and often a complex of many genes is required to produce a single recognizable attribute of the dog.

These genes function in pairs, one member of each pair being contributed by the father and the other member of the pair coming from the mother. The parents obtained these genes they hand on from their parents, and it is merely fortuitous which half of any pair of genes present in a dog's or a bitch's germ plasm may be passed on to any one of the progeny. Of any pair of its own genes, a dog or a bitch may contribute one member to one puppy and the other member to another puppy in the same litter or in different litters. The unknown number of pairs of genes is so great that there is an infinite number of combinations of them, which accounts for the differences we find between two full brothers or two full sisters. In fact, it depends upon the genes received whether a dog be a male or a female.

We know that the male dog contributes one and the bitch the

other of every pair of genes that unite to determine what the puppy will be like and what he will grow into. Thus, the parents make exactly equal contributions to the germ plasm or zygote from which every puppy is developed. It was long believed that the male dog was so much more important than the bitch in any mating that the excellence or shortcomings of the bitch might be disregarded. This theory was subsequently reversed and breeders considered the bitch to be more important than the dog. We now know that their contribution in every mating and in every individual puppy is exactly equal, and neither is to be considered more than the other.

There are two kinds of genes—the recessive genes and the dominant. And there are three kinds of pairs of genes: a recessive from the sire plus a recessive from the dam; a dominant from the sire plus a dominant from the dam; and a dominant from one parent plus a recessive from the other. It is the last combination that is the source of our trouble in breeding. When both members of a pair of genes are recessive, the result is a recessive attribute in the animal that carries them; when both members of the pair are dominant, the result is a pure dominant attribute; but when one member of the pair is recessive and the other member dominant, the result will be a wholly or only partially dominant attribute, which will breed true only half of the time. This explains why a dog or a bitch may fail to produce progeny that looks at all like itself.

If all the pairs of a dog's genes were purely dominant, we could expect him to produce puppies that resembled himself in all particulars, no matter what kind of mate he was bred to. Or if all his genes were recessive and he were mated to a bitch with all recessive genes, the puppies might be expected to look quite like the parents. However, a dog with mixed pairs of genes bred to a bitch with mixed pairs of genes may produce anything at all, puppies that bear no resemblance to either parent.

Long before the Mendelian laws were discovered, some dogs were known to be "prepotent" to produce certain characters, that is the characters would show up in their puppies irrespective of what their mates might be like. For instance, some dogs, themselves with dark eyes, might be depended upon never to produce a puppy with light eyes, no matter how light eyed the mate to which he was bred. This was true despite the fact that the dog's litter brother which had equally dark eyes, when bred to a light eyed bitch might produce a large percentage of puppies with light eyes.

Before it is decided to breed a bitch, it is well to consider whether she is worth breeding, whether she is good enough as an individual and whether she came from a good enough family to warrant the expectations that she will produce puppies worth the expense and trouble of raising. It is to be remembered that the bitch contributes exactly half the genes to each of her puppies; if she has not good genes to contribute, the time and money involved in breeding her and rearing her puppies will be wasted.

It is conceded that a bad or mediocre bitch when bred to an excellent dog will probably produce puppies better than herself. But while one is "grading up" from mediocre stock, other breeders are also grading upward from better stock and they will keep just so far ahead of one's efforts that one can never catch up with them. A merely pretty good bitch is no good at all for breeding. It is better to dispose of a mediocre bitch or to relegate her to the position of a family pet than to breed from her. It is difficult enough, with all the care and judgment one is able to muster, to obtain superlative puppies even from a fine bitch, without cluttering the earth with inferior puppies from just any old bitch.

If one will go into the market and buy the best possible bitch from the best possible family one's purse can afford and breed her sensibly to the best and most suitable stud dog one can find, success is reasonably sure. Even if for economy's sake, the bitch is but a promising puppy backed up by the best possible pedigree, it will require only a few months until she is old enough to be bred. From such a bitch, one may expect first-rate puppies at the first try, whereas in starting with an inferior bitch one is merely lucky if in two or three generations he obtains a semblance of the kind of dog he is trying to produce.

Assuming it is decided that the bitch is adequate to serve as a brood bitch, it becomes necessary to choose for her a mate in collaboration with which she may realize the ultimate of her possibilities. It is never wise to utilize for stud the family pet or the neighbor's pet just because he happens to be registered in the studbook or because his service costs nothing. Any dog short of the best and most suitable (wherever he may be and whoever may own

50

him) is an extravagance. If the bitch is worth breeding at all, she is worth shipping clear across the continent, if need be, to obtain for her a mate to enable her to realize her possibilities. Stud fees may range from fifty to one hundred dollars or even more. The average value of each puppy, if well reared, should at the time of weaning approximate the legitimate stud fee of its sire. With a good bitch it is therefore profitable to lay out as much as may be required to obtain the services of the best and most suitable stud dog—always assuming that he is worth the price asked. However, it is never wise to choose an inferior or unsuitable dog just because he is well ballyhooed and commands an exorbitant stud fee.

There are three considerations by which to evaluate the merits of a stud dog—his outstanding excellence as an individual, his pedigree and the family from which he derived, and the excellence or inferiority of the progeny he is known to have produced.

As an individual a good stud dog may be expected to be bold and aggressive (not vicious) and structurally typical of his breed, but without any freakish exaggerations of type. He must be sound, a free and true mover, possess fineness and quality, and be a gentleman of his own breed. Accidentally acquired scars or injuries such as broken legs should not be held against him, because he can transmit only his genes to his puppies and no such accidents impair his genes.

A dog's pedigree may mean much or little. One of two litter brothers, with pedigrees exactly alike, may prove to be a superlative show and stud dog, and the other worth exactly nothing for either purpose. The pedigree especially is not to be judged on its length, since three generations is at most all that is required, although further extension of the pedigree may prove interesting to a curious owner. No matter how well-bred his pedigree may show a dog to be, if he is not a good dog the ink required to write the pedigree was wasted.

The chief value of a pedigree is to enable us to know from which of a dog's parents, grandparents, or great-grandparents, he derived his merits, and from which his faults. In choosing a mate for him (or for her, as the case may be) one seeks to reinforce the one and to avoid the other. Let us assume that one of the grandmothers was upright in shoulder, whereas the shoulder should be well laid back; we can avoid as a mate for such a dog one with any

51

tendency to straight shoulders or one from straight shouldered ancestry. The same principle would apply to an uneven mouth, a light eye, a soft back, splayed feet, cowhocks, or to any other inherited fault. Suppose, on the other hand, that the dog himself, the parents, and all the grandparents are particularly nice in regard to their fronts; in a mate for such a dog, one desires as good a front as is obtainable, but if she, or some of her ancestors are not too good in respect to their fronts, one may take a chance anyway and trust to the good fronted dog with his good fronted ancestry to correct the fault. That then is the purpose of the pedigree as a guide to breeding.

A stud dog can best be judged, however, by the excellence of the progeny he is known to have produced, if it is possible to obtain all the data to enable the breeder to evaluate that record. A complete comparative evaluation is perhaps impossible to make, but one close enough to justify conclusions is available. Not only the number but the quality of the bitches to which the dog has been bred must enter into the consideration. A young dog may not have had the opportunity to prove his prowess in the stud. He may have been bred to few bitches and those few of indifferent merits, or his get may not be old enough as yet to hit the shows and establish a record for themselves or for their sire. Allowance may be made for such a dog.

On the other hand, a dog may have proved himself to be phenomenal in the show ring, or may have been made to seem phenomenal by means of the owner's ballyhoo and exploitation. Half of the top bitches in the entire country may have been bred to him upon the strength of his winning record. Merely from the laws of probability such a dog, if he is not too bad, will produce some creditable progeny. It is necessary to take into consideration the opportunities a dog has had in relation to the fine progeny he has produced.

That, however, is the chief criterion by which a good stud dog may be recognized. A dog which can sire two or three excellent puppies in every litter from a reasonably good bitch may be considered as an acceptable stud. If he has in his lifetime sired one or two champions each year, and especially if one or two of the lot are superlative champions, top members of their breed, he is a great stud dog. Ordinarily and without other considerations, such a dog

52

is to be preferred to one of his unproved sons, even though the son be as good or better an individual. In this way one employs genes one knows to produce what one wants. The son may be only hybrid dominant for his excellent qualities.

In the choice of a stud dog no attention whatever need be paid to claims that he sires numerically big litters. Unless the sire is deficient in sperm, the number of puppies in the litter, provided there are any puppies at all, depends entirely upon the bitch. At one service, a dog deposits enough spermatozoa to produce a million puppies, if there were so many ova to be fertilized. In any event, the major purpose should be to obtain good puppies, not large numbers of them.

There are three methods of breeding employed by experienced breeders—outcrossing, inbreeding, and line breeding. By outcrossing is meant the breeding together of mates of which no blood relationship can be traced. It is much favored by novice breeders, who feel that the breeding together of blood relatives is likely to result in imbecility, constitutional weakness, or some other kind of degeneration. Inbreeding is the mating together of closely related animals—father to daughter, mother to son, brother to sister, half brother to half sister. Some of the best animals ever produced have been bred from some such incestuous mating, and the danger from such practices, if they are carried out by persons who know what they are about, is minimal. Line breeding is the mating together of animals related one to another, but less closely—such as first cousins, grandsire to granddaughter, granddam to grandson, uncle to niece, or aunt to nephew.

Absolute outcrossing is usually impossible, since all the good dogs in any breed are more or less related—descended from some common ancestor in the fifth or sixth or seventh generation of their pedigrees. In any event, it is seldom to be recommended, since the results from it in the first generation of progeny are usually not satisfactory. It may be undertaken by some far-sighted and experienced breeder for the purpose of bringing into his strain some particular merit lacking in it and present in the strain of the unrelated dog. While dogs so bred may obtain an added vigor from what is known in genetics as *heterosis,* they are likely to manifest a coarseness and a lack of uniformity in the litter which is not to be found in more closely bred puppies. Good breeders never out-

53

cross if it is possible to obtain the virtues they want by sticking to their own strain. And when they do outcross, it is for the purpose of utilizing the outcrossed product for further breeding. It is not an end in itself.

Inbreeding (or incest breeding, as it is sometimes called) involves no such hazards as are and in the past have been attributed to it. It produces some very excellent dogs when correctly employed, some very bad ones even when correctly employed, and all bad ones when carelessly used. All the standard breeds of dogs were established as uniform breeds through intense inbreeding and culling over many generations. Inbreeding brings into manifestation undesirable recessive genes, the bearers of which can be discarded and the strain can thus be purged of its bad recessives.

Dogs of great soundness and excellence, from excellent parents and grandparents, all of them much alike, may be safely mated together, no matter how closely they may be related, with reasonable hope that most of the progeny will be sound and typical with a close resemblance to all the members of their ancestry. However, two such superlative and well-bred dogs are seldom to be found. It is the way to make progress rapidly and to establish a strain of dogs much alike and which breeds true. The amateur with the boldness and courage to try such a mating in the belief that his dogs are good enough for it is not to be discouraged. But if his judgment is not justified by the results, let him not complain that he has not been warned.

Line breeding is the safest course between the Scylla of outcrossing and the Charybdis of inbreeding for the inexperienced navigator in the sea of breeding. It, too, is to be used with care, because when it succeeds it partakes much of the nature of inbreeding. At any rate, its purpose is the pairing of like genes.

Here the pedigrees come into use. We examine the pedigree of the bitch to be bred. We hope that all the dogs named in it are magnificent dogs, but we look them over and choose the best of the four grandparents. We check this grandparent's breeding and find it good, as it probably is if it is itself a dog or bitch of great excellence. We shall assume that this best dog in the bitch's pedigree is the maternal grandsire. Then our bitch may be bred back to this particular grandsire, to his full brother if he has one of equal excellence, to his best son or best grandson. In such a fashion we

54

compound the genes of this grandsire, and hope to obtain some puppies with his excellences intensified.

The best name in the pedigree may be some other dog or bitch, in which case it is his or her germ plasm that is to be doubled to serve for the foundation of the pedigrees of the puppies of the projected litter.

In making a mating, it is never wise to employ two dogs with the same positive fault. It is wise to use two dogs with as many of the same positive virtues as it is possible to obtain. Neither should faults balance each other, as one with a front too wide, the other with a front too narrow; one with a sway back, the other roach backed. Rather, one member of the mating should be right where the other is wrong. We cannot trust to obtain the intermediate, if we overcompensate the fault of one mate with a fault of the other.

NEGOTIATIONS TO USE THE STUD DOG

Plans to use a stud dog should be laid far enough in advance to enable one to make sure that the services of the dog will be available when they are required. Most men with a dog at public stud publish "stud cards," on which are printed the dog's pedigree and pertinent data pertaining to its record. These should be requested for all the dogs one contemplates using. Most such owners reserve the right to refuse to breed their dogs to bitches they deem unsuitable for them; they wish to safeguard their dog's reputation as a producer of superior puppies, by choosing the bitches to which he shall be bred. Therefore, it is advisable to submit a description of the bitch, with or without a picture of her, and her pedigree to the stud dog's owner at the time the application to use him is made.

Notification should be sent to the owner of the dog as soon as the bitch begins to show in heat, and she should be taken or sent by air or by railway express to the dog's owner about the time she is first recognized to be in full heat and ready to breed. The stud dog's owner should be advised by telegram or telephone just how she has been sent and just when she may be expected, and instruction should be given about how she is to be returned.

Extreme care should be used in securely crating a bitch for shipment when she is in heat. Such bitches are prone to chew their way out of insecure boxes and escape to be bred by some vagrant mongrel. A card containing a statement of the bitch's condition should be attached to the crate as a warning to the carrier to assure her greater security.

MATING

The only time the bitch may become pregnant is during her period of oestruation, a time also variously referred to as the "oestrus," "the season," and as being in "heat." A bitch's first season usually occurs when she is between six and nine months of age, with the average age being eight months. In rare instances it may occur as early as five months or as late as thirteen months of age. After the first season, oestrus usually recurs at intervals of approximately six months, though this too is subject to variation. Also, the bitch's cycle may be influenced by factors such as a change of environment or a change of climate, and her cycle will, of course, be changed if it is interrupted by pregnancy. Most bitches again come in season four to six months after whelping.

There is a decided controversy among breeders as to the wisdom of breeding a bitch during her first season. Some believe a really fine bitch should be bred during her first season in order that she may produce as many puppies as possible during the fertile years of her life span. Others feel that definite physical harm results from breeding a bitch at her first season. Since a normal healthy bitch can safely produce puppies until she is about nine years old, she can comfortably yield eight to ten litters with rests between them in her life. Any breeder should be satisfied with this production from one animal. It seems wiser, therefore, to avoid the risk of any harm and pass her first season. Bitches vary in temperament and in the ages at which they reach sufficient maturity for motherhood and its responsibilities. As with the human animal, stability comes with age and a dam is much more likely to be a good mother if she is out of the puppy phase herself. If the bitch is of show quality, she might become a champion between her first and second heats if not bred.

Usually, oestruation continues for a period of approximately three weeks, but this too is subject to variation. Prior to the beginning of the oestrus, there may be changes in the bitch's actions and demeanor; she may appear restless, or she may become increasingly affectionate. Often there is increased frequency of urination and the bitch may be inclined to lick her external parts. The breeder should be alert for any signs of the approach of oestrus since the bitch must be confined and protected at this time in order to preclude the

57

possibility of the occurrence of a mating with any but the selected stud.

The first physical sign of oestrus is a bloody discharge of watery consistency. The mucous membrane lining the vulva becomes congested, enlarged, and reddened, and the external parts become puffy and swollen. The color of the discharge gradually deepens during the first day or two until it is a rich red color; then it gradually becomes lighter until by the tenth to twelfth day it has only a slightly reddish, or straw-colored, tinge. During the next day or so it becomes almost clear. During this same period, the swelling and hardness of the external parts gradually subside, and by the time the discharge has lost most of its color, the parts are softened and spongy. It is at this time that ovulation, the production of ripened ova (or eggs), takes place, although physical manifestations of oestrus may continue for another week.

A normal bitch has two ovaries which contain her ova. All the eggs she will produce during her lifetime are present in the ovaries at birth. Ordinarily, some of the ova ripen each time the bitch comes in season. Should a bitch fail to ovulate (produce ripened ova), she cannot, of course, become pregnant. Actually, only one ovary is necessary for ovulation, and loss of or damage to one ovary without impairment of the other will not prevent the bitch from producing puppies.

If fertilization does not occur, the ova (and this is also true of the sperm of the male) live only a short time—probably a couple of days at the most. Therefore, if mating takes place too long before or after ovulation, a bitch will not conceive, and the unfertilized ova will pass through the uterus into the vagina. Eventually they will either be absorbed or will pass out through the vulva by the same opening through which urination takes place. If fertilization does occur, the fertilized eggs become implanted on the inner surface of the uterus and grow to maturity.

Obviously, the breeder must exercise great care in determining when the dog and the bitch should be put together. Because the length of time between the beginning of the oestrus and the time of ovulation varies in different bitches, no hard and fast rule can be established, although the twelfth to fourteenth day is in most cases the correct time. The wise breeder will keep a daily record of the changes in the bitch's condition and will arrange to put the bitch and dog together when the discharge has become almost clear and the external parts are softened and spongy. If the bitch refuses the advances of the dog, it is preferable to separate the two, wait a day, then again permit the dog to approach the bitch.

Ordinarily, if the bitch is willing to accept the dog, fertilization of the ovum will take place. Usually one good service is sufficient, although two at intervals of twenty-four to forty-eight hours are often allowed.

Male dogs have glands on the penis which swell after passing the sphincter muscle of the vagina and "tie" the two animals together. The time may last for a period of a few minutes, a half hour, or occasionally up to an hour or more, but will end naturally when the locking glands have deflated the needful amount. While tying may increase the probability of success, in many cases no tie occurs, yet the bitches become pregnant.

Sperm are produced in the dog's testicles and are stored in the epididymis, a twisting tube at the side of the testicle. The occasional male dog whose testicles are not descended (a cryptorchid) is generally conceded to be sterile, although in a few instances it has been asserted that cryptorchids were capable of begetting progeny. The sterility in cryptorchids is believed to be due to the fact that the sperm are destroyed if the testicle remains within the abdominal cavity because the temperature is much higher there than in the normally descended testicle. Thus all sperm produced by the dog may be destroyed if both testicles are undescended. A monorchid (a dog with one testicle descended, the other undescended) may be fertile. Nevertheless, it is unwise to use a monorchid for stud purposes, because monorchidism is believed to be a heritable trait, and the monorchid, as well as the cryptorchid, is ineligible for the show ring.

After breeding, a bitch should be confined for a week to ten days to avoid mismating with another dog.

WHELPING CALENDAR

Find the month and date on which your bitch was bred in one of the left-hand columns. Directly opposite that date, in the right-hand column, is her expected date of whelping, bearing in mind that 61 days is as common as 63.

Date bred	Date due to whelp	Date bred	Date due to whelp	Date bred	Date due to whelp	Date bred	Date due to whelp	Date bred	Date due to whelp	Date bred	Date due to whelp	Date bred	Date due to whelp	Date bred	Date due to whelp	Date bred	Date due to whelp	Date bred	Date due to whelp	Date bred	Date due to whelp	Date bred	Date due to whelp
January	March	February	April	March	May	April	June	May	July	June	August	July	September	August	October	September	November	October	December	November	January	December	February
1	5	1	5	1	3	1	3	1	3	1	3	1	2	1	3	1	3	1	3	1	3	1	2
2	6	2	6	2	4	2	4	2	4	2	4	2	3	2	4	2	4	2	4	2	4	2	3
3	7	3	7	3	5	3	5	3	5	3	5	3	4	3	5	3	5	3	5	3	5	3	4
4	8	4	8	4	6	4	6	4	6	4	6	4	5	4	6	4	6	4	6	4	6	4	5
5	9	5	9	5	7	5	7	5	7	5	7	5	6	5	7	5	7	5	7	5	7	5	6
6	10	6	10	6	8	6	8	6	8	6	8	6	7	6	8	6	8	6	8	6	8	6	7
7	11	7	11	7	9	7	9	7	9	7	9	7	8	7	9	7	9	7	9	7	9	7	8
8	12	8	12	8	10	8	10	8	10	8	10	8	9	8	10	8	10	8	10	8	10	8	9
9	13	9	13	9	11	9	11	9	11	9	11	9	10	9	11	9	11	9	11	9	11	9	10
10	14	10	14	10	12	10	12	10	12	10	12	10	11	10	12	10	12	10	12	10	12	10	11
11	15	11	15	11	13	11	13	11	13	11	13	11	12	11	13	11	13	11	13	11	13	11	12
12	16	12	16	12	14	12	14	12	14	12	14	12	13	12	14	12	14	12	14	12	14	12	13
13	17	13	17	13	15	13	15	13	15	13	15	13	14	13	15	13	15	13	15	13	15	13	14
14	18	14	18	14	16	14	16	14	16	14	16	14	15	14	16	14	16	14	16	14	16	14	15
15	19	15	19	15	17	15	17	15	17	15	17	15	16	15	17	15	17	15	17	15	17	15	16
16	20	16	20	16	18	16	18	16	18	16	18	16	17	16	18	16	18	16	18	16	18	16	17
17	21	17	21	17	19	17	19	17	19	17	19	17	18	17	19	17	19	17	19	17	19	17	18
18	22	18	22	18	20	18	20	18	20	18	20	18	19	18	20	18	20	18	20	18	20	18	19
19	23	19	23	19	21	19	21	19	21	19	21	19	20	19	21	19	21	19	21	19	21	19	20
20	24	20	24	20	22	20	22	20	22	20	22	20	21	20	22	20	22	20	22	20	22	20	21
21	25	21	25	21	23	21	23	21	23	21	23	21	22	21	23	21	23	21	23	21	23	21	22
22	26	22	26	22	24	22	24	22	24	22	24	22	23	22	24	22	24	22	24	22	24	22	23
23	27	23	27	23	25	23	25	23	25	23	25	23	24	23	25	23	25	23	25	23	25	23	24
24	28	24	28	24	26	24	26	24	26	24	26	24	25	24	26	24	26	24	26	24	26	24	25
25	29	25	29	25	27	25	27	25	27	25	27	25	26	25	27	25	27	25	27	25	27	25	26
26	30	26	30	26	28	26	28	26	28	26	28	26	27	26	28	26	28	26	28	26	28	26	27
27	31	27	1 (May)	27	29	27	29	27	29	27	29	27	28	27	29	27	29	27	29	27	29	27	28
28	1 (Apr.)	28	2	28	30	28	30	28	30	28	30	28	29	28	30	28	30	28	30	28	30	28	1 (Mar)
29	2			29	31	29	1 (July)	29	31	29	31	29	30	29	31	29	1 (Dec.)	29	31	29	31	29	2
30	3			30	1 (June)	30	2	30	1 (Aug.)	30	1 (Sep.)	30	1 (Oct.)	30	1 (Nov.)	30	2	30	1 (Jan.)	30	1 (Feb.)	30	3
31	4			31	2			31	2			31	2	31	2			31	2			31	4

THE PREGNANCY AND WHELPING
OF THE BITCH

The "period of gestation" of the bitch, by which is meant the duration of her pregnancy, is usually estimated at sixty-three days. Many bitches, especially young ones, have their puppies as early as sixty days after they are bred. Cases have occurred in which strong puppies were born after only fifty-seven days, and there have been cases that required as many as sixty-six days. However, if puppies do not arrive by the sixty-fourth day, it is time to consult a veterinarian.

For the first five to six weeks of her pregnancy, the bitch requires no more than normal good care and unrestricted exercise. For that period, she needs no additional quantity of food, although her diet must contain sufficient amounts of all the food factors, as is stated in the division of this book that pertains to food. After the fifth to sixth week, the ration must be increased and the violence of exercise restricted. Normal running and walking are likely to be better for the pregnant bitch than a sedentary existence but she should not be permitted to jump, hunt, or fight during the latter half of her gestation. Violent activity may cause her to abort her puppies.

About a week before she is due to whelp, a bed should be prepared for her and she be persuaded to use it for sleeping. This bed may be a box of generous size, big enough to accommodate her with room for activity. It should be high enough to permit her to stand upright, and is better for having a hinged cover. An opening in one side will afford her ingress and egress. This box should be placed in a secluded location, away from any possible molestation by other dogs, animals, or children. The bitch must be made confident of her security in her box.

A few hours, or perhaps a day or two, before her whelping, the bitch will probably begin arranging the bedding of the box to suit herself, tearing blankets or cushions and nosing the parts into the corners. Before the whelping actually starts, however, it is best to substitute burlap sacking, securely tacked to the floor of the box. This is to provide traction for the puppies to reach the dam's breast.

The whelping may take place at night without any assistance from the owner. The box may be opened in the morning to reveal

61

the happy bitch nursing a litter of complacent puppies. But she may need some assistance in her parturition. If whelping is recognized to be in process, it is best to help the bitch.

As the puppies arrive, one by one, the enveloping membranes should be removed as quickly as possible, lest the puppies suffocate. Having removed the membrane, the umbilical cord should be severed with clean scissors some three or four inches from the puppy's belly. (The part of the cord attached to the belly will dry up and drop off in a few days.) There is no need for any medicament or dressing of the cord after it is cut.

The bitch should be permitted to eat the afterbirth if she so desires, and she normally does. If she has no assistance, she will probably remove the membrane and sever the cord with her teeth. The only dangers are that she may delay too long or may bite the cord too short. Some bitches, few of them, eat their newborn puppies (especially bitches not adequately fed during pregnancy). This unlikelihood should be guarded against.

As they arrive, it is wise to remove all the puppies except one, placing them in a box or basket lined and covered by a woolen cloth, somewhere aside or away from the whelping bed, until all have come and the bitch's activity has ceased. The purpose of this is to prevent her from walking or lying on the whelps, and to keep her from being disturbed by the puppies' whining. A single puppy should be left with the bitch to ease her anxiety.

It is best that the "midwife" be somebody with whom the bitch is on intimate terms and in whom she has confidence. Some bitches exhibit a jealous fear and even viciousness while they are whelping. Such animals are few, and most appear grateful for gentle assistance through their ordeal.

The puppies arrive at intervals of a few minutes to an hour until all are delivered. It is wise to call a veterinarian if the interval is greater than one hour. Though such service is seldom needed, an experienced veterinarian can usually be depended upon to withdraw with obstetrical forceps an abnormally presented puppy. It is possible, but unlikely, that the veterinarian will recommend a Caesarian section. This surgery in the dog is not very grave, but it should be performed only by an expert veterinarian. It is unnecessary to describe the process here, or the subsequent management of the patient, since, if a Caesarian section should be necessary, the veterinarian will provide all the needed instructions.

Some bitches, at or immediately after their whelping period, go into a convulsive paralysis, which is called *eclampsia*. This is unlikely if the bitch throughout her pregnancy has had an adequate measure of calcium in her rations. The remedy for eclampsia is the intravenous or intramuscular administration of parenteral calcium. The bitch suspected of having eclampsia should be attended by a veterinarian.

Assuming that the whelping has been normal and without untoward incident, all of the puppies are returned to the bitch, and put, one by one, to the breast, which strong puppies will accept with alacrity. The less handling of puppies for the first four or five hours of their lives, the better. However, the litter should be looked over carefully for possible defectives and discards, which should be destroyed as soon as possible. There is no virtue in rearing hare-lipped, crippled, or mismarked puppies.

It is usually unwise to destroy sound, healthy puppies just to reduce the number in the litter, since it is impossible to sort young puppies for excellence and one may be destroying the best member of the litter, a future champion. Unless a litter is extraordinarily numerous, the dam, if well fed, can probably suckle them all. If it is found that her milk is insufficient, the litter may be artificially fed or may be divided, and the surplus placed on a foster mother if it is possible to obtain one. The foster mother need not be of the same breed as the puppies, a mongrel being as good as any. She should be approximately the same size as the actual mother of the puppies, clean, healthy, and her other puppies should be of as nearly the same age as the ones she is to take over as possible. She should be removed from her own puppies (which may well be destroyed) and her breasts be permitted to fill with milk until she is somewhat uncomfortable, at which time her foster puppies can be put to her breasts and will usually be accepted without difficulty. Unless the services of the foster mother are really required, it is better not to use her.

The whelping bitch may be grateful for a warm meal even between the arrivals of her puppies. As soon as her chore is over, she should be offered food in her box. This should be of cereal and milk or of meat and broth, something sloppy. She will probably not leave her puppies to eat and her meals must be brought to her.

63

It is wise to give a mild laxative for her bowels, also milk of magnesia. She will be reluctant to get out of her box even to relieve herself for about two days, but she should be urged, even forced, to do so regularly. A sensible bitch will soon settle down to care for her brood and will seldom give further trouble. She should be fed often and well, all that she can be induced to eat during her entire lactation.

As a preventive for infections sometimes occurring after whelping, some experienced breeders and veterinarians recommend injecting the bitch with penicillin or another antibiotic immediately following the birth of the last puppy. Oral doses of the same drug may be given daily thereafter for the first week. It is best to consult your veterinarian about this treatment.

ACID MILK

Occasionally a bitch produces early milk (colostrum) so acid that it disagrees with, sometimes kills, her puppies. The symptoms of the puppies are whining, disquiet, frequently refusal to nurse, frailty, and death. It is true that all milk is slightly acid, and it should be, turning blue litmus paper immersed in it a very light pink. However, milk harmfully on the acid side will readily turn litmus paper a vivid red. It seems that only the first two or three days milk is so affected. Milk problems come also from mastitis and other infections in the bitch.

This is not likely to occur with a bitch that throughout her pregnancy has received an adequate supply of calcium phosphate regularly in her daily ration. That is the best way to deal with the situation—to see to the bitch's correct nutrition in advance of her whelping. The owner has only himself to blame for the bitch's too acid milk, since adequate calcium in advance would have neutralized the acid.

If it is found too late that her milk is too acid, the puppies must be taken from her breast and either given to a foster mother or artificially fed from bottle or by medicine dropper. Artificial feeding of very young puppies seldom is successful. Sometimes the acidity of the dam's milk can be neutralized by giving her large doses of bicarbonate of soda (baking soda), but the puppies should not be restored to her breasts until her milk ceases to turn litmus paper red.

If it is necessary to feed the puppies artificially, "Esbilac," a commercial product, or the following orphan puppy formula, may be used.

7 oz. whole milk
1 oz. cream (top milk)
1 egg yolk
2 tbsp. corn syrup
2 tbsp. lime water

REARING THE PUPPIES

Puppies are born blind and open their eyes at approximately the ninth day thereafter. If they were whelped earlier than the full sixty-three days after the breeding from which they resulted, the difference should be added to the nine days of anticipated blindness. The early eye color of young puppies is no criterion of the color to which the eyes are likely to change, and the breeder's anxiety about his puppies' having light eyes is premature.

In breeds that require the docking of the tail, this should be done on the third day and is a surgical job for the veterinarian. Many a dog has had his tail cut off by an inexperienced person, ruining his good looks and his possibility for a win in the show ring. Dew claws should be removed at the same time. There is little else to do with normal puppies except to let them alone and permit them to grow. The most important thing about their management is their nutrition, which is discussed in another chapter. The first two or three weeks, they will thrive and grow rapidly on their mother's milk, after which they should have additional food as described.

Puppies sleep much of the time, as do other babies, and they should not be frequently awakened to be played with. They grow more and more playful as they mature.

After the second week their nails begin to grow long and sharp. The mother will be grateful if the puppies' nails are blunted with scissors from time to time so that in their pawing of the breast they do not lacerate it. Sharp nails tend to prompt the mother to wean the whelps early, and she should be encouraged to keep them with her as long as she will tolerate them. Even the small amount of milk they can drain from her after the weaning process is begun is the

65

best food they can obtain. It supplements and makes digestible the remainder of their ration.

Many bitches, after their puppies are about four weeks of age, eat and regurgitate food, which is eaten by the puppies. This food is warmed and partly digested in the bitch's stomach. This practice, while it may appear digusting to the novice keeper of dogs, is perfectly normal and should not be discouraged. However, it renders it all the more necessary that the food of the bitch be sound, clean, and nutritious.

It is all but impossible to rear a litter of puppies without their becoming infested with roundworms. Of course, the bitch should be wormed, if she harbors such parasites, before she is bred, and her teats should be thoroughly washed with mild soap just before she whelps to free them from the eggs of roundworms. Every precaution must be taken to reduce the infestation of the puppies to a minimum. But, in spite of all it is possible to do, puppies will have roundworms. These pests hamper growth, reduce the puppies' normal resistance to disease, and may kill them outright unless the worms are eliminated. The worming of puppies is discussed in the chapter entitled "Intestinal Parasites and Their Control."

External Vermin
and Parasites

U NDER this heading the most common external parasites will be given consideration. Fleas, lice, ticks, and flies are those most commonly encountered and causing the most concern. The external parasite does not pose the problem that it used to before we had the new "miracle" insecticides. Today, with DDT, lindane, and chlordane, the course of extermination and prevention is much easier to follow. Many of the insecticide sprays have a four to six weeks residual effect. Thus the premises can be sprayed and the insect pests can be quite readily controlled.

FLEAS

Neglected dogs are too often beset by hundreds of blood-thirsty fleas, which do not always confine their attacks to the dogs but also sometimes feast upon their masters. Unchecked, they overrun kennels, homes, and playgrounds. Moreover, they are the intermediate hosts for the development of the kind of tapeworm most frequently found in dogs, as will be more fully discussed under the subject of *Intestinal Parasites.* Fleas are all-round bad actors and nuisances. Although it need hardly concern us in America, where the disease is not known to exist, fleas are the recognized and only vectors of bubonic plague.

There are numerous kinds and varieties of fleas, of which we shall discuss here only the three species often found on dogs. These are the human flea (*Pulex irritans*), the dog flea (*Ctenocephalides canis*), and the so-called chicken flea or sticktight flea (*Echidnophaga gallinacea*).

Of these the human flea prefers the blood of man to that of the dog, and unless humans are also bothered, are not likely to be found on the dog. They are small, nearly black insects, and occur mostly in the Mississippi Valley and in California. Their control is the same as for the dog flea.

The dog flea is much larger than his human counterpart, is dark brown in color and seldom bites mankind. On an infested dog these dog fleas may be found buried in the coat of any part of the anatomy, but their choicest habitat is the area of the back just forward from the tail and over the loins. On that part of a badly neglected dog, especially in summer, fleas by the hundreds will be found intermixed with their dung and with dried blood. They may cause the dog some discomfort or none. It must not be credited that because a dog is not kept in a constant or frequent agitation of scratching that he harbors no fleas. The coats of pet animals are soiled and roughened by the fleas and torn by the scratching that they sometimes induce. Fleas also appear to be connected with summer eczema of dogs; at least the diseased condition of the skin often clears up after fleas are eradicated.

Although the adults seldom remain long away from the dog's body, fleas do not reproduce themselves on the dog. Rather, their breeding haunts are the debris, dust, and sand of the kennel floor, and especially the accumulations of dropped hair, sand, and loose soil of unclean sleeping boxes. Nooks and cracks and crannies of the kennel may harbor the eggs or maggot-like larvae of immature fleas.

This debris and accumulation must be eliminated—preferably by incineration—after which all possible breeding areas should be thoroughly sprayed with a residual effect spray.

The adult dog may be combed well, then bathed in a detergent solution, rinsed thoroughly in warm water, and allowed to drip fairly dry. A solution of Pine Oil (1 oz. to a quart of water) is then used as a final rinse. This method of ridding the dog of its fleas is ideal in warm weather. The Pine Oil imparts a pleasant odor

68

to the dog's coat and the animal will enjoy being bathed and groomed.

The same procedure may be followed for young puppies except that the Pine Oil solution should be rinsed off. When bathing is not feasible, then a good flea powder—one containing lindane—should be used.

Sticktight fleas are minute, but are to be found, if at all, in patches on the dog's head and especially on the ears. They remain quiescent and do not jump, as the dog fleas and human fleas do. Their tiny heads are buried in the dog's flesh. To force them loose from the area decapitates them and the heads remain in the skin which is prone to fester from the irritation. They may be dislodged by placing a cotton pad or thick cloth well soaked in ether or alcohol over the flea patch, which causes them immediately to relinquish their hold, after which they can be easily combed loose and destroyed.

These sticktights abound in neglected, dirty, and abandoned chicken houses, which, if the dogs have access to them, should be cleaned out thoroughly and sprayed with DDT.

Fleas, while a nuisance, are only a minor problem. They should be eliminated not only from the dog but from all the premises he inhabits. Dogs frequently are reinfested with fleas from other dogs with which they play or come in contact. Every dog should be occasionally inspected for the presence of fleas, and, if any are found, immediate means should be taken to eradicate them.

LICE

There are even more kinds of lice than of fleas, although as they pertain to dogs there is no reason to differentiate them. They do not infest dogs, except in the events of gross neglect or of unforeseen accident. Lice reproduce themselves on the body of the dog. To rid him of the adult lice is easy. The standard Pine Oil solution used to kill fleas will also kill lice. However, the eggs or "nits" are harder to remove. Weather permitting, it is sometimes best to have the dog clipped of all its hair. In heavily infested dogs this is the only sure way to cope with the situation. When the hair is clipped, most of the "nits" are removed automatically. A good commercial flea and louse powder applied to the skin will then keep the situation under control.

69

Rare as the occurrence of lice upon dogs may be, they must be promptly treated and eradicated. Having a dog with lice can prove to be embarrassing, for people just do not like to be around anything lousy. Furthermore, the louse may serve as the intermediate host of the tapeworm in dogs.

The dog's quarters should be thoroughly sprayed with a residual spray of the same type recommended for use in the control of fleas. The problem of disinfecting kennel and quarters is not as great as it is in the case of fleas, for the louse tends to stay on its host, not leaving the dog as the flea does.

TICKS

The terms "wood ticks" and "dog ticks," as usually employed, refer to at least eight different species, whose appearances and habits are so similar that none but entomologists are likely to know them apart. It is useless to attempt to differentiate between these various species here, except to warn the reader that the Rocky Mountain spotted fever tick (*Dermacentor andersoni*) is a vector of the human disease for which it is named, as well as of rabbit fever (tularemia), and care must be employed in removing it from dogs lest the hands be infected. Some one or more of these numerous species are to be found in well nigh every state in the Union, although there exist wide areas where wood ticks are seldom seen and are not a menace to dogs.

All the ticks must feed on blood in order to reproduce themselves. The eggs are always deposited on the ground or elsewhere after the female, engorged with blood, has dropped from the dog or other animal upon which she has fed. The eggs are laid in masses in protected places on the ground, particularly in thick clumps of grass. Each female lays only one such mass, which contains 2500 to 5000 eggs. The development of the American dog tick embraces four stages: the egg, the larva or seed tick, the nymph, and the adult. The two intermediate stages in the growth of the tick are spent on rodents, and only in the adult stage does it attach itself to the dog. Both sexes affix themselves to dogs and to other animals and feed on their blood; the males do not increase in size, although the female is tremendously enlarged as she gorges. Mating occurs while the female is feeding. After some five to thirteen days, she drops from her host, lays her eggs and dies. At no time do ticks feed on anything except the blood of animals.

The longevity and hardihood of the tick are amazing. The larvae and nymphs may live for a full year without feeding, and the adults survive for more than two years if they fail to encounter a host to which they may attach. In the Northern United States the adults are most active in the spring and summer, few being found after July. But in the warmer Southern states they may be active the year around.

Although most of the tick species require a vegetative cover and wild animal hosts to complete their development, at least one species, the brown tick (*Rhipicephalus sanguinius*), is adapted to life in the dryer environment of kennels, sheds, and houses, with the dog as its only necessary host. This tick is the vector of canine piroplasmosis, although this disease is at this time almot negligible in the United States.

This brown dog tick often infests houses in large numbers, both immature and adult ticks lurking around baseboards, window casings, furniture, the folds of curtains, and elsewhere. Thus, even dogs kept in houses are sometimes infested with hundreds of larvae, nymphs, and adults of this tick. Because of its ability to live in heated buildings, the species has become established in many Northern areas. Unlike the other tick species, the adult of the brown dog tick does not bite human beings. However, also unlike the other ticks, it is necessary not only to rid the dogs of this particular tick but also to eliminate the pests from their habitat, especially the dogs' beds and sleeping boxes. A spray with a 10% solution of DDT suffices for this purpose. Fumigation of premises seldom suffices, since not only are brown dog ticks very resistant to mere fumigation, but the ticks are prone to lurk around entry ways, porches and outbuildings, where they cannot be reached with a fumigant. The spraying with DDT may not penetrate to spots where some ticks are in hiding, and it must be repeated at intervals until all the pests are believed to be completely eradicated.

Dogs should not be permitted to run in brushy areas known to be infested with ticks, and upon their return from exercise in a place believed to harbor ticks, dogs should be carefully inspected for their presence.

If a dog's infestation is light, the ticks may be picked individually

71

from his skin. To make tick release its grip, dab with alcohol or a drop of ammonia. If the infestation is heavy, it is easier and quicker to saturate his coat with a derris solution (one ounce of soap and two ounces of derris powder dissolved in one gallon of water). The derris should be of an excellent grade containing at least 3% of rotenone. The mixture may be used and reused, since it retains its strength for about three weeks if it is kept in a dark place.

If possible, the dip should be permitted to dry on the dog's coat. It should not get into a dog's eyes. The dip will not only kill the ticks that are attached to the dog, but the powder drying in the hair will repel further infestation for two or three days and kill most if not all the boarders. These materials act slowly, requiring sometimes as much as twenty-four hours to complete the kill.

If the weather is cold or the use of the dip should be otherwise inconvenient, derris powder may be applied as a dust, care being taken that it penetrates the hair and reaches the skin. Breathing or swallowing derris may cause a dog to vomit, but he will not be harmed by it. The dust and liquid should be kept from his eyes.

Since the dog is the principal host on which the adult tick feeds and since each female lays several thousand eggs after feeding, treating the dog regularly will not only bring him immediate relief but will limit the reproduction of the ticks. Keeping underbrush, weeds, and grass closely cut tends to remove protection favorable to the ticks. Burning vegetation accomplishes the same results.

Many of the ticks in an infested area may be killed by the thorough application of a spray made as follows: Four tablespoonfuls of nicotine sulphate (40% nicotine) in three gallons of water. More permanent results may be obtained by adding to this solution four ounces of sodium fluorides, but this will injure the vegetation.

Besides the ticks that attach themselves to all parts of the dog, there is another species that infests the ear specifically. This pest, the spinose ear tick, penetrates deep into the convolutions of the ear and often causes irritation and pain, as evidenced by the dog's scratching its ears, shaking its head or holding it on one side. One part derris powder (5% rotenone) mixed with ten parts medicinal mineral oil and dropped into the ear will kill spinose ear ticks. Only a few drops of the material is required, but it is best to massage the base of the ear to make sure the remedy penetrates to the deepest part of the ear to reach all the ticks.

72

FLIES

Flies can play havoc with dogs in outdoor kennels, stinging them and biting the ears until they are raw. Until recently the only protection against them was the screening of the entire kennel. The breeding places of flies, which are damp filth and stagnant garbage, are in most areas now happily abated, but the chief agent for control of the pest is DDT.

A spray of a 10% solution of DDT over all surfaces of the kennel property may be trusted to destroy all the flies that light on those surfaces for from two weeks to one month. It must, of course, be repeated from time to time when it is seen that the efficacy of the former treatment begins to diminish.

Intestinal Parasites and Their Control

THE varieties of worms that may inhabit the alimentary tract of the dog are numerous. Much misapprehension exists, even among experienced dog keepers, about the harm these parasites may cause and about the methods of getting rid of them. Some dog keepers live in terror of these worms and continually treat their dogs for them whether they are known to be present or not; others ignore the presence of worms and do nothing about them. Neither policy is justified.

Promiscuous dosing, without the certainty that the dog harbors worms or what kind he may have, is a practice fraught with danger for the well-being of the animal. All drugs for the expulsion or destruction of parasites are poisonous or irritant to a certain degree and should be administered only when it is known that the dog is infested by parasites and what kind. It is hardly necessary to say that when a dog is known to harbor worms he should be cleared of them, but in most instances there is no such urgency as is sometimes manifested.

It may be assumed that puppies at weaning time are more or less infested with intestinal roundworms or ascarids (*Toxocara canis*) and that such puppies need to be treated for worms. It is all but impossible to rear a litter of puppies to weaning age free from those parasites. Once the puppies are purged of them, it is amazing to see the spurt of their growth and the renewal of their thriftiness.

74

Many neglected puppies surmount the handicap of their worms and at least some of them survive. This, however, is no reason that good puppies—puppies that are worth saving—should go unwormed and neglected.

The ways to find out that a dog actually has worms are to see some of the worms themselves in the dog's droppings or to submit a sample of his feces to a veterinarian or to a biological laboratory for microscopic examination. From a report of such an examination, it is possible to know whether or not a dog is a host to intestinal parasites at all and intelligently to undertake the treatment and control of the specific kind he may harbor.

All of the vermifuges, vermicides, and anthelmintic remedies tend to expel other worms besides the kind for which they are specifically intended, but it is better to employ the remedy particularly effective against the individual kind of parasite the dog is known to have, and to refrain from worm treatment unless or until it is known to be needed.

ROUNDWORMS

The ascarids, or large intestinal roundworms, are the largest of the worm parasites occurring in the digestive tract of the dog, varying in length from 1 to 8 inches, the females being larger than the males. The name "spool worms," which is sometimes applied to them, is derived from their tendency to coil in a springlike spiral when they are expelled, either from the bowel or vomited, by their hosts. There are at least two species of them which frequently parasitize dogs: *Toxocara canis* and *Toxascaris leonina,* but they are so much alike except for some minor details in the life histories of their development that it is not practically necessary for the dog keeper to seek to distinguish between them.

Neither specie requires an intermediate host for its development. Numerous eggs are deposited in the intestinal tract of the host animal; these eggs are passed out by the dog in his feces and are swallowed by the same or another animal, and hatching takes place in its small intestine. Their development requires from twelve to sixteen days under favorable circumstances.

It has been shown that puppies before their birth may be infested by roundworms from their mother. This accounts for the occasional finding of mature or nearly mature worms in very young puppies. It cannot occur if the mother is entirely free from worms, as she should be.

These roundworms are particularly injurious to young puppies. The commonest symptoms of roundworm infestation are general unthriftiness, digestive disturbances, and bloat after feeding. The hair grows dead and lusterless, and the breath may have a peculiar sweetish odor. Large numbers of roundworms may obstruct the intestine, and many have been known to penetrate the intestinal wall. In heavy infestations the worms may wander into the bile ducts, stomach, and even into the lungs and upper respiratory passages where they may cause pneumonia, especially in very young animals.

The control of intestinal roundworms depends primarily upon prompt disposal of feces, keeping the animals in clean quarters and on clean ground, and using only clean utensils for feed and water. Dampness of the ground favors the survival of worm eggs and larvae. There is no known chemical treatment feasible for the destruction of eggs in contaminated soil, but prolonged exposure to sunlight

76

and drying has proved effective.

Numerous remedies have been in successful use for roundworms, including turpentine, which has a recognized deleterious effect upon the kidneys; santonin, an old standby; freshly powdered betel nut and its derivative, arecoline, both of which tend to purge and sicken the patient; oil of chenopodium, made from American wormseed; carbon tetrachloride, widely used as a cleaning agent; tetrachlorethylene, closely related chemically to the former, but less toxic; and numerous other medicaments. While all of them are effective as vermifuges or vermicides, if rightly employed, to each of them some valid objection can be interposed.

In addition to the foregoing, there are other vermifuges available for treatment of roundworms. Some may be purchased without a prescription, whereas others may be procured only when prescribed by a veterinarian.

HOOKWORMS

Hookworms are the most destructive of all the parasites of dogs. There are three species of them—*Ancylostoma caninum, A. braziliense,* and *Uncinaria stenocephalia*—all to be found in dogs in some parts of the United States. The first named is the most widespread; the second found only in the warmer parts of the South and Southwest; the last named, in the North and in Canada. All are similar one to another and to the hookworm that infests mankind (*Ancylostoma uncinariasis*). For purposes of their eradication, no distinction need be made between them.

It is possible to keep dogs for many years in a dry and well drained area without an infestation with hookworms, which are contracted only on infested soils. However, unthrifty dogs shipped from infested areas are suspect until it is proved that hookworm is not the cause of their unthriftiness.

Hookworm males seldom are longer than half an inch, the females somewhat larger. The head end is curved upward, and is equipped with cutting implements, which may be called teeth, by which they attach themselves to the lining of the dog's intestine and suck his blood.

The females produce numerous eggs which pass out in the dog's feces. In two weeks or a little more these eggs hatch, the worms pass through various larval stages, and reach their infective stage. Infection of the dog may take place through his swallowing the organism, or by its penetration of his skin through some lesion. In the latter case the worms enter the circulation, reach the lungs, are coughed up, swallowed, and reach the intestine where their final development occurs. Eggs appear in the dog's feces from three to six weeks after infestation.

Puppies are sometimes born with hookworms already well developed in their intestines, the infection taking place before their birth. Eggs of the hookworm are sometimes found in the feces of puppies only thirteen days old. Assumption is not to be made that all puppies are born with hookworms or even that they are likely to become infested, but in hookworm areas the possibility of either justifies precautions that neither shall happen.

Hookworm infestation in puppies and young dogs brings about a condition often called kennel anemia. There may be digestive

78

disturbances and blood streaked diarrhea. In severe cases the feces may be almost pure blood. Infested puppies fail to grow, often lose weight, and the eyes are sunken and dull. The loss of blood results in an anemia with pale mucous membranes of the mouth and eyes. This anemia is caused by the consumption of the dog's blood by the worms and the bleeding that follows the bites. The worms are not believed to secrete a poison or to cause damage to the dog except loss of blood.

There is an admitted risk in worming young puppies before weaning time, but it is risk that must be run if the puppies are known to harbor hookworms. The worms, if permitted to persist, will ruin the puppies and likely kill them. No such immediacy is needful for the treatment of older puppies and adult dogs, although hookworm infestation will grow steadily worse until it is curbed. It should not be delayed and neglected in the belief or hope that the dog can cure himself.

If treatment is attempted at home, there are available three fairly efficacious and safe drugs that may be used: normal butyl chloride, hexaresorcinal, and methyl benzine.

If a dog is visibly sick and a diagnosis of hookworm infestation has been made, treatment had best be under professional guidance.

Brine made by stirring common salt (sodium chloride) into boiling water, a pound and a half of salt to the gallon of water, will destroy hookworm infestation in the soil. A gallon of brine should be sufficient to treat eight square feet of soil surface. One treatment of the soil is sufficient unless it is reinfested.

TAPEWORMS

The numerous species of tapeworm which infest the dog may, for practical purposes, be divided into two general groups, the armed forms and the unarmed forms. Species of both groups resemble each other in their possession of a head and neck and a chain of segments. They are, however, different in their life histories, and the best manner to deal with each type varies. This is unfortunately not well understood, since to most persons a tapeworm is a tapeworm.

The armed varieties are again divided into the single pored forms of the genera *Taenia, Multiceps,* and *Echinococcus,* and the double pored tapeworm, of which the most widespread and prevalent among dogs in the United States is the so-called dog tapeworm, *Dipylidium caninum.* This is the variety with segments shaped like cucumber-seeds. The adult rarely exceeds a foot in length, and the head is armed with four or five tiny hooks. For the person with well cared for and protected dogs, this is the only tapeworm of which it is necessary to take particular cognizance.

The dog tapeworm requires but a single intermediate host for its development, which in most cases is the dog flea or the biting louse. Thus, by keeping dogs free from fleas and lice the major danger of tapeworm infestation is obviated.

The tapeworm is bi-sexual and requires the intermediate host in order to complete its life cycle. Segments containing the eggs of the tapeworm pass out with the stool, or the detached proglottid may emerge by its own motile power and attach itself to the contiguous hair. The flea then lays its eggs on this segment, thus affording sustenance for the larva. The head of the tapeworm develops in the lung chamber of the baby flea. Thus, such a flea, when it develops and finds its way back to a dog, is the potential carrier of tapeworm. Of course, the cycle is complete when the flea bites the dog and the dog, in biting the area to relieve the itching sensation, swallows the flea.

Since the egg of the tapeworm is secreted in the segment that breaks off and passes with the stool, microscopic examination of the feces is of no avail in attempting to determine whether tapeworms infest a dog. It is well to be suspicious of a finicky eater— a dog that refuses all but the choicest meat and shows very little

80

appetite. The injury produced by this armed tapeworm to the dog that harbors it is not well understood. Frequently it produces no symptoms at all, and it is likely that it is not the actual cause of many of the symptoms attributed to it. At least, it is known that a dog may have one or many of these worms over a long period of time and apparently be no worse for their presence. Nervous symptoms or skin eruptions, or both, are often charged to the presence of tapeworm, which may or may not be the cause of the morbid condition.

Tapeworm-infested dogs sometimes involuntarily pass segments of worms and so soil floors, rugs, furniture, or bedding. The passage by dogs of a segment or a chain of segments via the anus is a frequent cause of the dog's itching, which he seeks to allay by sitting and dragging himself on the floor by his haunches. The segments or chains are sometimes mistakenly called pinworms, but pinworms are a kind of roundworm to which dogs are not subject.

Despite that they may do no harm, few dogs owners care to tolerate tapeworms in their dogs. These worms, it has been definitely established, are not transmissible from dog to dog or to man. Without the flea or the louse, it is impossible for the adult dog tapeworm to reproduce itself, and by keeping dogs free from fleas and lice it is possible to keep them also free from dog tapeworm.

The various unarmed species of tapeworm find their intermediate hosts in the flesh and other parts of various animals, fish, crustacians and crayfish. Dogs not permitted to eat raw meats which have not been officially inspected, never have these worms, and it is needless here to discuss them at length. Hares and rabbits are the intermediate hosts to some of these worms and dogs should not be encouraged to feed upon those animals.

Little is known of the effects upon dogs of infestations of the unarmed tapeworms, but they are believed to be similar to the effects (if any) of the armed species.

The prevention of tapeworm infestation may be epitomized by saying: Do not permit dogs to swallow fleas or lice nor to feed upon uninspected raw meats. It is difficult to protect dogs from such contacts if they are permitted to run at large, but it is to be presumed that persons interested enough in caring for dogs to read this book will keep their dogs at home and protect them.

The several species of tapeworm occurring in dogs are not all removable by the same treatment. The most effective treatment for the removal of the armed species, which is the one most frequently found in the dogs, is arecoline hydrobromide. This drug is a drastic purgative and acts from fifteen to forty-five minutes after its administration. The treatment should be given in the morning after the dog has fasted overnight, and food should be withheld for some three hours after dosing.

Arecoline is not so effective against the double-pored tapeworm as against the other armed species, and it may be necessary to repeat the dose after a few days waiting, since some of the tapeworm heads may not be removed by the first treatment and regeneration of the tapeworm may occur in a few weeks. The estimatedly correct dosage is not stated here, since the drug is so toxic that the dosage should be estimated for the individual dog by a competent veterinarian, and it is better that he should be permitted to administer the remedy and control the treatment.

WHIPWORMS

The dog whipworm (*Trichuris vulpis*) is so called from its fancied resemblance to a tiny blacksnake whip, the front part being slender and hairlike and the hinder part relatively thick. It rarely exceeds three inches in its total length. Whipworms in dogs exist more or less generally throughout the world, but few dogs in the United States are known to harbor them. They are for the most part confined to the caecum, from which they are hard to dislodge, but sometimes spill over into the colon, whence they are easy to dislodge.

The complete life history of the whipworm is not well established, but it is known that no intermediate host is required for its development. The eggs appear to develop in much the same way as the eggs of the large roundworm, but slower, requiring from two weeks to several months for the organisms to reach maturity.

It has not as yet been definitely established that whipworms are the true causes of all the ills of which they are accused. In many instances they appear to cause little damage, even in heavy infestations. A great variety of symptoms of an indefinite sort have been ascribed to whipworms, including digestive disturbances, diarrhea, loss of weight, nervousness, convulsions, and general unthriftiness, but it remains to be proved that whipworms were responsible.

To be effective in its removal of whipworms, a drug must enter the caecum and come into direct contact with them; but the entry of the drug into this organ is somewhat fortuitous, and to increase the chances of its happening, large doses of a drug essentially harmless to the dog must be used. Normal butyl chloride meets this requirement, but it must be given in large doses. Even then, complete clearance of whipworms from the caecum may not be expected; the best to be hoped is that their numbers will be reduced and the morbid symptoms will subside.

Before treatment the dog should be fasted for some eighteen hours, although he may be fed two hours after being treated. It is wise to follow the normal butyl chloride in one hour with a purgative dose of castor oil. This treatment, since it is not expected to be wholly effective, may be repeated at monthly intervals.

The only known means of the complete clearance of whipworms from the dog is the surgical removal of the caecum, which of course should be undertaken only by a veterinary surgeon.

HEART WORMS

Heart worms (*Dirofilaria immitis*) in dogs are rare. They occur largely in the South and Southeast, but their incidence appears to be increasing and cases have been reported along the Atlantic Seaboard as far north as New York. The various species of mosquitoes are known to be vectors of heart worms, although the flea is also accused of spreading them.

The symptoms of heart worm infestation are somewhat vague, and include coughing, shortness of breath and collapse. In advanced cases, dropsy may develop. Nervous symptoms, fixity of vision, fear of light, and convulsions may develop. However, all such symptoms may occur from other causes and it must not be assumed because a dog manifests some of these conditions that he has heart worms. The only way to be sure is a microscopic examination of the blood and the presence or absence of the larvae. Even in some cases where larvae have been found in the blood, post mortem examinations have failed to reveal heart worms in the heart.

Both the diagnosis and treatment of heart worm are functions of the veterinarian. They are beyond the province of the amateur. The drug used is a derivative from antimony known as fuadin, and many dogs are peculiarly susceptible to antimony poisoning. If proper treatment is used by a trained veterinarian, a large preponderance of cases make a complete recovery. But even the most expert of veterinarians may be expected to fail in the successful treatment of a percentage of heart worm infestations. The death of some of the victims is to be anticipated.

LESS FREQUENTLY FOUND WORMS

Besides the intestinal worms that have been enumerated, there exist in some dogs numerous other varieties and species of worms which are of so infrequent occurrence that they require no discussion in a book for the general dog keeper. These include, esophageal worms, lungworms, kidney worms, and eye worms. They are in North America, indeed, so rare as to be negligible.

COCCIDIA

Coccidia are protozoic, microscopic organisms. The forms to which the dog is a host are *Isospora rivolta, I. bigeminia* and *I. felis.* Coccidia eggs, called *oocysts,* can be carried by flies and are picked up by dogs as they lick themselves or eat their stools.

These parasides attack the intestinal wall and cause diarrhea. They are particularly harmful to younger puppies that have been weaned, bringing on fever, running eyes, poor appetite and debilitation as well as the loose stools.

The best prevention is scrupulous cleanliness of the puppy or dog, its surroundings and its playmates whether canine or human. Flies should be eliminated as described in the preceding chapter and stools removed promptly where the dog cannot touch it.

Infection can be confirmed by microscopic examination of the stool. Treatment consists of providing nourishing food, which should be force-fed if necessary, and whatever drug the veterinarian recommends. Puppies usually recover, though occasionally their teeth may be pitted as in distemper.

A dog infected once by one form develops immunity to that form but may be infected by another form.

Skin Troubles

THERE is a tendency on the part of the amateur dog keeper to consider any lesion of the dog's skin to be mange. Mange is an unusual condition in clean, well fed, and well cared for dogs. Eczema occurs much more frequently and is often more difficult to control.

MANGE OR SCABIES

There are at least two kinds of mange that effect dogs—sarcoptic mange and demodectic or red mange, the latter rare indeed and difficult to cure.

Sarcoptic mange is caused by a tiny spider-like mite (*Sarcoptes scabiei canis*) which is similar to the mite that causes human scabies or "itch." Indeed, the mange is almost identical with scabies and is transmissible from dog to man. The mite is approximately 1/100th of an inch in length and without magnification is just visible to acute human sight.

Only the female mites are the cause of the skin irritation. They burrow into the upper layers of the skin, where each lays twenty to forty eggs, which in three to seven days hatch into larvae. These larvae in turn develop into nymphs which later grow into adults. The entire life cycle requires from fourteen to twenty-one days for completion. The larvae, nymphs, and males do not burrow into the skin, but live under crusts and scabs on the surface.

The disease may make its first appearance on any part of the dog's body, although it is usually first seen on the head and muzzle, around the eyes, or at the base of the ears. Sometimes it is first noticed in the armpits, the inner parts of the thighs, the lower abdomen or on the front of the chest. If not promptly treated it may cover the whole body and an extremely bad infestation may cause the death of the dog after a few months.

Red points which soon develop into small blisters are the first signs of the disease. These are most easily seen on the unpigmented parts of the skin, such as the abdomen. As the female mites burrow into the skin, there is an exudation of serum which dries and scabs. The affected parts soon are covered with bran-like scales followed with grayish crusts. The itching is intense, especially in hot weather or after exercise. The rubbing and scratching favor secondary bacterial infections and the formation of sores. The hair may grow matted and fall out, leaving bare spots. The exuded serum decomposes and gives rise to a peculiar mousy odor which increases as the disease develops and which is especially characteristic.

Sarcoptic mange is often confused with demodectic (red) mange, ringworm, or with simple eczema. If there is any doubt about the diagnosis, a microscopic examination of the scrapings of the lesions will reveal the true facts.

It is easy to control sarcoptic mange if it is recognized in its earlier stages and treatment is begun immediately. Neglected, it may be very difficult to eradicate. If it is considered how rapidly the causative mites reproduce themselves, the necessity for early treatment becomes apparent. That treatment consists not only of medication of the dog but also of sterilization of his bedding, all tools and implements used on him, and the whole premises upon which he has been confined. Sarcoptic mange is easily and quickly transmissible from dog to dog, from area to area on the same dog, and even from dog to human.

In some manner which is not entirely understood, an inadequate or unbalanced diet appears to predispose a dog to sarcoptic mange, and few dogs adequately fed and cared for ever contract it. Once a dog has contracted mange, however, improvement in the amount of quality of his food seems not to hasten his recovery.

There are various medications recommended for sarcoptic mange, sulphur ointment being the old standby. However, it is messy,

87

difficult to use, and not always effective. For the treatment of sarcoptic mange, there are available today such insecticides as lindane, chlordane, and DDT. The use of these chemicals greatly facilitates treatment and cure of the dogs affected with mange and those exposed to it.

A bath made by dissolving four ounces of derris powder (containing at least 5% rotenone) and one ounce of soap in one gallon of water has proved effective, especially if large areas of the surface of the dog's skin are involved. All crusts and scabs should be removed before its application. The solution must be well scrubbed into the skin with a moderately stiff brush and the whole animal thoroughly soaked. Only the surplus liquid should be taken off with a towel and the remainder must be permitted to dry on the dog. This bath should be repeated at intervals of five days until all signs of mange have disappeared. Three such baths will usually suffice.

The advantage of such all over treatment is that it protects uninfected areas from infection. It is also a precautionary measure to bathe in this solution uninfected dogs which have been in contact with the infected one.

Isolated mange spots may be treated with oil of lavender. Roll a woolen cloth into a swab with which the oil of lavender can be applied and rubbed in thoroughly for about five minutes. This destroys all mites with which the oil of lavender comes into contact.

Even after a cure is believed to be accomplished, vigilance must be maintained to prevent fresh infestations and to treat new spots immediately if they appear.

DEMODECTIC OR RED MANGE

Demodectic mange, caused by the wormlike mite *Demodex canis,* which lives in the hair follicles and the sebaceous glands of the skin, is difficult to cure. It is a baffling malady of which the prognosis is not favorable. The life cycle of the causative organism is not well understood, the time required from the egg to maturity being so far unknown. The female lays eggs which hatch into young of appearance similar to that of the adult, except that they are smaller and have but three pairs of legs instead of four.

One peculiar feature about demodectic mange is that some dogs appear to be genetically predisposed to it while others do not contract it whatever their contact with infected animals may be. Young animals seem to be especially prone to it, particularly those with short hair. The first evidence of its presence is the falling out of the hair on certain areas of the dog. The spots may be somewhat reddened, and they commonly occur near the eyes, on the hocks, elbows, or toes, although they may be on any part of the dog's body. No itching occurs at the malady's inception, and it never grows so intense as in sarcoptic mange.

In the course of time, the hairless areas enlarge, and the skin attains a copper hue; in severe cases it may appear blue oi leadish gray. During this period the mites multiply and small pustules develop. Secondary invasions may occur to complicate the situation. Poisons are formed by the bacteria in the pustules, and the absorption of toxic materials deranges the body functions and eventually affects the whole general health of the dog, leading to emaciation, weakness, and the development of an acrid, unpleasant odor.

This disease is slow and subtle in its development, runs a casual course, and frequently extends over a period of two or even three years. Unless it is treated, it usually terminates in death, although spontaneous recovery occasionally occurs, especially if the dog has been kept on a nourishing diet. As in other skin diseases, correct nutrition plays a major part in recovery from demodectic mange, as it plays an even larger part in its prevention.

It is possible to confuse demodectic mange with sarcoptic mange, fungus infection, acne, or eczema. A definite diagnosis is possible only from microscopic examination of skin scrapings and of material from the pustules. The possibility of demodectic mange, particularly in its earlier stages, is not negated by the failure to find the mites under the microscope, and several examinations may be necessary to arrive at a definite diagnosis.

The prognosis is not entirely favorable. It may appear that the mange is cured and a new and healthy coat may be re-established only to have the disease manifest itself in a new area, and the whole process of treatment must be undertaken afresh.

In the treatment of demodectic mange, the best results have been obtained by the persistent use of benzine hexachloride, chlordane, rotenone, and 2-mercapto benzothiazole. Perseverance is necessary, but even then failure is possible.

EAR MITES OR EAR MANGE

The mites responsible for ear mange (*Ododectes cynotis*) are considerably larger than the ones which cause sarcoptic mange. They inhabit the external auditory canal and are visible to the unaided eye as minute, slowly moving, white objects. Their life history is not known, but is probably similar to that of the mite that causes sarcoptic mange.

These mites do not burrow into the skin, but are found deep in the ear canal, near the eardrum. Considerable irritation results from their presence, and the normal secretions of the ear are interfered with. The ear canal is filled with inflammatory products, modified ear wax, and mites, causing the dog to scratch and rub its ears and to shake its head. While ear mange is not caused by incomplete washing or inefficient drying of the ears, it is encouraged by such negligence.

The ear mange infestation is purely local and is no cause for anxiety. An ointment containing benzine hexachloride is very effective in correcting this condition. The ear should be treated every third or fourth day.

ECZEMA

Eczema is probably the most common of all ailments seen in the dog. Oftentimes it is mistaken for mange or ringworm, although there is no actual relationship between the conditions. Eczema is variously referred to by such names as "hot spots," "fungitch," and "kennel itch."

Some years ago there was near-unanimity of opinion among dog people that the food of the animal was the major contributing factor of eczema. Needless to say, the manufacturers of commercial dog foods were besieged with complaints. Some research on the cause of eczema placed most of the blame on outside environmental factors, and with some help from other sources it was found that a vegetative organism was the causative agent in a great majority of the cases.

Some dogs do show an allergic skin reaction to certain types of protein given to them as food, but this is generally referred to as the "foreign protein" type of dermatitis. It manifests itself by raising numerous welts on the skin, and occasionally the head, face, and ears will become alarmingly swollen. This condition can be controlled by the injection of antihistamine products and subsequent dosage with antihistaminic tablets or capsules such as chlortrimenton or benedryl. Whether "foreign protein" dermatitis is due to an allergy or whether it is due to some toxin manufactured and elaborated by the individual dog is a disputed point.

Most cases of eczema start with reddening of the skin in certain parts. The areas most affected seem to be the region along the spine and at the base of the tail. In house dogs this may have its inception from enlarged and plugged anal glands. The glands when full and not naturally expressed are a source of irritation. The dog will rub his hind parts on the grass in order to alleviate the itching sensation. Fleas, lice, and ticks may be inciting factors, causing the dog to rub and roll in the grass in an attempt to scratch the itchy parts.

In hunting dogs, it is believed that the vegetative cover through which the dogs hunt causes the dermatitis. In this class of dogs the skin becomes irritated and inflamed in the armpits, the inner surfaces of the thighs, and along the belly. Some hunting dogs are bedded down in straw or hay, and such dogs invariably show a

91

general reddening of the skin and a tendency to scratch.

As a general rule, the difference between moist and dry eczema lies in the degree to which the dog scratches the skin with his feet or chews it with his teeth. The inflammation ranges from a simple reddening of the skin to the development of papules, vesicles, and pustules with a discharge. Crusts and scabs like dandruff may form, and if the condition is not treated, it will become chronic and then next to impossible to treat with any success. In such cases the skin becomes thickened and may be pigmented. The hair follicles become infected, and the lesions are constantly inflamed and exuding pus.

When inflammation occurs between the toes and on the pads of the feet, it closely resembles "athletes foot" in the human. Such inflammation generally causes the hair in the region to turn a reddish brown. The ears, when they are affected, emit a peculiar moldy odor and exude a brownish black substance. It is thought that most cases of canker of the ear are due to a primary invasion of the ear canal by a vegetative fungus. If there is a pustular discharge, it is due to the secondary pus-forming bacteria that gain a foothold after the resistance of the parts is lowered by the fungi.

Some breeds of dogs are more susceptible to skin ailments than are others. However, all breeds of dogs are likely to show some degree of dermatitis if they are exposed to causative factors.

Most cases of dermatitis are seen in the summer time, which probably accounts for their being referred to as "summer itch" or "hot spots." The warm moist days of summer seem to promote the growth and development of both fleas and fungi. When the fleas bite the dog, the resulting irritation causes the dog to scratch or bite to alleviate the itch. The area thus becomes moist and makes a perfect place for fungi spores to propagate. That the fungi are the cause of the trouble seems evident, because most cases respond when treated externally with a good fungicide. Moreover, the use of a powder containing both an insecticide and a fungicide tends to prevent skin irritation. Simply dusting the dog once or twice a week with a good powder of the type mentioned is sound procedure in the practice of preventive medicine.

(Editor's note: I have had some success with hydrogen peroxide in treating mild skin troubles. Saturate a cotton pad with a mixture of 2 parts 3% hydrogen peroxide to 1 part boiled water. Apply,

92

but do NOT rub, to affected skin. Let dry naturally and when *completely* dry apply an antiseptic talcum powder like Johnson & Johnson's Medicated Powder. When this treatment was suggested to my veterinarian, he confirmed that he had had success with it. If the skin irritation is not noticeably better after two of these treatments, once daily, the case should be referred to a veterinarian.)

RINGWORM

Ringworm is a communicable disease of the skin of dogs, readily transmissible to man and to other dogs and animals. The disease is caused by specific fungi, which are somewhat similar to ordinary molds. The lesions caused by ringworm usually first appear on the face, head, or legs of the dog, but they may occur on any part of the surface of his body.

The disease in dogs is characterized by small, circular areas of dirty gray or brownish-yellow crusts or scabs partially devoid of hair, the size of a dime. As the disease progresses, the lesions increase both in size and in number and merge to form larger patches covered with crusts containing broken off hair. A raw, bleeding surface may appear when crusts are broken or removed by scratching or rubbing to relieve itching. In some cases, however, little or no itching is manifested. Microscopic examination and culture tests are necessary for accurate diagnosis.

If treatment of affected dogs is started early, the progress of the disease can be immediately arrested. Treatment consists of clipping the hair from around the infected spots, removing the scabs and painting the spots with tincture of iodine, five percent salicylic acid solution, or other fungicide two or three times weekly until recovery takes place. In applying these remedies it is well to cover the periphery of the circular lesion as well as its center, since the spots tend to expand outward from their centers. Scabs, hair, and debris removed from the dog during his treatments should be burned to destroy the causative organisms and to prevent reinfection. Precautions in the handling of animals affected with ringworm should be observed to preclude transmission to man and other animals. Isolation of affected dogs is not necessary if the treatment is thorough.

93

COAT CARE

Skin troubles can often be checked and materially alleviated by proper grooming. Every dog is entitled to the minimum of weekly attention to coat, skin and ears; ideally, a daily stint with brush and comb is highly recommended. Frequent examination may catch skin disease in its early stages and provide a better chance for a quick cure.

The outer or "guard" hairs of a dog's coat should glint in the sunlight. There should be no mats or dead hair in the coat. Wax in the outer ear should be kept at a minimum.

It is helpful to stand the dog on a flat, rigid surface off the floor at a height convenient to the groomer. Start at the head and ears brushing briskly *with* the lay of short hair, *against* the lay of long hair at first then with it. After brushing, use a fine comb with short teeth on fine, short hair and a coarse comb with long teeth on coarse or long hair. If mats cannot be readily removed with brush or comb, use barber's thinning shears and cut into the matted area several times until mat pulls free easily. Some mats can be removed with the fingers if one has the patience to separate the hair a bit at a time.

After brushing and combing, run your palms over the dog's coat from head to tail. Natural oils in your skin will impart sheen to your dog's coat.

The ears of some dogs secrete and exude great amounts of wax. Frequent examination will determine when your dog's ears need cleaning. A thin coating of clean, clear wax is not harmful. But a heavy accumulation of dirty, dark wax needs removal by cotton pads soaked in diluted hydrogen peroxide (3% cut in half with boiled water), or alcohol or plain boiled water if wax is not too thick.

There are sprays, "dry" bath preparations and other commercial products for maintaining your dog's coat health. Test them first, and if they are successful, you may find them beneficial time-savers in managing your dog's coat.

First Aid

JOHN STEINBECK, the Nobel Prize winning author, in *Travels with Charley in Search of America* bemoans the lack of a good, comprehensive book of home dog medicine. Charley is the aged Poodle that accompanies his illustrious author-owner on a motor tour of the U.S.A.

As in human medicine, most treatment and dosing of dogs are better left in the experienced, trained hands and mind of a professional—in this case, the veterinarian. However, there are times and situations when professional aid is not immediately available and an owner's prompt action may save a life or avoid permanent injury. To this purpose, the following suggestions are given.

The First Aid Kit

For instruments keep on hand a pair of tweezers, a pair of pliers, straight scissors, a rectal thermometer, a teaspoon, a tablespoon, and swabs for cotton.

For dressings, buy a container of cotton balls, a roll of cotton and a roll of 2″ gauze. Strips of clean, old sheets may come in handy.

For medicines, stock ammonia, aspirin, brandy, 3% hydrogen peroxide, bicarbonate of soda, milk of bismuth, mineral oil, salt, tea, vaseline, kaopectate, baby oil and baby talcum powder.

Handling the Dog for Treatment

Approach any injured or sick dog calmly with reassuring voice and gentle, steady hands. If the dog is in pain, slip a gauze or sheet strip noose over its muzzle tying the ends first under the throat and then back of the neck. Make sure the dog's lips are not caught between his teeth, but make noose around muzzle *tight*.

If the dog needs to be moved, grasp the loose skin on the back of the neck with one hand and support chest with the other hand. If the dog is too large to move in this manner, slide him on a large towel, blanket or folded sheet which may serve as a stretcher for two to carry.

If a pill or liquid is to be administered, back the dog in a corner in a sitting position. For a pill, pry back of jaws apart with thumb and forefinger of one hand and with the same fingers of your other hand place pill as far back in dog's throat as possible; close and hold jaws, rubbing throat to cause swallowing. If dog does not gulp, hold one hand over nostrils briefly; he will gulp for air and swallow pill. For liquids, lift the back of the upper lip and tip spoon into the natural pocket formed in the rear of the lower lip; it may be necessary to pull this pocket out with forefinger. Do not give liquids by pouring directly down the dog's throat; this might choke him or make the fluid go down the wrong way.

After treatment keep dog quiet, preferably in his bed or a room where he cannot injure himself or objects.

Bites and Wounds

Clip hair from area. Wash gently with pure soap and water or hydrogen peroxide. If profuse bleeding continues, apply sheet strip or gauze tourniquet between wound and heart but nearest the wound. Release tourniquet briefly at ten-minute intervals. Cold water compresses may stop milder bleeding.

For insect bites and stings, try to remove stinger with tweezers or a dab of cotton, and apply a few drops of ammonia. If dog is in pain, give aspirin at one grain per 10 pounds. (An aspirin tablet is usually 5 grains.)

Burns

Clip hair from area. Apply strong, lukewarm tea (for its tannic acid content) on a sheet strip compress. Vaseline may be used for slight burns. Give aspirin as recommended if dog is in pain. Keep him warm if he seems to be in shock.

Constipation

Give mineral oil: one-quarter teaspoon up to 10 pounds; half teaspoon from 10 to 25 pounds; full teaspoon from 25 to 75 pounds; three-quarters tablespoon over 75 pounds.

Diarrhea

Give kaopectate in same doses by size as indicated for mineral oil above, but repeat within four and eight hours.

Fighting

Do not try forcibly to separate dogs. If available throw a pail of cold water on them. A sharp rap on the rump of each combatant with a strap or stick may help. A heavy towel or blanket dropped over the head of the aggressor, or a newspaper twisted into a torch, lighted and held near them, may discourage the fighters. If a lighted newspaper is used, be careful that sparks do not fall or blow on dogs.

Fits

Try to get the dog into a room where he cannot injure himself. If possible, cover him with a towel or blanket. When the fit ends, give aspirin one grain for every 10 pounds.

Nervousness

Remove cause or remove the dog from the site of the cause. Give the recommended dose of aspirin. Aspirin acts as a tranquilizer.

Poisoning

If container of the poison is handy, use recommended antidote printed thereon. Otherwise, make a strong solution of household salt in water and force as much as possible into the dog's throat using the lip pocket method. Minutes count with several poisons; if veterinarian cannot be reached immediately, try to get dog to an MD or registered nurse.

Shock

If dog has chewed electric cord, protect hand with rubber glove or thick dry towel and pull cord from socket. If dog has collapsed, hold ammonia under its nose or apply artificial respiration as follows: place dog on side with its head low, press on abdomen and rib cage, releasing pressure at one- or two-second intervals. Keep dog warm.

Stomach Upsets

For mild stomach disorders, milk of bismuth in same doses as recommended for mineral oil under *Constipation* will be effective. For more severe cases brandy in the same doses but diluted with an equal volume of water may be helpful.

Swallowing Foreign Objects

If object is still in mouth or throat, reach in and remove it. If swallowed, give strong salt solution as for *Poisoning*. Some objects that are small, smooth or soft may not give trouble.

Porcupines and Skunks

Using tweezers or pliers, twist quills one full turn and pull out. Apply hydrogen peroxide to bleeding wounds. For skunk spray, wash dog in tomato juice.

WARNING! Get your dog to a veterinarian *soonest* for severe bites, wounds, burns, poisoning, fits and shock.

98

Internal Canine Diseases
and Their Management

THE word *management* is employed in this chapter heading rather than *treatment,* since the treatment of disease in the dog is the function of the veterinarian, and the best counsel it is possible to give the solicitous owner of a sick dog is to submit the case to the best veterinarian available and to follow his instructions implicitly. In general, it may be said, the earlier in any disease the veterinarian is consulted, the more rapid is the sick animal's recovery and the lower the outlay of money for the services of the veterinarian and for the medicine he prescribes.

Herein are presented some hints for the prevention of the various canine maladies and for their recognition when they occur. In kennel husbandry, disease is a minor problem, and, if preventive methods are employed, it is one that need not be anticipated.

DISTEMPER

Distemper, the traditional bugbear of keeping dogs, the veritable scourge of dog-kind, has at long last been well conquered. Compared with some years ago when "over distemper" was one of the best recommendations for the purchase of a dog, the incidence of distemper in well-bred and adequately cared for dogs is now minimal.

The difference between then and now is that we now have available preventive sera, vaccines, and viruses, which may be employed to forestall distemper before it ever appears. There are valid differences of opinion about which of these measures is best to use and at what age of the dog they are variously indicated. About the choice of preventive measures and the technique of administering them, the reader is advised to consult his veterinarian and to accept his advice. There can be no doubt, however, that any person with a valued or loved young dog should have him immunized.

For many years most veterinarians used the so-called "three-shot" method of serum, vaccine and virus, spaced two weeks apart after the puppy was three or four months old, for permanent immunization. For temporary immunization lasting up to a year, some veterinarians used only vaccine; this was repeated annually if the owner wished, though since a dog was considered most susceptible to distemper in the first year of his life, the annual injection was often discontinued. Under both these methods, serum was used at two-week intervals from weaning to the age when permanent or annual immunization was given.

Until 1950 living virus, produced by the methods then known to and used by laboratories, was considered too dangerous to inject without the preparation of the dog for it by prior use of serum or vaccine (killed virus). Then, researchers in distemper developed an attenuated or weakened live virus by injecting strong virus into egg embryos and other intermediate hosts. The weakened virus is now often used for permanent, one-shot distemper immunization of puppies as young as eight weeks.

Today certain researchers believe that the temporary immunity given by the bitch to her young depends on her own degree of immunity. If she has none, her puppies have none; if she has maximum immunity, her puppies may be immune up to the age of 12 weeks or more. By testing the degree of the bitch's immunity early in her pregnancy, these researchers believe they can determine the proper age at which her puppies should receive their shots.

The veterinarian is best qualified to determine the method of distemper immunization and the age to give it.

Canine distemper is an acute, highly contagious, febrile disease caused by a filterable virus. It is characterized by a catarrhal inflammation of all the mucous membranes of the body, frequently accompanied by nervous symptoms and pustular eruptions of the skin. Its human counterpart is influenza, which, though not identical with distemper, is very similar to it in many respects. Distemper is so serious and complicated a disease as to require expert attention; when a dog is suspected of having it, a veterinarian should be consulted immediately. It is the purpose of this discussion of the malady rather to describe it that its recognition may be possible than to suggest medication for it or means of treating it.

Distemper is known in all countries and all parts of the United States in all seasons of the year, but it is most prevalent during the winter months and in the cold, damp weather of early spring and late autumn. No breed of dogs is immune. Puppies of low constitutional vigor, pampered, overfed, unexercised dogs, and those kept in overheated, unventilated quarters contract the infection more readily and suffer more from it than hardy animals, properly fed and living in a more natural environment. Devitalizing influences which decrease the resistance of the dog, such as rickets, parasitic infestations, unsanitary quarters, and especially an insufficient or unbalanced diet, are factors predisposing to distemper.

While puppies as young as ten days or two weeks have been known to have true cases of distemper, and very old dogs in rare instances, the usual subjects of distemper are between two months (after weaning) and full maturity at about eighteen months. The teething period of four to six months is highly critical. It is believed that some degree of temporary protection from distemper is passed on to a nursing litter through the milk of the mother.

As was first demonstrated by Carré in 1905 and finally established by Laidlaw and Duncan in their work for the Field Distemper Fund in 1926 to 1928, the primary causative agent of distemper is a filterable virus. The clinical course of the disease may be divided into two parts, produced respectively by the primary Carré filterable virus and by a secondary invasion of bacterial organisms which produce serious complicating conditions usually associated with the disease. It is seldom true that uncomplicated Carré distemper would cause more than a fever with malaise and indisposition if the secondary bacterial invasion could be avoided. The primary disease but prepares the ground for the secondary invasion which produces the havoc and all too often kills the patient.

Although it is often impossible to ascertain the source of infection

101

in outbreaks of distemper, it is known that the infection may spread from affected to susceptible dogs by either direct or indirect contact. The disease, while highly infectious throughout its course, is especially easy to communicate in its earliest stages, even before clinical symptoms are manifested. The virus is readily destroyed by heat and by most of the common disinfectants in a few hours, but it resists drying and low temperatures for several days, and has been known to survive freezing for months.

The period of incubation (the time between exposure to infection and the development of the first symptoms) is variable. It has been reported to be as short as three days and as long as two weeks. The usual period is approximately one week. The usual course of the disease is about four weeks, but seriously complicated cases may prolong themselves to twelve weeks.

The early symptoms of distemper, as a rule, are so mild and subtle as to escape the notice of any but the most acute observer. These first symptoms may be a rise in temperature, a watery discharge from the eyes and nose, an impaired appetite, a throat-clearing cough, and a general sluggishness. In about a week's time the symptoms become well marked, with a discharge of mucus or pus from the eyes and nose, and complications of a more or less serious nature, such as broncho-pneumonia, hemorrhagic inflammation of the gastro-intestinal tract, and disturbances of the brain and spinal cord, which may cause convulsions. In the early stages of distemper the body temperature may suddenly rise from the normal 101°F. to 103°. Shivering, dryness of the nostrils, a slight dry cough, increased thirst, a drowsy look, reluctance to eat, and a desire to sleep may follow. Later, diarrhea (frequently streaked with blood or wholly of blood), pneumonia, convulsions, paralysis, or chorea (a persistent twitching condition) may develop. An inflammation of the membranes of the eye may ensue; this may impair or destroy the sight through ulceration or opacity of the cornea. Extreme weakness and great loss of body weight occur in advanced stages.

All, any, or none of these symptoms may be noticeable. It is believed that many dogs experience distemper in so mild a form as to escape the owner's observation. Because of its protean and obscure nature and its strong similarity to other catarrhal affections, the diagnosis of distemper, especially in its early stages, is difficult. In young dogs that are known to have been exposed to the disease,

102

a rise of body temperature, together with shivering, sneezing, loss of appetite, eye and nasal discharge, sluggishness, and diarrhea (all or any of these symptoms), are indicative of trouble.

There is little specific that can be done for a dog with primary distemper. The treatment is largely concerned with alleviating the symptoms. No drug or combination of drugs is known at this time that has any specific action on the disease. Distemper runs a definite course, no matter what is done to try to cure it.

Homologous anti-distemper serum, administered subcutaneously or intravenously by the veterinarian, is of value in lessening the severity of the attack. The veterinarian may see fit to treat the secondary pneumonia with penicillin or one of the sulpha drugs, or to allay the secondary intestinal infection with medication. It is best to permit him to manage the case in his own way. The dog is more prone to respond to care in his own home and with his own people, if suitable quarters and adequate nursing are available to him. Otherwise, he is best off in a veterinary hospital.

The dog affected with distemper should be provided with clean, dry, warm but not hot, well ventilated quarters. It should be given moderate quantities of nourishing, easily digested food—milk, soft boiled eggs, cottage cheese, and scraped lean beef. The sick dog should not be disturbed by children or other dogs. Discharges from eyes and nose should be wiped away. The eyes may be bathed with boric acid solution, and irritation of the nose allayed with greasy substances such as petrolatum. The dog should not be permitted to get wet or chilled, and he should have such medication as the veterinarian prescribes and no other.

When signs of improvement are apparent, the dog must not be given an undue amount of food at one meal, although he may be fed at frequent intervals. The convalescing dog should be permitted to exercise only very moderately until complete recovery is assured.

In the control of distemper, affected animals should be promptly isolated from susceptible dogs. After the disease has run its course, whether it end in recovery or death, the premises where the patient has been kept during the illness should be thoroughly cleaned and disinfected, as should all combs, brushes, or other utensils used on the dog, before other susceptible dogs are brought in. After an apparent recovery has been made in the patient, the germs are present for about four weeks and can be transmitted to susceptible dogs.

CHOREA OR ST. VITUS DANCE

A frequent sequela of distemper is chorea, which is characterized by a more or less pronounced and frequent twitching of a muscle or muscles. There is no known remedy for the condition. It does not impair the usefulness of a good dog for breeding, and having a litter of puppies often betters or cures chorea in the bitch. Chorea is considered a form of unsoundness and is penalized in the show ring. The condition generally becomes worse.

ECLAMPSIA OR WHELPING TETANY

Convulsions of bitches before, during, or shortly after their whelping are called eclampsia. It seldom occurs to a bitch receiving a sufficient amount of calcium and vitamin D in her diet during her pregnancy. The symptoms vary in their severity for nervousness and mild convulsions to severe attacks which may terminate in coma and death. The demands of the nursing litter for calcium frequently depletes the supply in the bitch's system.

Eclampsia can be controlled by the hypodermic administration of calcium gluconate. Its recurrence is prevented by the addition to the bitch's ration of readily utilized calcium and vitamin D.

RICKETS, OR RACHITIS

The failure of the bones of puppies to calcify normally is termed rickets, or more technically rachitis. Perhaps more otherwise excellent puppies are killed or ruined by rickets than by any other disease. It is essentially a disease of puppies, but the malformation of the skeleton produced by rickets persists through the life of the dog.

The symptoms of rickets include lethargy, arched neck, crouched stance, knobby and deformed joints, bowed legs, and flabby muscles. The changes characteristic of defective calcification in the puppy are most marked in the growth of the long bones of the leg, and at the cartilaginous junction of the ribs. In the more advanced stages of rickets the entire bone becomes soft and easily deformed or broken. The development of the teeth is also retarded.

Rickets results from a deficiency in the diet of calcium, phosphorus, or vitamin D. It may be prevented by the inclusion of sufficient amounts of those substances in the puppy's diet. It may also be cured, if not too far advanced, by the same means, although distortions in the skeleton that have already occurred are seldom rectified. The requirements of vitamin D to be artificially supplied are greater for puppies raised indoors and with limited exposure to sunlight or to sunlight filtered through window glass.

(It is possible to give a dog too much vitamin D, but very unlikely without deliberate intent.)

Adult dogs that have had rickets in puppyhood and whose recovery is complete may be bred from without fear of their transmission to their puppies of the malformations of their skeletons produced by the disease. The same imbalance or absence from their diet that produced rickets in the parent may produce it in the progeny, but the disease in such case is reproduced and not inherited.

The requirements of adult dogs for calcium, phosphorus, and vitamin D are much less than for puppies and young dogs, but a condition called osteomalacia, or late rickets, is sometimes seen in grown dogs as the result of the same kind of nutritional deficiency that causes rickets in puppies. In such cases a softening of the bones leads to lameness and deformity. The remedy is the same as in the rickets of puppyhood, namely the addition of calcium, phosphorus, and vitamin D to the diet. It is especially essential that bitches during pregnancy and lactation have included in their diets ample amounts of these elements, both for their own nutrition and for the adequate skeletal formations of their fetuses and the development of their puppies.

BLACKTONGUE

Blacktongue (the canine analogue of pellagra in the human) is no longer to be feared in dogs fed upon an adequate diet. For many years, it was a recognized scourge among dogs, and its cause and treatment were unknown. It is now known to be caused solely by the insufficiency in the ration of vitamin B complex and specifically by an insufficiency of nicotinic acid. (Nicotinic acid is vitamin B_2, formerly known as vitamin G.)

Blacktongue may require a considerable time for its full development. It usually begins with a degree of lethargy, a lack of appetite for the kind of food the dog has been receiving, constipation, often with spells of vomiting, and particularly with a foul odor from the mouth. As the disease develops, the mucous membranes of the mouth, gums, and tongue grow red and become inflamed, with purple splotches of greater or lesser extent, especially upon the front part of the tongue, and with ulcers and pustules on the lips and the lining of the cheeks. Constipation may give way to diarrhea as the disease develops. Blacktongue is an insidious malady, since its development is so gradual.

This disease is unlikely to occur except among dogs whose owners are so unenlightened, careless, or stingy as to feed their dogs exclusively on a diet of cornmeal mush, salt pork, cowpeas, sweet potatoes, or other foodstuffs that are known to be responsible for the development of pellagra in mankind. Blacktongue is not infectious or contagious, although the same deficiency in the diet of dogs may produce the malady in all the inmates throughout a kennel.

Correct treatment involves no medication as such, but consists wholly in the alteration of the diet to include foods which are good sources of the vitamin B complex, including nicotinic acid; such food as the muscles of beef, mutton, or horse, dried yeast, wheat germ, milk, eggs, and especially fresh liver. As an emergency treatment, the hypodermic injection of nicotinic acid may be indicated. Local treatments of the mouth, its cleansing and disinfection, are usually included, although they will avail nothing without the alteration in the diet.

LEPTOSPIROSIS OR CANINE TYPHUS

Leptospirosis, often referred to as canine typhus, is believed to be identical with Weil's disease (infectious jaundice) in the human species. It is not to be confused with non-infectious jaundice in the dog, which is a mere obstruction in the bile duct which occurs in some liver and gastric disorders. Leptospirosis is a comparatively rare disease as yet, but its incidence is growing and it is becoming more widespread.

It is caused by either of two spirocheates, *Leptospira canicola* or *Leptospira icterohenorrhagiae*. These causative organisms are found in the feces or urine of infected rats, and the disease is transmitted to dogs by their ingestion of food fouled by those rodents. It is therefore wise in rat infested houses to keep all dog food in covered metal containers to which it is impossible for rats to gain access. It is also possible for an ill dog to transmit the infection to a well one, and, it is believed, to man. Such cases, however, are rare.

Symptoms of leptospirosis include a variable temperature, vomiting, loss of appetite, gastroenteritis, diarrhea, jaundice and depression. Analysis of blood and urine may be helpful toward diagnosis. The disease is one for immediate reference to the veterinarian whenever suspected.

Prognosis is not entirely favorable, especially if the disease is neglected in its earlier stages. Taken in its incipience, treatment with penicillin has produced excellent results, as has antileptospiral serum and vaccine.

Control measures include the extermination of rats in areas where the disease is known to exist, and the cleaning and disinfection of premises where infected dogs have been kept.

INFECTIOUS HEPATITIS

This is a virus disease attacking the liver. Apparently it is not the same virus that causes hepatitis in humans. Symptoms include an unusual thirst, loss of appetite, vomiting, diarrhea, pain causing the dog to moan, anemia and fever. The afflicted dog may try to hide.

The disease runs a fast course and is often fatal. A dog recovering from it may carry the virus in his urine for a long period, thus infecting other dogs months later.

Serum and vaccine are available to offer protection. A combination for distemper and hepatitis is now offered.

TURNED-IN OR TURNED-OUT EYELIDS

When the eyelid is inverted, or turned-in, it is technically termed entropion. When the eyelid is turned-out, it is referred to as extropion. Both conditions seem to be found in certain strains of dogs and are classified as being heritable. Both conditions may be corrected by competent surgery. It is possible to operate on such cases and have complete recovery without scar formation. However, cognizance should be taken of either defect in a dog to be used for breeding purposes.

CONJUNCTIVITIS OR INFLAMMATION OF THE EYE

Certain irritants, injuries or infections, and many febrile diseases, such as distemper, produce conjunctivitis, an inflammation of the membranes lining the lids of the dog's eyes. At first there is a slight reddening of the membranes and a watery discharge. As the condition progresses, the conjunctivae become more inflamed looking and the color darkens. The discharge changes consistency and color, becoming muco-purulent in character and yellow in color. The eyelids may be pasted shut and granulation of the lids may follow.

When eye infection persists for an extended period of time, the cornea sometimes becomes involved. Ulcers may develop, eventually penetrating the eyeball. When this happens, the condition becomes very painful and, even worse, often leads to the loss of vision.

Home treatment, to be used only until professional care may be had, consists of regular cleaning of the eye with a 2% boric acid solution and the application of one of the antibiotic eye ointments.

When anything happens to the dog's eye, it is always best to seek professional help and advice.

RABIES

This disease, caused by a virus, is transmissible to all warm blooded animals, and the dog seems to be the number one disseminator of the virus. However, outbreaks of rabies have been traced to wild animals—the wolf, coyote, or fox biting a dog which in turn bites people, other dogs, or other species of animals.

The virus, which is found in the saliva of the rabid animal, enters the body only through broken skin. This usually is brought about by biting and breaking the skin, or through licking an open cut on the skin. The disease manifests itself clinically in two distinct forms. One is called the "furious type" and the other the "dumb type." Both types are produced by the same strain of virus.

The disease works rather peculiarly on the dog's disposition and

108

character. The kindly old dog may suddenly become ferocious; just the reverse may also occur, the mean, vicious dog becoming gentle and biddable. At first the infected dog wants to be near his master, wants to lick his hand or his boots; his appetite undergoes a sudden change, becoming voracious, and the animal will eat anything—stones, bits of wood, even metal. Soon there develops a sense of wanderlust, and the dog seems to wish to get as far away as possible from his owner.

In all rabid animals there is an accentuation of the defense mechanisms. In other words, the dog will bite, the cat will hiss and claw, the horse will bite and kick, and the cow will attack anything that moves.

An animal afflicted with rabies cannot swallow because there is usually a paralysis of the muscles of deglutinition. The animal, famished for a drink, tries to bite the water or whatever fluid he may be attempting to drink. The constant champing of the jaws causes the saliva to become mixed and churned with air, making it appear whipped and foamy. In the old days when a dog "frothed at the mouth," he was considered "mad." There is no doubt but what some uninfected dogs have been suspected of being rabid and shot to death simply because they exhibited these symptoms.

One of the early signs of rabies in the dog is the dropping of the lower jaw. This is a sign of rabies of the so-called "dumb type." The animal has a "faraway" look in his eyes, and his voice or bark has an odd pitch. Manifesting these symptoms, the dog is often taken to the clinic by the owner, who is sure the dog has a bone in the throat. The hind legs, and eventually the whole hindquarters, subsequently become paralyzed, and death ensues.

Many commonwealths have passed laws requiring that all dogs be vaccinated against rabies, and usually, a vaccination certificate must be presented before a dog license may be issued. The general enforcement of this law alone would go a long way toward the eradication of rabies.

Some will ask why a dog must be impounded as a biter when he has taken a little "nip" at someone and merely broken the skin—if this must be done, they cannot understand the "good" of the vaccination. But the vaccination does not give the dog the right to bite. Statistics show that rabies vaccination is effective in about 88% of the cases. All health authorities wish it were 100% effective, thus eliminating a good deal of worry from their minds. Because the vaccination is not 100% effective, we cannot take a chance on the vaccine alone. The animal must be impounded and under the daily supervision of a qualified observer, generally for a period of fourteen days. It is pretty well recognized that if the bite was provocated by rabies, the biting animal will develop clinical symptoms in that length of time; otherwise, he will be released as "clinically normal."

THE SPAYING OF BITCHES

The spaying operation, technically known as an ovariectomy, is the subject of a good deal of controversy. It is an operation that has its good and its bad points.

Spayed bitches cannot be entered in the show ring, and of course can never reproduce their kind. However, under certain circumstances, the operation is recommended by veterinarians. If the operation is to be performed, the bitch should preferably be six to eight months of age. At this age, she has pretty well reached the adolescent period; time enough has been allowed for the endocrine balance to become established and the secondary sex organs to develop.

Mechanical difficulties sometimes arise in the urinary systems of bitches that have been operated on at three or four months of age. In a very small percentage of the cases, loss of control of the sphincter muscles of the bladder is observed. But this can readily be corrected by an injection of the female hormone stilbestrol.

There are many erroneous ideas as to what may happen to the female if she is spayed. Some people argue that the disposition will be changed, that the timid dog may become ferocious, and, strangely enough, that the aggressive animal will become docile. Some breeders say that the spayed bitch will become fat, lazy, and lethargic. According to the records that have been kept on bitches following the spaying operation, such is not the case. It is unjust to accuse the spaying operation when really the dog's owner is at fault—he just feeds the dog too much.

THE CASTRATION OF DOGS

This operation consists of the complete removal of the testes. Ordinarily the operation is not encouraged. Circumstances may attenuate the judgment, however. Castration may be necessary to correct certain pathological conditions such as a tumor, chronic prostatitis, and types of perineal troubles. Promiscuous wetting is sometimes an excuse for desexing.

It must be remembered that as with the spayed bitch, the castrated dog is barred from the show ring.

ANAL GLANDS

On either side of the anus of the dog is situated an anal gland, which secretes a lubricant that better enables the dog to expel the contents of the rectum. These glands are subject to being clogged, and in them accumulates a fetid mass. This accumulation is not, strictly speaking, a disease—unless it becomes infected and purulent. Almost all dogs have it, and most of them are neglected without serious consequences. However, they are better if they are relieved. Their spirits improve, their eyes brighten, and even their coats gradually grow more lively if the putrid mass is occasionally squeezed out of the anus.

This is accomplished by seizing the tail with the left hand, encircling its base with the thumb and forefinger of the right hand, and pressing the anus firmly between thumb and finger. The process results in momentary pain to the dog and often causes him to flinch, which may be disregarded. A semi-liquid of vile odor is extruded from the anus. The operation should be repeated at intervals of from one week to one month, depending on the rapidity of glandular accumulation. No harm results from the frequency of such relief, although there may be no apparent results if the anal glands are kept free of their accumulations.

If this process of squeezing out of the glands is neglected, the glands sometimes become infected and surgery becomes necessary. This is seldom the case, but, if needful at all, it must be entrusted to a skillful veterinary surgeon.

111

METRITIS

Metritis is the acute or chronic inflammation of the uterus of the bitch and may result from any one of a number of things. Perhaps the most common factor, especially in eight- to twelve-year-old bitches, is pseudocyesis, or false pregnancy. Metritis often follows whelping; it may be the result of a retained placenta, or of infection of the uterus following the manual or instrument removal of a puppy.

The term pyometria is generally restricted to cases where the uterus is greatly enlarged and filled with pus. In most such cases surgery must be resorted to in order to effect a cure.

SIDING
TONGUE &
GROOVE

ASSEMBLED VIEW

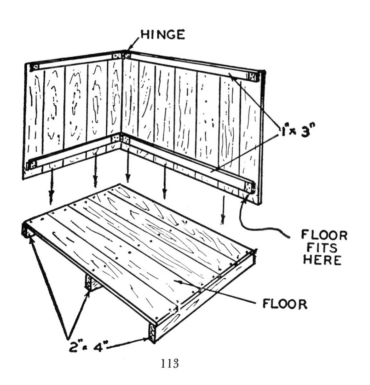

HINGE

1" x 3"

FLOOR
FITS
HERE

FLOOR

2" x 4"

113

Housing for Dogs

EVERY owner will have, and will have to solve, his own problems about providing his dog or dogs with quarters best suited to the dog's convenience. The special circumstances of each particular owner will determine what kind of home he will provide for his dogs. Here it is impossible to provide more than a few generalities upon the subject.

Little more need be said than that fit quarters for dogs must be secure, clean, dry, and warm. Consideration must be given to convenience in the care of kennel inmates by owners of a large number of dogs, but by the time one's activities enlarge to such proportions one will have formulated one's own concept of how best to house one's dogs. Here, advice will be predicated upon the maintenance of not more than three or four adult dogs with accommodations for an occasional litter of puppies.

First, let it be noted that dogs are not sensitive to aesthetic considerations in the place they are kept; they have no appreciation of the beauty of their surroundings. They do like soft beds of sufficient thickness to protect them from the coldness of the floors. These beds should be secluded and covered to conserve body heat. A box or crate of adequate size to permit the dog to lie full length in it will suffice. The cushion may be a burlap bag stuffed with shredded paper, *not straw, hay, or grass*. Paper is recommended, for its use will reduce the possibility of the dog's developing skin trouble.

114

Most dogs are allergic to fungi found on vegetative matter such as straw, hay, and grass. Wood shavings and excelsior may be used with impunity.

The kennel should be light, except for a retiring place; if sunshine is available at least part of the day, so much the better. Boxes in a shed or garage with secure wire runs to which the dogs have ready access suffice very well, are very inexpensive, and are easy to plan and to arrange. The runs should be made of wire fencing strong enough that the dogs are unable to tear it with their teeth and high enough that the dogs are unable to jump or climb over it. In-turning flanges of wire netting at the tops of the fences tend to obviate jumping. Boards, rocks, or cement buried around the fences forestall burrowing to freedom.

These pens need not be large, if the dogs are given frequent respites from their captivity and an opportunity to obtain needed exercise. However, they should be large enough to relieve them of the aspect of cages. Concrete floors for such pens are admittedly easy to keep clean and sanitary. However, they have no resilience, and the feet of dogs confined for long periods on concrete floors are prone to spread and their shoulders to loosen. A further objection to concrete is that it grows hot in the summer sunshine and is very cold in winter. If it is used for flooring at all, a low platform of wood, large enough to enable the dogs to sprawl out on it full length, should be provided in each pen.

A well drained soil is to be preferred to concrete, if it is available; but it must be dug out to the depth of three inches and renewed occasionally, if it is used. Otherwise, the accumulation of urine will make it sour and offensive. Agricultural limestone, applied monthly and liberally, will "sweeten" the soil.

Gates, hinges, latches, and other hardware must be trustworthy. The purpose of such quarters is to confine the dogs and to keep them from running at large; unless they serve such a purpose they are useless. One wants to know when one puts a dog in his kennel, the dog will be there when one returns. An improvised kennel of old chicken wire will not suffice for one never knows whether it will hold one's dogs or not.

Frequently two friendly bitches may be housed together, or a dog housed with a bitch. Unless one is sure of male friendships, it is seldom safe to house two adult male dogs together. It is better, if possible, to provide a separate kennel for each mature dog. But, if the dogs can be housed side by side with only a wire fence between them, they can have companionship without rancor. Night barking can be controlled by confining the dogs indoors or by shutting them up in their boxes.

Adult dogs require artificial heat in only the coldest of climates, if they are provided with tight boxes placed under shelter. Puppies need heat in cold weather up until weaning time, and even thereafter if they are not permitted to sleep together. Snuggled together in a tight box with shredded paper, they can withstand much cold without discomfort. All dogs in winter without artificial heat should have an increase of their rations—especially as pertains to fat content.

Whatever artificial heat is provided for dogs should be safe, foolproof, and dog-proof. Caution should be exercised that electric wiring is not exposed, that stoves cannot be tipped over, and that it is impossible for sparks from them to ignite the premises. Many fires in kennels, the results of defective heating apparatus or careless handling of it, have brought about the deaths of the inmates. It is because of them that this seemingly unnecessary warning is given.

No better place for a dog to live can be found than the home of its owner, sharing even his bed if permitted. So is the dog happiest. There is a limit, however, to the number of dogs that can be tolerated in the house. The keeper of a small kennel can be expected to alternate his favorite dogs in his own house, thus giving them a respite to confinement in a kennel. Provision must be made for a place of exercise and relief at frequent intervals for dogs kept in the house. An enclosed dooryard will serve such a purpose, or the dog may be exercised on a lead with as much benefit to the owner as to the dog.

That the quarters of the dog shall be dry is even more important than that they shall be warm. A damp, drafty kennel is the cause of much kennel disease and indisposition. It is harmless to permit a dog to go out into inclement weather of his own choice, if he is provided with a sheltered bed to which he may retire to dry himself.

By cleanness, sanitation is meant—freedom from vermin and bacteria. A little coat of dust or a degree of disorder does not discommode the dog or impair his welfare, but the best dog keepers are orderly persons. They at least do not permit bedding and old

116

bones to accumulate in a dog's bed, and they take the trouble to spray with antiseptic or wash with soap and water their dog's house at frequent intervals. The feces in the kennel runs should be picked up and destroyed at least once, and better twice, daily. Persistent filth in kennels can be counted on as a source of illness sooner or later. This warning appears superfluous, but it isn't; the number of ailing dogs kept in dirty, unsanitary kennels is amazing. It is one of the axioms of keeping dogs that their quarters must be sanitary or disease is sure to ensue.

GOOD DOG KEEPING PRACTICES

Pride of ownership is greatly enhanced when the owner takes care to maintain his dog in the best possible condition at all times. And meticulous grooming not only will make the dog look better but also will make him feel better. As part of the regular, daily routine, the grooming of the dog will prove neither arduous nor time consuming; it will also obviate the necessity for indulging in a rigorous program designed to correct the unkempt state in which too many owners permit their dogs to appear. Certainly, spending a few minutes each day will be well worth while, for the result will be a healthier, happier, and more desirable canine companion.

THAT DOGGY ODOR

Many persons are disgusted to the point of refusal to keep a dog by what they fancy is a "doggy odor." Of course, almost everything has a characteristic odor—everyone is familiar with the smell of the rose. No one would want the dog to smell like a rose, and, conversely, the world wouldn't like it very well if the rose smelled doggy. The dog must emit a certain amount of characteristic odor or he wouldn't be a dog. That seems to be his God-given grant. However, when the odor becomes too strong and obnoxious, then it is time to look for the reason. In most cases it is the result of clogged anal glands. If this be the case, all one must do to rid the pet of his odor is to express the contents of these glands and apply to the anal region a little soap and water.

If the odor is one of putrefaction, look to his mouth for the trouble. The teeth may need scaling, or a diseased root of some one or two teeth that need to be treated may be the source of the odor. In some dogs there is a fold or a crease in the lower lip near the lower canine tooth, and this may need attention. This spot is favored by fungi that cause considerable damage to the part. The smell here is somewhat akin to the odor of human feet that have been attacked by the fungus of athlete's foot.

The odor may be coming from the coat if the dog is heavily infested with fleas or lice. Too, dogs seem to enjoy the odor of dead fish and often roll on a foul smelling fish that has been cast up on the beach. The dog with a bad case of otitis can fairly "drive you out of the room" with this peculiar odor. Obviously, the way to rid the dog of odor is to find from whence it comes and then take steps to eliminate it. Some dogs have a tendency toward excessive flatulence (gas). These animals should have a complete change of diet and with the reducing of the carbohydrate content, a teaspoon of granular charcoal should be added to each feeding.

BATHING THE DOG

There is little to say about giving a bath to a dog, except that he shall be placed in a tub of warm (not hot) water and thoroughly scrubbed. He may, like a spoiled child, object to the ordeal, but if handled gently and firmly he will submit to what he knows to be inevitable.

The water must be only tepid, so as not to shock or chill the dog. A bland, unmedicated soap is best, for such soaps do not irritate the skin or dry out the hair. Even better than soap is one of the powdered detergents marketed especially for this purpose. They rinse away better and more easily than soap and do not leave the coat gummy or sticky.

It is best to begin with the face, which should be thoroughly and briskly washed with a cloth. Care should be taken that the cleaning solvent does not get into the dog's eyes, not because of the likelihood of causing permanent harm, but because such an experience is unpleasant to the dog and prone to prejudice him against future baths. The interior of the ear canals should be thoroughly cleansed until they not only look clean but also until no unpleasant odor comes from them. The head may then be rinsed and dried before proceeding to the body. Especial attention should be given to the drying of the ears, inside and outside. Many ear infections arise from failure to dry the canals completely.

With the head bathed and the surplus water removed from that part, the body must be soaked thoroughly with water, either with a hose or by dipping the water from the bath and pouring it over the dog's back until he is totally wetted. Thereafter, the soap or detergent should be applied and rubbed until it lathers freely. A stiff brush is useful in penetrating the coat and cleansing the skin. It is not sufficient to wash only the back and sides—the belly, neck, legs, feet, and tail must all be scrubbed thoroughly.

If the dog is very dirty, it may be well to rinse him lightly and repeat the soaping process and scrub again. Thereafter, the dog must be rinsed with warm (tepid) water until all suds and soil come away. If a bath spray is available, the rinsing is an easy matter. If the dog must be rinsed in standing water, it will be needful to renew it two or three times.

When he is thoroughly rinsed, it is well to remove such surplus water as may be squeezed with the hand, after which he is enveloped with a turkish towel, lifted from the tub, and rubbed until he is dry. This will probably require two or three dry towels. In the process of drying the dog, it is well to return again and again to the interior of the ears.

THE DOG'S TEETH

The dog, like the human being, has two successive sets of teeth, the so-called milk teeth or baby teeth, which are shed and replaced later by the permanent teeth. The temporary teeth, which begin to emerge when the puppy is two and a half to three weeks of age, offer no difficulty. The full set of milk teeth (consisting usually of six incisors and two canines in each jaw, with four molars in the upper jaw and six molars in the lower jaw) is completed usually just before weaning time. Except for some obvious malformation, the milk teeth may be ignored and forgotten about.

At about the fourth month the baby teeth are shed and gradually replaced by the permanent teeth. This shedding and replacement process may consume some three or four months. This is about the most critical period of the dog's life—his adolescence. Some constitutionally vigorous dogs go through their teething easily, with no

119

seeming awareness that the change is taking place. Others, less vigorous, may suffer from soreness of the gums, go off in flesh, and require pampering. While they are teething, puppies should be particularly protected from exposure to infectious diseases and should be fed on nutritious foods, especially meat and milk.

The permanent teeth normally consist of 42—six incisors and two canines (fangs) in each jaw, with twelve molars in the upper jaw and fourteen in the lower jaw. Occasionally the front molars fail to emerge; this deficiency is considered by most judges to be only a minor fault, if the absence is noticed at all.

Dentition is a heritable factor in the dog, and some dogs have soft, brittle and defective permanent teeth, no matter how excellent the diet and the care given them. The teeth of those dogs which are predisposed to have excellent sound ones, however, can be ruined by an inferior diet prior to and during the period of their eruption. At this time, for the teeth to develop properly, a dog must have an adequate supply of calcium phosphate and vitamin D, besides all the protein he can consume.

Often the permanent teeth emerge before the shedding of the milk teeth, in which case the dog may have parts of both sets at the same time. The milk teeth will eventually drop out, but as long as they remain they may deflect or displace the second teeth in the process of their growth. The incisors are the teeth in which a malformation may result from the late dropping of the baby teeth. When it is realized just how important a correct "bite" may be deemed in the show ring, the hazards of permitting the baby teeth to deflect the permanent set will be understood.

The baby teeth in such a case must be dislodged and removed. The roots of the baby teeth are resorbed in the gums, and the teeth can usually be extracted by firm pressure of thumb and finger, although it may be necessary to employ forceps or to take the puppy to the veterinarian.

The permanent teeth of the puppy are usually somewhat overshot, by which is meant that the upper incisors protrude over and do not play upon the lower incisors. Maturity may be trusted to remedy this apparent defect unless it is too pronounced.

An undershot mouth in a puppy, on the other hand, tends to grow worse as the dog matures. Whether or not it has been caused by the displacement of the permanent teeth by the persistence of the milk teeth, it can sometimes be remedied (or at least bettered) by frequent hard pressure of the thumb on the lower jaw, forcing the lower teeth backward to meet the upper ones. Braces on dog teeth have seldom proved efficacious, but pressure and massage are worth trying on the bad mouth of an otherwise excellent puppy.

High and persistent fevers, especially from the fourth to the ninth month, sometimes result in discolored, pitted, and defective teeth, commonly called "distemper teeth." They often result from maladies other than distemper. There is little that can be done for them. They are unpleasant to see and are subject to penalty in the show ring, but are serviceable to the dog. Distemper teeth are not in themselves heritable, but the predisposition for their development appears to be. At least, at the teething age, the offspring from distemper toothed ancestors seem to be especially prone to fevers which impair their dentition.

Older dogs, especially those fed largely upon carbohydrates, tend to accumulate more or less tartar upon their teeth. The tartar generally starts at the gum line on the molars and extends gradually to the cusp. To rectify this condition, the dog's teeth should be scaled by a veterinarian.

The cleanliness of a dog's mouth may be brought about and the formation of tartar discouraged by the scouring of the teeth with a moist cloth dipped in a mixture of equal parts of table salt and baking soda.

A large bone given the dog to chew on or play with tends to prevent tartar from forming on the teeth. If tartar is present, the chewing and gnawing on the bone will help to remove the deposit mechanically. A bone given to puppies will act as a teething ring and aid in the cutting of the permanent teeth. So will beef hide strips you can buy in pet shops.

CARE OF THE NAILS

The nails of the dog should be kept shortened and blunted right down to the quick—never into the quick. If this is not done, the toes may spread and the foot may splay into a veritable pancake. Some dogs have naturally flat feet, which they have inherited. No pretense is made that the shortening of the nails of such a foot will obviate the fault entirely and make the foot beautiful or serviceable.

121

It will only improve the appearance and make the best of an obvious fault. Short nails do, however, emphasize the excellence of a good foot.

Some dogs keep their nails short by digging and friction. Their nails require little attention, but it is a rare dog whose foot cannot be bettered by artificially shortening the nails.

Nail clippers are available, made especially for the purpose. After using them, the sides of the nail should be filed away as much as is possible without touching the quick. Carefully done, it causes the dog no discomfort. But, once the quick of a dog's nail has been injured, he may forever afterward resent and fight having his feet treated or even having them examined.

The obvious horn of the nail can be removed, after which the quick will recede to permit the removal of more horn the following week. This process may be kept up until the nail is as short and blunt as it can be made, after which nails will need attention only at intervals of six weeks or two months.

Some persons clip the nails right back to the toes in one fell swoop, disregarding injury to the quick and pain of the dog. The nails bleed and the dog limps for a day or two, but infection seldom develops. Such a procedure should not be undertaken without a general anesthetic. If an anesthetic is used, this forthright method does not prejudice the dog against having his feet handled.

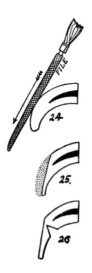

NAIL TRIMMING
ILLUSTRATED
The method here illustrated is to take a sharp file and stroke the nail downwards in the direction of the arrow, as in Figure 24, until it assumes the shape in Figure 25, the shaded portion being the part removed, a three-cornered file should then be used on the underside just missing the quick, as in Figure 26, and the operation is then complete, the dog running about quickly wears the nail to the proper shape.

Care for
the Old Dog

FIRST, how old is old, in a dog? Some breeds live longer than others, as a general rule. The only regularity about dog ages at death is their irregularity breed to breed and dog to dog.

The dog owner can best determine senility in his canine friend by the dog's appearance and behavior. Old dogs "slow down" much as humans do. The stairs are a little steeper, the breath a little shorter, the eye dimmer, the hearing usually a little harder.

As prevention is always better than cure, a dog's life may be happily and healthfully extended if certain precautionary steps are taken. As the aging process becomes quite evident, the owner should become more considerate of his dog's weaknesses, procrastinations and lapses. A softer, drier, warmer bed may be advisable; a foam rubber mattress will be appreciated. If a kennel dog has been able to endure record-breaking hot or cold, torrential or desert-dry days, he may in his old age appreciate spending his nights at least in a warm, comfy human house. And if the weather outside is frightful during the day, he should—for minimum comfort and safety—be brought inside before pneumonia sets in.

The old dog should NOT be required or expected to chase a ball, or a pheasant, or one of his species of different sex. The old bitch should not continue motherhood.

123

If many teeth are gone or going, foods should be softer. The diet should be blander—delete sweet or spicy or heavy tidbits—and there should be less of it, usually. The older dog needs less fat, less carbohydrate and less minerals unless disease and convalescence dictate otherwise. DON'T PERMIT AN OLD DOG TO GET FAT! It's cruel. The special diet known as PD or KD may be in order, if the dog has dietary troubles or a disease concomitant with old age. The veterinarian should be asked about PD or KD diets. Vitamin B-12 and other vitamin reinforcements may help.

The dog diseases of old age parallel many of the human illnesses. Senior male dogs suffer from prostate trouble, kidney disease and cancer. Senior bitches suffer from metritis and cancer. Both sexes suffer blindness, deafness and paralysis. Dogs suffer from heart disease; I know one old dog that is living an especially happy old age through the courtesy of digitalis. If the symptoms of any disease manifest themselves in an old dog the veterinarian MUST be consulted.

Many dog owners are selfish about old dogs. In their reluctance to lose faithful friends, they try to keep their canine companions alive in terminal illnesses, such as galloping cancer. If the veterinarian holds little or no promise for recovery of a pet from an illness associated with old age, or if the pet suffers, the kindest act the owner can perform is to request euthanasia. In this sad event, the kindest step the owner may take in *his* interest is to acquire a puppy or young dog of the same breed immediately. Puppies have a wonderful way of absorbing grief!

Glossary of Dog Terms

Achilles tendon: The large tendon attaching the muscle of the calf in the second thigh to the bone below the hock; the hamstring.

A.K.C.: The American Kennel Club.

Albino: An animal having a congenital deficiency of pigment in the skin, hair, and eyes.

American Kennel Club: A federation of member show-giving and specialty clubs which maintains a stud book, and formulates and enforces rules under which dog shows and other canine activities in the United States are conducted. Its address is 51 Madison Ave., New York, N. Y. 10010.

Angulation: The angles of the bony structure at the joints, particularly of the shoulder with the upper arm (front angulation), or the angles at the stifle and the hock (rear angulation).

Anus: The posterior opening of the alimentary canal through which the feces are discharged.

Apple head: A rounded or domed skull.

Balance: A nice adjustment of the parts one to another; no part too big or too small for the whole organism; symmetry.

Barrel: The ribs and body.

Bitch: The female of the dog species.

Blaze: A white line or marking extending from the top of the skull (often from the occiput), between the eyes, and over the muzzle.

Brisket: The breast or lower part of the chest in front of and between the forelegs, sometimes including the part extending back some distance behind the forelegs.

Burr: The visible, irregular inside formation of the ear.

Butterfly nose: A nose spotted or speckled with flesh color.

Canine: (Noun) Any animal of the family *Canidae*, including dogs, wolves, jackals, and foxes.
(Adjective) Of or pertaining to such animals; having the nature and qualities of a dog.

Canine tooth: The long tooth next behind the incisors in each side of each jaw; the fang.

Castrate: (Verb) Surgically to remove the gonads of either sex, usually said of the testes of the male.

Character: A combination of points of appearance, behavior, and disposition

125

contributing to the whole dog and distinctive of the individual dog or of its particular breed.

Cheeky: Having rounded muscular padding on sides of the skull.

Chiseled: (Said of the muzzle) modeled or delicately cut away in front of the eyes to conform to breed type.

Chops: The mouth, jaws, lips, and cushion.

Close-coupled: Short in the loins.

Cobby: Stout, stocky, short-bodied; compactly made; like a cob (horse).

Coupling: The part of the body joining the hindquarters to the parts of the body in front; the loin; the flank.

Cowhocks: Hocks turned inward and converging like the presumed hocks of a cow.

Croup: The rear of the back above the hind limbs; the line from the pelvis to the set-on of the tail.

Cryptorchid: A male animal in which the testicles are not externally apparent, having failed to descend normally, not to be confused with a castrated dog.

Dentition: The number, kind, form, and arrangement of the teeth.

Dewclaws: Additional toes on the inside of the leg above the foot; the ones on the rear legs usually removed in puppyhood in most breeds.

Dewlap: The pendulous fold of skin under the neck.

Distemper teeth: The discolored and pitted teeth which result from some febrile disease.

Down in (or on) pastern: With forelegs more or less bent at the pastern joint.

Dry: Free from surplus skin or flesh about mouth, lips, or throat.

Dudley nose: A brown or flesh-colored nose, usually accompanied by eye-rims of the same shade and light eyes.

Ewe-neck: A thin sheep-like neck, having insufficient, faulty, or concave arch.

Expression: The combination of various features of the head and face, particularly the size, shape, placement and color of eyes, to produce a certain impression, the outlook.

Femur: The heavy bone of the true thigh.

Fetlock or Fetlock joint: The joint between the pastern and the lower arm; sometimes called the "knee," although it does not correspond to the human knee.

Fiddle front: A crooked front with bandy legs, out at elbow, converging at pastern joints, and turned out pasterns and feet, with or without bent bones of forearms.

Flews: The chops; pendulous lateral parts of the upper lips.

Forearm: The part of the front leg between the elbow and pastern.

Front: The entire aspect of a dog, except the head, when seen from the front; the forehand.

Guard hairs: The longer, smoother, stiffer hairs which grow through the undercoat and normally conceal it.

Hackney action: The high lifting of the front feet, like that of a Hackney horse, a waste of effort.

Hare-foot: A long, narrow, and close-toed foot, like that of the hare or rabbit.

Haw: The third eyelid, or nictitating membrane, especially when inflamed.

Height: The vertical distance from withers at top of shoulder blades to floor.

Hock: The lower joint in the hind leg, corresponding to the human ankle; sometimes, incorrectly, the part of the hind leg, from the hock joint to the foot.

Humerus: The bone of the upper arm.

Incisors: The teeth adapted for cutting; specifically, the six small front teeth in each jaw between the canines or fangs.

126

Knuckling over: Projecting or bulging forward of the front legs at the pastern joint; incorrectly called knuckle knees.

Leather: Pendant ears.

Lippy: With lips longer or fuller than desirable in the breed under consideration.

Loaded: Padded with superfluous muscle (said of such shoulders).

Loins: That part on either side of the spinal column between the hipbone and the false ribs.

Molar tooth: A rear, cheek tooth adapted for grinding food.

Monorchid: A male animal having but one testicle in the scrotum; monorchids may be potent and fertile.

Muzzle: The part of the face in front of the eyes.

Nictitating membrane: A thin membrane at the inner angle of the eye or beneath the lower lid, capable of being drawn across the eyeball. This membrane is frequently surgically excised in some breeds to improve the expression.

Occiput or occipital protuberance: The bony knob at the top of the skull between the ears.

Occlusion: The bringing together of the opposing surfaces of the two jaws; the relation between those surfaces when in contact.

Olfactory: Of or pertaining to the sense of smell.

Out at elbow: With elbows turned outward from body due to faulty joint and front formation, usually accompanied by pigeon-toes; loose-fronted.

Out at shoulder: With shoulder blades loosely attached to the body, leaving the shoulders jutting out in relief and increasing the breadth of the front.

Overshot: Having the lower jaw so short that the upper and lower incisors fail to meet; pig-jawed.

Pace: A gait in which the legs move in lateral pairs, the animal supported alternatively by the right and left legs.

Pad: The cushion-like, tough sole of the foot.

Pastern: That part of the foreleg between the fetlock or pastern joint and the foot; sometimes incorrectly used for pastern joint or fetlock.

Period of gestation: The duration of pregnancy, about 63 days in the dog.

Puppy: Technically, a dog under a year in age.

Quarters: The two hind legs taken together.

Roach-back: An arched or convex spine, the curvature rising gently behind the withers and carrying over the loins; wheel-back.

Roman nose: The convex curved top line of the muzzle.

Scapula: The shoulder blade.

Scissors bite: A bite in which the incisors of the upper jaw just overlap and play upon those of the lower jaw.

Slab sides: Flat sides with insufficient spring of ribs.

Snipey: Snipe-nosed, said of a muzzle too sharply pointed, narrow, or weak.

Spay: To render a bitch sterile by the surgical removal of her ovaries; to castrate a bitch.

Specialty club: An organization to sponsor and forward the interests of a single breed.

Specialty show: A dog show confined to a single breed.

Spring: The roundness of ribs.

Stifle or stifle joint: The joint next above the hock, and near the flank, in the hind leg; the joint corresponding to the knee in man.

Stop: The depression or step between the forehead and the muzzle between the eyes.

Straight hocks: Hocks lacking bend or angulation.

Straight shoulders: Shoulder formation with blades too upright, with angle greater than 90° with bone of upper arm.

Substance: Strength of skeleton, and weight of solid musculature.

Sway-back: A spine with sagging, concave curvature from withers to pelvis.

Thorax: The part of the body between the neck and the abdomen, and supported by the ribs and sternum.

Throaty: Possessing a superfluous amount of skin under the throat.

Undercoat: A growth of short, fine hair, or pile, partly or entirely concealed by the coarser top coat which grows through it.

Undershot: Having the lower incisor teeth projecting beyond the upper ones when the mouth is closed; the opposite to overshot; prognathous; underhung.

Upper arm: The part of the dog between the elbow and point of shoulder.

Weaving: Crossing the front legs one over the other in action.

Withers: The part between the shoulder bones at the base of the neck; the point from which the height of a dog is usually measured.

(End of Part II. Please see Contents page for total number of pages in book.)